# REAL WORLD ALGEBRA

## *Understanding the Power of Mathematics*

**Edward Zaccaro**

*Hickory Grove Press*

## About the Author

Ed lives outside of Dubuque, Iowa with his wife and three children. He has been involved in education in various forms since graduating from Oberlin College in 1974. Ed has taught students of all ages and abilities, but his focus for the past ten years has been working with mathematically gifted students at the elementary and middle school level. When unable to find sufficient curriculum and materials for his students, he began to develop his own, resulting in the following collection of books:

- *Primary Grade Challenge Math*
- *Challenge Math for the Elementary and Middle School Student*
- *Real World Algebra*
- *The Ten Things All Future Mathematicians and Scientists Must Know
  (But are Rarely Taught)*

From 1996-2001, Ed served on the School Board for the Dubuque Community School District. He has presented at state and national conferences in the areas of mentoring and gifted education.

Ed credits his interest in math to his father, Luke N. Zaccaro, who was a college math professor for his entire career.

Cover designed by Wilderness Graphics, Dubuque, Iowa.

Phone: 563-583-4767
E-mail: challengemath@aol.com
http://www.challengemath.com

Library of Congress Control Number: 2001097032
ISBN: 0-9679915-2-8

*This book is dedicated to my students,
whose passion for math and science
is the reason that I teach.*

# Contents

# Recognizing and Honoring Academic Brilliance

Can you imagine what it feels like for an athlete to have hundreds of parents and class-mates cheering for him or her. Add to that the newspaper articles, trophies, medals, and other awards. This kind of reinforcement pushes athletes to excel. It is unlikely that this kind of motivating environment will ever become routine for those students who excel in math and science. Because there are precious few opportunities for gifted children to be formally recognized and honored, it is important that teachers make students feel that their gifts are something to be treasured.

For several years I have been recognizing and honoring my students by handing out "Einstein Awards" for problem solving brilliance. I'd like to share an experience that shows the impact this kind of recognition can have on children. During a workshop I was conducting at a neighboring district, one of the children solved a difficult problem with a very clever and insightful solution, for which she was given an Einstein Award. The next day, her teacher said that the child's parents had called and mentioned that their child felt that the Einstein Award was "the best thing that ever happened to her".

Some might say that this was a sad commentary on this child's life, but at that moment, the power and importance of recognizing and honoring academic brilliance in children became apparent. Children who have a special capacity for math must learn to treasure and value their gift.

## Einstein Award

*"This award is given for brilliant insight and extraordinary problem solving"*

Name: _____

# Introduction

Disaster struck Apollo 13 when it was 200,000 miles from earth. A routine journey to the moon suddenly became perilous when an oxygen tank aboard the service module exploded. As precious oxygen and power began draining away from the spacecraft, NASA and the astronauts of Apollo 13 struggled to find a way to bring their crippled vehicle safely back to earth. Throughout the 4-day drama, as problem after problem arose, the astronauts depended on mathematicians and engineers to save their lives. The intellectual brilliance of these professionals helped avert a national tragedy.

While the story of Apollo 13 is fairly well known, the important role of algebra in the rescue is not. The problem-solving power of algebra was used throughout the mission as NASA struggled with oxygen levels, carbon dioxide poisoning, engine thrust and reentry angles.

Algebra is the most powerful problem-solving tool ever invented. It was used during the Apollo 13 rescue, and it has also been relied on during the development of much of our civilization. Unfortunately, many people are frightened and confused by algebra symbols and letters because they don't understand that algebra is simply a different language---a math language.

*Real World Algebra* begins by explaining how to turn words into the math language of algebra. Once students are comfortable working with the language of algebra, they easily step into working with equations and then real problem-solving. Soon they will not only be "translating" complex problems into algebra and solving them, but they will appreciate the many uses of algebra.

# The Language of Algebra

When I was a small girl, my grandmother taught me the secrets of the most powerful problem-solving method ever invented. She called it algebra and she told me that the key to learning algebra was to remember that it is just like learning a foreign language. The only difference is that algebra is not a spoken language like French or Spanish, it is a math language.

We used to spend hours in her attic using an old algebra machine that she built to translate word problems into the math language of algebra. I know now that Grandma was really doing the translating, not the machine, but it sure seemed real back then. We would send a problem through the machine like the one shown below.

> Sara is 30 years older than Luke who is 6 years older than Dan. If the total of their ages is 84 years, how old is Dan?

Grandma and I would call one of the ages $n$. In this problem, we had the letter $n$ stand for Dan's age because he was the youngest. We would write Dan is $n$ on the machine and then start putting what we knew about the other people through the machine to change the information into the math language of algebra.

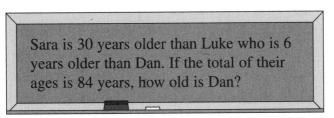

Luke is 6 years older than Dan → Dan is $n$ → $n + 6$

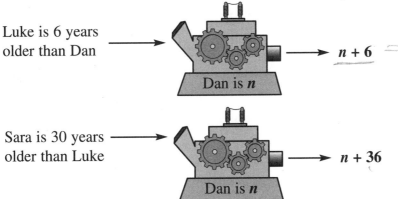

Sara is 30 years older than Luke → Dan is $n$ → $n + 36$

After we translated the words into the math language of algebra, the problem took only a few seconds to solve. (You will see how to solve algebra problems in chapter 2). After a few months of using the algebra machine, I found that I could translate problems into the math language of algebra without the help of Grandma's machine. Now I am using algebra to help build buildings, design cars, and help our space program be successful. Have fun using the math language of algebra. It will make you a great problem solver!!

I've heard that algebra is so amazing that it is almost like magic. What is algebra, and can it really allow me to solve very difficult problems?

Algebra is just like a foreign language, but it is a math language. Watch me turn a math problem into the math language called algebra. Don't get scared by all the fancy letters though, I'll teach you how to "speak" algebra later. All I want to do now is show you how powerful algebra really is.

That was unbelievable! I would have spent all day doing guess and check. You have really confused me, but I really want to learn algebra now.

## Math Problem

Luke is twice as old as Dan, who is 5 years younger than Rachel. Sara is 9 years older than twice Luke's age and all their ages add up to 94. How old is Dan?

## Math Language of Alegebra

$$n + 2n + n + 5 + 4n + 9 = 94$$

$$8n + 14 = 94$$

$$n = 10$$

Dan is 10 years old

Before you can learn algebra, you have to learn how to change words into algebra. We call this turning words into algebraic expressions. Look at the sentence I wrote and watch how easy it is to change it into an algebraic expression. Whenever you don't know something, you use a letter to take its place. We will be using the same letter so it isn't too confusing. We will use the letter *n*.

| Sentence |
| --- |
| Kristin had $17 and then she found a bag of money. |

| Algebraic Expression |
| --- |
| 17 + n |

That's easy, you just put in an *n* for the amount of money in the bag because you don't know how much it is. I think I'll be able to learn the language of algebra pretty quickly!

That was pretty easy. Try this one: If I said Jordan was twice as old as Steve, what expressions would you write for each of the children?

I see how to do that. I would call Steve *n* because I don't know his age. I would then call Jordan *2n* because he is twice as old as Steve. If Steve had a brother three times his age, I would call him *3n*.

*Always call the smallest unknown **n**. If we didn't do that in the last example we would have called Jordan **n**, and Steve would have been ¹/2 **n**. There's nothing wrong with having fractions in our expressions, but it makes them a little bit messy.*

Look at the sentences below and the translations into the language of algebra. See if you can understand why the algebraic expressions are written the way they are.

| Sentences | Algebraic Expressions |
|---|---|
| Jill is three years older than Nancy | Expression for Nancy: **n**<br>Expression for Jill: **n + 3** |
| Rick weighs 56 pounds more than Ed | Expression for Ed: **n**<br>Expression for Rick: **n + 56** |
| Three consecutive numbers | Expression for the smallest: **n**<br>Expression for the next number: **n + 1**<br>Expression for the largest: **n + 2** |
| Three consecutive even numbers | Expression for the smallest: **n**<br>Expression for the next number: **n + 2**<br>Expression for the largest: **n + 4** |

These were easy. The three consecutive even numbers almost fooled me, but then I realized that even numbers are two away from each other.

Now you can tell people that you know another language. I think it's fun turning sentences into the math language of algebra.

**Match the words on the left with the expressions on the right.**

Steve had an unknown amount of money in his pocket. He then lost $23. What is the expression that shows how much money he has now?     _____

Adam found a bag of money that he split with 22 friends. What is the expression that shows the amount of money that each person has? (Don't forget to include Adam.)     _____

Rachel found a box with money in it. What is the expression for this money?     _____

Steve cashed his paycheck and then found $23. What is the expression that shows how much money Steve has now?     _____

A dog lost 15 pounds. What is the expression that shows the dog's current weight?     _____

Ryan weighs 6 times as much as his dog. What is an expression for Ryan's weight if you call his dog's weight $n$?     _____

What is an expression for the value of an unknown number of dimes?     _____

Jamie is 7 years older than Nancy. What is an expression for Jamie's age if Nancy is called $n$?     _____

Fritz is 6 years older than twice his brothers age. What is an expression for Fritz's age if his brother's age is called $n$?     _____

What is an expression for the circumference of a circle with a diameter of $n$ inches?     _____

What is an expression for the value of an unknown number of half-dollars?     _____

If there are 4 times as many dimes in a pile of coins as there are nickels, what is the expression for the number of dimes if you call the number of nickels $n$?     _____

$n \div 23$

$n - 23$

$n + 23$

$n - 15$

$n$

$\pi n$

$4n$

$6n$

$10n$

$50n$

$2n + 6$

$n + 7$

## The Language of Algebra                                    Level 1

1) A horse cost $900 more than the saddle. Write an expression for the saddle and one for the horse.

2) Nicki can throw a ball 5 times farther than Eric. Write an expression for the distance Eric can throw the ball and an expression for the distance Nicki can throw the ball.

3) Briana's weight is four times that of her baby sister. Write an expression for each of their weights.

4) Write an expression for the number of feet in an unknown number of yards.

5) Write an expression for the number of hours in an unknown number of days.

6) Write an expression for the perimeter of a square where each side is called *n*.

7) Write an expression for the value of an unknown number of nickels.

8) Write expressions for three consecutive numbers. Hint: Call the smallest number n.

9) Bob weighs 17 pounds more than Steve. Write expressions for each of their weights.

10) A math book weighs 2 pounds more than a science book. Write expressions for the weight of each book.

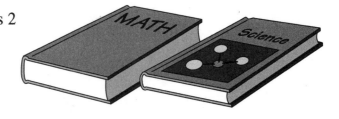

## The Language of Algebra                                    Level 2

1) Dave worked **n** hours for $8 per hour. Write an expression for the amount of money Dave earned.

2) Write an expression for the value of a pile of quarters.

3) Write an expression for the area of a square with sides that are each **n** feet long.

4) Write an expression for 3 consecutive multiples of 5 with **n** being the smallest number.

5) Stacy brought her entire savings account to the store. She spent $50 on a dress and then she found $18 on the sidewalk on her way home. Write an expression for the amount of money Stacy has left.

6) Write an expression for the distance a car traveling at 65 mph goes in an unknown number of hours.

7) Sara earns $580 more than one half of Karen's salary. Write an expression for Sara's salary where **n** stands for Karen's salary.

**n**

8) Write an expression for the diameter of a circle with a circumference of **n**.

9) Write an expression for the number of hours in an unknown number of seconds.

10) If a hat and coat together cost $185 and the hat cost **n** dollars, write an expression for the cost of the coat.

1) Write an expression for the perimeter of a rectangle that has a length which is three times its width.

2) Warren has twice as many quarters as dimes and twice as many nickels as quarters. Write an expression for the number of quarters, the number of dimes, and the number of nickels.

3) Write an expression for the value of the quarters, dimes and nickels in the previous problem.

4) A farmer has 50 pigs and an unknown number of cows on his farm. Write an expression for the number of legs on the farm where *n* is the number of cows. (Make sure you include the farmer.)

5) Dan receives $9 per hour plus a bonus of $55 each week. Write an expression for the amount of money Dan makes in a year (52 weeks) if he works the same number of hours each week.

6) Write an expression for the average of 4 consecutive even numbers where *n* is the smallest number.

7) A garden's length is five times its width. Write an expression for the number of sections of 10 foot fence that are needed for this garden.

8) A farmer has pigs and chickens. If the farmer has 75 total animals, write an expression for the number of chickens.    Pigs: *n*
Chickens:

9) Write an expression for the radius of a circle with a circumference of *n*.

10) Write an expression for the number of revolutions a tire with a circumference of *n* feet makes when it travels one mile.

# Solving Equations

When I first learned algebra from my grandmother, I made a terrible mistake that I have never forgotten. One of the most important rules of algebra is that you can do whatever you want to one side of an equation as long as you are fair and do the same thing to the other side of the equation. In a moment of carelessness, I forgot this rule.

> You can do whatever you want to one side of the equation as long as you are fair and do it to the other side.

The equation I was working with was fairly simple: $n - 12 = 36$. I wanted the $n$ to be all alone on one side of the equation so I added $12$ to the left side of the equation. Now the $n$ was all alone because $-12 + 12 = 0$. Unfortunately, in my hurry to solve the equation, I forgot the most important algebra rule and forgot to also add $12$ to the right side of the equation. As you probably guessed, the result was horrendous. Not only did the equation get unbalanced and tip over, but the right side of the equation was so upset about the unfairness of my action that it started to cry uncontrollably.

> I knew you liked the left side more than my side.

$$n - 12 + 12 = 36$$

It took that equation a long time to forgive me for that mistake, but I am happy to report that for the last 20 years I have always been fair to both sides of every equation I work with. So my advice to you is please be fair to both sides of an equation. Feel free to do whatever you want to one side of an equation to help you solve it, but remember to also do exactly the same thing to the other side. I don't want another equation to go through the pain of what I did 20 years ago.

When we turn problems into algebra, we now know that it is almost like we are changing the words into a different language.

I started the day with $85. After I found a bag of money, I had $143. How much money was in the bag?

Since I know how to speak Algebra, I can turn your problem into the math language of algebra. $85 plus some number equals $143. I could write that as an equation as: $85 + n = 143$

Before we learn how to turn problems into equations, we need to know how to solve equations. To solve algebraic equations, you must go through three steps. **The first step is called collecting.** When we collect, we gather together things that are the same. Look at the following equation:

**$5n + 3n + 25 + 10 + 5 = 120$**

I can collect the *n*'s because they are the same.

You can also collect the 25 and 10 and 5 because they are the same. (They are all numbers.)

The new equation becomes:

**8n + 40 = 120**

**The second step is called getting the *n*'s all by themselves.**

Why doesn't the 8n want the 40 with it?

I don't know, but the n's always want to be alone on their side of the equation.

The **40** is preventing the **8n** from being by itself, so we will subtract it.

**8n + 40 = 120**

**-40**

That doesn't seem right. Can we just subtract the 40 because it is in the way?

That's a good point! That doesn't seem fair to the other side of the equation.

*There is a very important rule in algebra. The rule says that you can do whatever you want to one side of the equation as long as you do the exact same thing to the other side.*

So we are allowed to subtract 40 from the left side of the equation as long as we do the exact same thing to the other side.

$$8n + 40 = 120$$
$$\phantom{8n}-40 \quad -40$$

**8n = 80** is our new equation

**The third step is called just one *n*.** We don't want **8*n***, we don't want **5*n***, we don't want **100*n***, we always want plain old just one *n*.

To turn the 8 into a 1, we simply divide both sides by 8 (Remember the fairness rule)

$$\frac{8n}{8} = \frac{80}{8}$$

$\frac{8}{8}$ of course is equal to 1 so 1*n* or **n = 10**

I know the number 8 caused us a problem, but why can't we just subtract it.

Anytime you have a number next to n you must divide to get rid of it. You can never just subtract it. Remember that 8n means 8 x n.

| Let's look at another example:  7n + 11n - 7 + 15 = 62 | | |
|---|---|---|
| Step 1 (Collecting) | **18*n* + 8 = 62** | |
| Step 2 (Isolating *n*) | 18*n* + 8 = 62  − 8    −8 | |
| | **18*n* = 54** | |
| Step 3 ( Just 1 *n*) | $\frac{18n}{18} = \frac{54}{18}$ | *n* = 3 |

 *When you solve equations, you must remember to go through the three steps. In addition, you must always follow the fairness rule of algebra. You can do anything you want to one side of the equation, as long as you are fair and do it to the other side.*

Use the three steps to find the value of $n$ in the following problems:

1) $n + 5 = 30$

2) $2n + 7 = 42$

3) $5n + 4n + 7 + 8 = 24$

4) $6n - 2n + 10 - 4 = 26$

5) $12n + 5 + 3n - 1 = 49$

6) $2n + 9 = 23$

7) $5n + 4 = 49$

8) $n + 6 + 3n = 30$

9) $19n - 1 + 2n + 7 = 111$

10) $5n + 10 + 5 + 6n - 7 = 85$

## Rules of Algebra

(1) Collect
(2) Isolating the $n$'s
(3) Just one $n$

Sometimes I get equations that are a little tricky. Look at this one.

If I subtract 8 from each side, the -8 won't disappear, it will turn into -16. Watch what I do to get rid of the -8.

$$6n - 8 = 22$$

We want to make the -8 turn into zero.
All we need to do is add 8 to both sides.

$$6n - 8 = 22$$
$$+8 \quad +8$$

$$6n = 30$$

$$\frac{6n}{6} = \frac{30}{6} \quad \text{or} \quad n = 5$$

Let's look at another problem:

$$9n - 5 = 67$$

| Step 1 (Collecting) | **No collecting needed** |
|---|---|
| Step 2 (Isolating) | $9n - 5 = 67$ <br> $+ 5 \quad +5$ <br><br> $9n = 72$ |
| Step 3 (Just one n) | $\frac{9n}{9} = \frac{72}{9}$ <br><br> $n = 8$ |

Find the value of *n* in the following problems:

1) $5n - 16 = 9$

2) $2n + 8n - 10 = 10$

3) $15n - 4 - 5n - 9 = 27$

4) $18n - 7 = 29$

5) $8n + 10 - 6n - 15 = 9$

6) $19n + 6 + 5n - 31 = 203$

**Use your ability to turn words into the language of algebra and then try and solve the equations that you make. If it is too hard, don't worry, we will learn how to turn problems into the language of algebra in the next chapter.**

1) If you take 7 away from three times a number, you would get 236. What is the number?

2) Scott and Jacob are splitting $92. They agreed that Scott would get $6 less than Jacob. How much money will Scott receive?

3) Josh earned $72 less than his sister who earned $93 more than her mom. If they earned a total of $504, how much did Josh earn?

4) A baseball cost $8.47 less than a basketball. If together they cost $19.11, how much does the basketball cost?

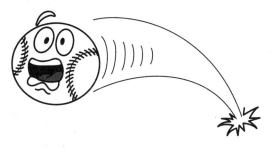

5) If Jacob tripled his money and then spent $67 he would have the same amount of money as Erin. If Erin has $269, how much money does Jacob have?

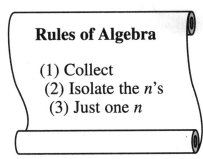

**Rules of Algebra**

(1) Collect
(2) Isolate the $n$'s
(3) Just one $n$

There is another type of equation that can be difficult to solve.

$$\frac{1}{8}n = 7$$

I know I want to turn $\frac{1}{8}n$ into just n. If I could only turn the $\frac{1}{8}$ into 1, then I would be able to solve the problem.

If you multiply both sides by 8, look what happens.

$$\frac{8}{1} \times \frac{1}{8}n = \frac{7}{1} \times \frac{8}{1}$$

Becomes ⟶ $\frac{8}{8}n = 56$

Becomes ⟶ $1n = 56$

$\frac{8}{8}n$ is equal to 1n, so you figured out how to change $\frac{1}{8}n$ into n.

That was pretty easy. What would you do if you had an equation like $\frac{3}{4}n = 12$?

$$\frac{3}{4}n = 12$$

I need to multiply $\frac{3}{4}$ by something to turn it into 1.

Every fraction has a special fraction friend called a reciprocal that can turn the fraction into one. Look at the fractions and their reciprocals shown below and see if you can figure out how each fraction's reciprocal was found.

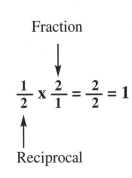

Fraction     Fraction     Fraction     Fraction

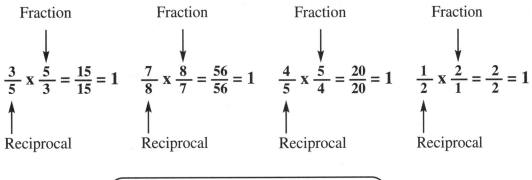

$$\frac{3}{5} \times \frac{5}{3} = \frac{15}{15} = 1 \qquad \frac{7}{8} \times \frac{8}{7} = \frac{56}{56} = 1 \qquad \frac{4}{5} \times \frac{5}{4} = \frac{20}{20} = 1 \qquad \frac{1}{2} \times \frac{2}{1} = \frac{2}{2} = 1$$

Reciprocal     Reciprocal     Reciprocal     Reciprocal

I know how to find the reciprocal. You simply turn the fraction upside down. The reciprocal of $\frac{3}{4}$ is $\frac{4}{3}$

$$\frac{4}{3} \times \frac{3}{4}n = \frac{12}{1} \times \frac{4}{3}$$

$$\frac{12}{12}n = \frac{48}{3}$$

$$n = 16$$

*The reciprocal of a number is found by turning the fraction upside down. Whole numbers and mixed numbers also have reciprocals. The reciprocal of the number 13 is $^1/_{13}$. The reciprocal of 12 $^2/_3$ is $^3/_{38}$*

Solve the following equations by finding the reciprocal to help you get "just one *n*". Remember to get the *n*'s by themselves on their side of the equation before you find the reciprocal.

1) $\frac{1}{8}n = 64$

6) $\frac{2}{7}n - 10 = 14$

2) $\frac{1}{5}n + 5 = 7$

7) $\frac{3}{8}n - 1 = 2$

3) $\frac{1}{2}n + 12 = 22$

8) $\frac{n}{10} = 5$     Hint: $\frac{n}{10}$ is the same as $\frac{1}{10}n$

4) $\frac{3}{2}n + 7 = 19$

9) $\frac{n}{6} = 25$     Hint: $\frac{n}{6}$ is the same as $\frac{1}{6}n$

5) $\frac{4}{5}n + 6 = 22$

10) $\frac{n}{3} + 25 = 30$

---

There is another type of algebra problem you will need to know how to solve. Look at this problem : **8n + 5 = 3n + 30**

Step 1 (Collecting)     No collecting necessary

Step 2 (Isolating *n*)  **8n + 5 = 3n + 30**
                     **−5          −5**
                      **8n = 3n + 25**

> Why don't we use the fairness rule and subtract 3n from both sides of the equation?

> We have a problem here. We don't want *n*'s on both sides of the equation.

$$8n = 3n + 25$$
$$-3n \quad -3n$$

$$5n = 25$$

Step 3 (Just 1 *n*)     $\frac{5}{5}n = \frac{25}{5}$

$$n = 5$$

*You always want all your n's to be on one side of the equation. When you are trying to decide what n's to get rid of, it is a good idea to always remove the smaller one. If you had to choose between 2n and 7n, you would subtract 2n from both sides of the equation. If you had to choose between 4n and -7n, you would of course remove the -7n because it is smaller.*

Now you have **four** algebra equation solving steps to go through. Go through the four steps and find what **n** is equal to in the following equations.

1) $2n - 8 = 3n + 3$

2) $4n - 5 = 2n + 17$

3) $3n + 10 + 15 = 2n + 50$

4) $5n = 3n + 50$

5) $2n + 5 + 7n + 8 = 6n + 25$

6) $8n + 17 = 9n - 8$

7) $8 + 32n = 31n + 17$

8) $-9 + 16n = 5n + 13$

9) $-7n = 2n + 36$

10) $-6n - 9 = -2n + 53$

### Rules of Algebra

(1) Collect
(2) Get the *n*'s on one side
(3) Isolate the *n*'s
(4) Just one *n*

**Use your ability to turn words into the language of algebra and then try and solve the equations that you make. If it is too hard, don't worry, we will learn how to turn problems into the language of algebra in the next chapter.**

1) The weight of three bricks plus 22 pounds is equal to the weight of five bricks minus 12 pounds. What is the weight of one brick?

2) Joey gave a hint to his friends who were trying to think of his secret number. Six more than five times my number is equal to 994 less than six times my number. What is Joey's secret number?

3) Half of a number is equal to twice the number minus 96. What is the number?

 4) If you double the length of one leg of a right triangle and then add three inches you will get the length of the hypotenuse. You can also determine the length of the hypotenuse by tripling the length of this leg of the triangle and then subtracting two inches. What is the length of the hypotenuse of this triangle?

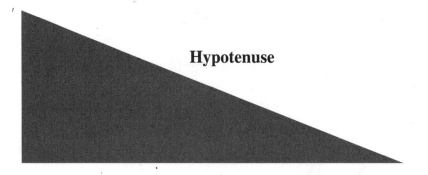

**Hypotenuse**

5) The cost of four math books plus a science book is $4 more than the cost of two math books plus three science books. If a science book cost $22.95, what is the cost of a math book?

## Solving Equations        Level 1

1) $n + 5 = 30$

2) $2n + 7 = 41$

3) $5n - 16 = 39$

4) $2n + 6 + 7n + 4 = 100$

5) $16n - 6 + 3n + 9 = 79$

6) $3n - 7 = 2n + 8$

7) $4n - 9 + 2n - 6 - 7n = 6n - 36$

8) $\frac{1}{2}n - 9 = 2n - 36$

9) $\frac{n}{100} = \frac{5}{8}$

10) $2n - n = 5 - n$

**Rules of Algebra**

(1) Collect
(2) Get the *n*'s on one side
(3) Isolate the *n*'s
(4) Just one *n*

1) $\dfrac{2}{n} = \dfrac{1}{2}$

6) $\dfrac{n}{2} = \dfrac{n}{4} + 3$

2) $\dfrac{1}{4}n = \dfrac{1}{8}n + 8$

7) $90n = \dfrac{1}{2}$

3) $3n + 6 - \dfrac{1}{2}n + 10 = 36$

8) $\dfrac{n}{2} + \dfrac{n}{4} + \dfrac{n}{8} = 14$

4) $15 + \dfrac{n}{8} = 17$   Hint: $\dfrac{n}{8}$ is the same as $\dfrac{1}{8}n$

9) $\dfrac{n}{2} = \dfrac{2}{n}$

5) $3n + 5 = -4$

10) $\dfrac{7}{8}n + \dfrac{1}{8} = 21\dfrac{1}{8}$

**Rules of Algebra**

(1) Collect
(2) Get the *n*'s on one side
(3) Isolate the *n*'s
(4) Just one *n*

1) $2\frac{1}{2}n + \frac{3}{8} = 6n - 4\frac{1}{2} + \frac{1}{4}n - 28\frac{7}{8}$

6) $\frac{n}{1} + n + \frac{n}{2} + \frac{n}{3} + \frac{n}{6} = 1$

2) $\frac{1}{n} + \frac{2}{n} + \frac{3}{n} = 1$

7) $\frac{n^2}{1} = \frac{1}{n^2}$

3) $3n^2 + 19 = 382$

8) $\frac{1}{n+1} + \frac{9}{10} = 1$

4) $16n^3 + 4600 - n^3 = 4615$

9) $n + \frac{n}{2} + \frac{2n}{n} + 3 = 20$

5) $\frac{1}{8}n + 35 = -\frac{1}{4}n + 41$

10) $8^{n-1} = 512$

**Rules of Algebra**

(1) Collect
(2) Get the *n*'s on one side
(3) Isolate the *n*'s
(4) Just one *n*

## Fun with Formulas

There are many common formulas that we use. One of these is the formula for the circumference of a circle. $C = \pi D$   What if we already knew the circumference of the circle and wanted to know the diameter? In that case we would have to use what we know about algebra and try and get the **D** all alone on one side of the equation.

| Step 1: Write the equation | $C = \pi D$ |
|---|---|
| Step 2: Isolate **D** | $\dfrac{C}{\pi} = \dfrac{\pi D}{\pi}$ |
| Step 3: | $\dfrac{C}{\pi} = D$ |

Try to isolate the variable that is asked for in the following formulas.

1) **Area of a circle**

$A = \pi r^2$              $r =$

If you know the area, what is the radius equal to?

2) **Area of a trapezoid**

$A = \dfrac{1}{2}h(b_1 + b_2)$      $h =$

If you know the area and both bases of the trapezoid, what is the height equal to?

3) **Time/Distance formula**

$D = R \times T$           $R =$

If you know the time and the distance, what is the rate?

4) **Volume of a rectangular prism**

$V = L \times W \times H$           $H =$

If you know the volume, length, and width, what is the height equal to?

5) **Area of a triangle**

$A = \dfrac{1}{2}bh$                $b =$

If you know the area and the height of the triangle, what is the base equal to?

6) **Volume of a sphere**

$V = \dfrac{4}{3}\pi r^3$              $r =$

If you know the volume of the sphere, what is the radius of the sphere equal to?

# Using Algebra to Solve Problems

The principal suddenly appeared in front of Briana's math class. He looked back and forth at the surprised expressions before him. He then stepped forward and whispered a strange poem.

> I have riddles that might
> Make you shake with fright
> Because the math that you need
> To give you the speed
> To have a chance to succeed
> Is difficult indeed

He then stepped back, turned, and suddenly left the room. As he left, a small scroll fell to the floor. On the scroll were these words:

*Those classes that want an extra two hours of recess with which to play must determine my age from the hints that I give you today. Take heed though, for your time is not free. In five minutes I'll return for your answer to see.*

*My age is four times my grandson's age. My son is 11 years younger than my daughter and my daughter is 30 years older than my grandson. The total of our ages is 196 years. How old am I?*

The class read the hints and was instantly discouraged. They really wanted the extra recess time, but the only way they knew how to do the problem was by using guess and check. It was clear to the class that it would be impossible to solve the problem in less than five minutes.

While the class complained loudly, Briana worked furiously at her desk. Suddenly, the principal came crashing through the door. He looked around the room as he slowly spoke four words: "What is my age?" The class sat silently as the principal again asked for his age. He then turned and started to leave the room when Briana shouted from the back of the room, "You are 84 years old."

As the principal turned to face the class, a look of disbelief came over his face. He never expected anyone to solve such a difficult problem in so little time. He then placed a certificate on Briana's desk that granted the entire class an extra two hours of recess.

As the principal hurried from the room, the children crowded around Briana trying to find out how she was able to solve the problem.

You've probably guessed that the girl in the story was me when I was in elementary school. And I imagine that you also figured out that I used algebra to solve the problem.

I was thinking that was you, but how does algebra allow you to solve difficult problems so quickly?

Before I show you how to do that problem, let's start with some easier algebra problems. The first thing we want to do is turn this problem into the language of algebra.

Larry weighs 50 pounds more than Steve. Together they weigh 130 pounds. What does Steve weigh?

**Language of algebra:**
Steve $\longrightarrow n$
Larry $\longrightarrow n + 50$

We call Steve *n* because he weighs the least. And because Larry weighs 50 pounds more than Steve, it is easy to see that his weight would be *n* + 50.

The problem says that if we add their weights, we'll get 130 pounds. Therefore the equation must be: n + n + 50 =130

Now we can use what we know about solving equations to get the answer. That was pretty easy.

| Equation: $n + n + 50 = 130$ | |
|---|---|
| Step 1 (collecting) | $2n + 50 = 130$ |
| Step 2 (Isolating the $n$) | $2n + 50 = 130$  $\quad -50 \quad -50$  $2n = 80$ |
| Step 3 (Just one $n$) | $\frac{2n}{2} = \frac{80}{2}$ or $n = 40$ |

Look at this slightly harder problem.

Dan had twice as much money as Scott. Steve had $8 more than Dan. If their money added up to $108, how much money did Scott have?

**Language of Algebra:**    Scott    $n$         (Scott had the smallest amount)

Dan      $2n$        (Dan had twice Scott's money)

Steve    $2n + 8$    (Steve had $8 more than Dan)

**Equation:**    $n + 2n + 2n + 8 = 108$

| Step 1 (Collecting) | $5n + 8 = 108$ |

Step 2 (Isolating $n$)

$$5n + 8 = 108$$
$$\phantom{5n + 8}{-8}\quad{-8}$$
$$5n + 0 = 100$$

| Step 3 (Just 1 $n$) | $\dfrac{5n}{5} = \dfrac{100}{5}$    $n = 20$ |

Try the problems on the next page. Remember to first change the problem into the math language of algebra by writing expressions. Next make an equation and then solve it.

**Rules of Algebra**

(1) Collect
(2) Get the $n$'s on one side
(3) Isolate the $n$'s
(4) Just one $n$

**Use your ability to turn words into the language of algebra and then solve the equations that you make.**

1) Nathan is 5 years older than Dan. If the total of their ages is 19, how old is Dan?

2) A horse is 45 pounds more than six times its rider's weight. If they weigh a total of 710 pounds, how much does the horse weigh?

3) Jordan is twice the age of Luke who is 5 years older than Erin. If the total of their ages is 59, how old is Erin?

4) A truck, its driver and its load weigh 43,320 pounds. The truck weighs 230 times the weight of the driver and the load is 30 pounds more than three times the driver's weight. What is the weight of the load?

5) The first side of a triangle is 7 inches longer than its shortest side. The longest side of the triangle is 8 inches longer than its shortest side. If the perimeter of the triangle is 30 inches, how long is the longest side?

6) A carpenter cut a 16 foot board into three pieces. The longest side is 5 feet longer than the shortest piece. If the remaining piece is 3 feet shorter than the longest piece, how long is each board?

7) A class of 34 children has two more girls than triple the number of boys. How many girls are there in the class?

8) The sum of three consecutive numbers is 264. What is the smallest number?

9) Steve weighs 18 pounds more than Ryan. If their weight totals 144 pounds, how much does Ryan weigh?

10) Because the moon's gravity is much less than the earth's, an individual standing on the earth would weigh 6 times what she would weigh on the moon. Kate weighs twice as much as Stephanie when they stand on the moon. If the total of their weights on the moon is 36 pounds, what does Stephanie weigh on the earth?

Now I think you are ready to solve the problem that earned my class two hours of extra recess.

My age is four times my grandson's age. My son is 11 years younger than my daughter and my daughter is 30 years older than my grandson. The total of our ages is 196 years. How old am I?

**Language of Algebra:**  Grandson    $n$
Daughter    $n + 30$
Son    $n + 19$
Principal    $4n$

**Equation:**    $n + n + 30 + n + 19 + 4n = 196$

| Step 1 | $7n + 49 = 196$ |
|--------|-----------------|

Step 2    $7n + 49 = 196$
$-49$    $-49$

$7n = 147$

| Step 3 | $\frac{7n}{7} = \frac{147}{7}$    $n = 21$ |
|--------|-------------------------------------------|

The grandson is 21 years old. Therefore the principal is 4 times as old, which is 84 years of age. Now I can see how you solved it so fast.

## Algebra Problems                                                     Level 1

1) A glove and a ball together cost $85. If the glove cost $75 more than the ball, what is the cost of the ball?

2) Ryan weighs twice as much as Steve and the total of their weights is 195 pounds. How much does Steve weigh?

3) A truck and its load weigh 22,800 pounds. If the load weighs 12,400 pounds more than the truck, how much does the truck weigh?

4) If 36 is added to four times a number, the value is equal to seven times that number. What is the number?

5) Four consecutive numbers add up to 154. What is the smallest number?

6) Luke is three years older than Rachel who is three years older than Daniel. If their ages add up to 51, how old is Luke?

7) Scott was paid $7 per hour plus a bonus of $18.50 per day. On a certain day Scott was paid $64. How many hours did he work on that day?

8) Erin had $35 more than Angie who had 3 times as much money as Jacob. If they had $196 altogether, how much money did Jacob have?

9) There are two numbers whose sum is 144. One number is three times as large as the other number. What is the smallest number?

10) Four consecutive multiples of 15 add up to 390. What is the largest number?

**Algebra Problems**                                    **Level 2**

1) The sales tax on a book was $1.74. If the sales tax was 5%, what was the cost of the book before taxes?

2) Six consecutive multiples of 5 add up to 765. What is the largest number?

3) The perimeter of a square is 64 inches. What is its area?

4) Stephanie had a pile of dimes and quarters that had a value of $6.75. If there were twice as many dimes as quarters, how many quarters did Stephanie have?

5) A rectangle's length is 6 times its width. If its perimeter is 126 feet, what is the length of the rectangle?

6) Jordan drove his car at 60 mph for the same number of hours that Luke drove his car at 52 mph.  If Jordan ended up driving 92 miles more than Luke, how many hours did they each drive?

7) If Kate triples her height, she will be as tall as if she added 147.5 inches to half her height. How tall is Kate?

8) What is the area of the small rectangle if the perimeter of the large rectangle is 64 feet?  The sides of the rectangles are shown.

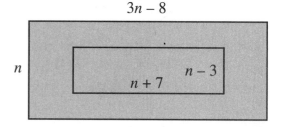

9) Nathan and Marissa each worked the same number of hours last week. Nathan is paid $8 per hour plus a weekly bonus of $33 while Marissa is paid $9 per hour with no bonus. If they worked an equal number of hours and were paid an equal amount of money last week, how many hours did they each work that week?

10) One side of a triangle is 5 inches shorter than the second side which is 3 inches shorter than the longest side. If the perimeter of the triangle is 31 inches, how long is the shortest side?

## Algebra Problems                    Einstein Level

1) A group of ducks and cows are in a field. They have a total of 65 heads and 226 legs. How many ducks are in the field?

2) A rectangle's length is equal to eight times its width. If the area of the rectangle is 392 square inches, what is the width of the rectangle?

3) The Campbell's were trying to decide which phone company they would sign up with. Company A charges $.07 per minute with no monthly fee. Company B charges $.04 per minute and also charges an $8.31 per month fee. How many minutes per month must the Campbells talk on the phone to make Company B the best buy?

4) Kirsten is 4 times Claire's age. Emily is 6 years older than Claire and 6 years younger than Zack. If Anna is twice as old as Claire and the total of their ages is 81, how old is Kirsten?

5) The distance between Westboro and Eastboro is 327.75 miles. Isaac heads west from Eastboro at 60 mph and Travis travels east from Westboro at 35 mph. If they leave at 12:00 noon, what time will they meet on the road?

**Westboro**                                    **Eastboro**

6) A pile of 68 coins consists of quarters and dimes. If the value of the pile is $15.05, how many dimes are there?

7) Claire and Anna were both saving for airline tickets to Washington D.C. On December 1st, Claire was $95 short of the amount she needed and Anna was $83 short of the amount she needed. If they combined their money, they had exactly enough for one ticket. How much did the airline ticket cost?

8) Zack charged the wrong tax on his first day at work at a hardware store. The correct tax was 6% but he charged 7%. Zack collected a total of $1342.85 using the wrong tax rate. (This total was for tax and purchased items). How much money should Zack have collected if he charged the correct tax?

9) Kate rode her scooter from her home to her school while Fritz drove from school to Kate's house in his car. Kate rides her scooter at 12 mph and Fritz drives his car at 40 mph. If they both left at 8:00 and the distance between the school and Kate's house is 10.4 miles, what time will they cross paths?

10) Ed added 32 inches to $\frac{1}{8}$ of Nancy's height. Steve doubled Nancy's height and then subtracted 88 inches. If Steve and Ed ended up with the same numbers, how tall is Nancy?

# Negative Numbers

Long ago in a faraway land, a group of mathematicians lived on a secluded piece of land called Integer Island. This was a time long before algebra was invented. The people who lived on Integer Island had two passions. The first, of course, was math. The second was collecting the rare shiny stones that could be found on the island.

The mathematicians who lived on Integer Island had a peculiar ritual that occurred every evening as the sun disappeared into the ocean. They would make signs to hang around their necks that told how many shiny stones they owned.

One evening, during the ritual, a serious problem arose. Mr. Polygon could not figure out what to write on his sign to show the other inhabitants of Integer Island how many shiny stones he owned. Mr. Polygon never did own many shiny stones, but this night was different. Due to an unfortunate accident on a recent fishing trip, he had to pay Mr. Amoeba 12 shiny stones. The problem was that Mr. Polygon only owned 5 shiny stones.

Now you might not think that this would be a problem, but the lowest number ever used on Integer Island was zero. Mr. Polygon's dilemma forced them to invent numbers even lower than zero. This was how negative numbers came to be on Integer Island.

At first all the mathematicians were very annoyed with Mr. Polygon because he forced them to use a number that was strange to them. Then something wonderful happened. All the islanders soon realized that negative numbers made math much more interesting. They spent months discovering how positive and negative number could be mixed together in different ways during addition, subtraction, multiplication, and division. After a while, several of the elders on Integer Island discovered several rules that made working with negative numbers much easier.

A grand ceremony was held and a giant plaque was unveiled with the rules permanently carved in stone. To help people understand the rules, examples were even carved underneath each rule. To honor their discovery, all the inhabitants of Integer Island decided to call all negative and positive whole numbers integers. (They also decided to call zero an integer.)

The only rule people had trouble understanding was the last rule. To show people the meaning of the rule, Mr. Amoeba decided to take away some of the debt that Mr. Polygon owed him. Mr. Polygon started with a -7 stone debt and Mr. Amoeba took away a three stone debt.

**-7 -(-3) means -7 + 3 = -4**

**Rules for working with negative numbers**

When you multiply or divide with two negative numbers, the answer will be positive.
**-7 x -5 = 35**

When you multiply or divide with one negative and one positive number, the answer will be negative.
**-8 x 6 = -48**

When you add or subtract with negative and positive numbers, you pretend they are money and then use common sense.
**-$8 + $5 = -$3**

When you subtract a negative number, you change the two negatives into a positive.
**8-(-5)  changes to  8 + 5 = 13**

# Adding and Subtracting Negative numbers

I always get confused when I use negative numbers. I am starting to feel like I'll never understand them. Are there any rules I can use to help me?

There are a few rules for when you use negative numbers, but most of the time plain old common sense will tell you the correct answer.

If I give you a number like -5, that is like saying someone owes $5. Look at the problems below and see how easy it is to find the answers by using my amoeba friends who owe money. Don't let the parenthesis frighten you, they are only there to separate the numbers we are adding.

$$(-5) + (-8) = ?$$

I owe $5

I owe $8

The answer is -13 because together they owe $13.

$$-5 \quad + \quad -8 \quad = -13$$

The parenthesis are really bothering me. You wrote the problem (-5) + (-8) Is it okay if I write it as -5 -8 ?

You can write it that way if you want. -5 -8 also equals -13. Look at the next two problems.

(-12) + (5) = ?

I owe $12

I have $5

$-12 + 5 = -7$

If they combine the money they owe with the money they have, my amoeba friends end up owing $7. The answer is therefore -7.

(-21) + (-7) + (32) = ?

I owe $21

I owe $7

I have $32

$-21 + -7 + 32$

If you combine the amounts of owed money with money they have, you would get $4. This is because when the $28 debt is paid from the $32, the amoebas end up with $4.

*There is a very confusing type of negative number problem. This is where negative numbers are subtracted. For example:  6-(-2)  The easiest way to do these problems is to remember that if you have two negative signs right next to each other, then they turn into a positive sign. 6 - (-2)  turns into 6 +2*

Example 1:  - (-5)  turns into +5

Example 2:  - ( -2*n*) turns into 2*n*

Example 3:  -18 – (-6) turns into -18 + 6 = -12

Example 4:  -5 -7 =  -12

Example 4 is not two negative signs next to each other. This is two negative numbers next to each other so the signs don't change to a positive.

Try the following problems using Einstein's rule. Remember that two negative numbers next to each other aren't positive: (-5) + (-7) = -12 Einstein's rule says that when two negative signs are next to each other, they turn into a positive sign: 5 - (-3)  = 5+3 =8

1)  5 + (-11) =

2)  -12 - (5) =

3) -10 - 10 =

4)  14 - (-6) =

5)  12*n* - 8*n* =

6) 15*n* - (-*n*) =

7)  (-19) + (-7) =

8) 14 + (-5) + (-6) + (-3) =

9) 16 - (-6) - (-10) =

10) -18*n* + (-9*n*) -6 - (17) =

# Multiplying and Dividing  Negative Numbers

Can you figure out how to multiply and divide negative numbers by using common sense?

Yes!  Just like adding and subtracting negative numbers, common sense will help quite a bit. Look at the problem below that my amoeba friends are helping with.

$$5 \times (-4) = ?$$

We each owe $4

| −4 | −4 | −4 | −4 | −4 |

The total amount of debt is $20 so 5 x (-4) = -20

That seems easy enough, but how does division with negative numbers work?

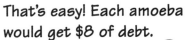

$$-32 \div 4 = ?$$

If you have a debt of $32 that you want to divide among 4 amoebas, how much debt would each amoeba get?

That's easy! Each amoeba would get $8 of debt.

$$-32 \div 4 = -8$$

That makes sense, but what happens if you multiply or divide a negative number by a negative number? What is the answer to (-5) x (-6)?

If you multiply or divide a negative number by another negative number, your answer will be positive. (-5) x (-6) = 30

*There are two very simple rules to follow when you are multiplying or dividing with negative numbers. If both numbers are negative, then your answer will be positive. If one number is positive and one number is negative, the answer is negative.*

Examples:

- $(-5) \times (-3) = 15$

- $(-4) \times (-2) = 8$

- $-2n \times -8 = 16n$

- $(-12) \div (-2) = 6$

- $\dfrac{-18n}{-6} = 3n$

- $\dfrac{-24}{-2} = 12$

- $-1 \times -n = n$

**Rules**

positive x negative = negative
negative x negative = positive

Try the following problems. Remember to follow the two simple rules for multiplying or dividing with negative numbers:

1) $(-5) \times (-2) =$

2) $(-5) \times (-n) =$

3) $145 \div (-2) =$

4) $\dfrac{-168}{-3}$

5) $-8n \times (-1) =$

6) $-2(45)$

7) $-8 \times 8 =$

8) $\dfrac{145}{-145}$

9) $(-n) \times (-n) =$

10) $-8 \times 5n =$

## Negative Numbers                                              Level 1

1) The coldest temperature ever recorded in Antarctica is approximately -120°F. The coldest temperature in Iowa is approximately -40°F. What is the difference between the two temperatures?

2) Travis was in debt $70 while his friend Collin had $48. If Joey was in debt $12, what is the total amount of money the three friends have?

3) The daytime temperature on a January day in Fargo, North Dakota was 15°F. At midnight the temperature dropped to -17°F. How many degrees did the temperature drop?

4) Marissa lived in Colorado at an elevation of 9827 feet. Nathan lives at a location 84 feet below sea level. How many feet higher is Marissa's location than Nathan's?

5) A football player carried the ball 5 times during a game. He gained 15 yards on the first play, gained 11 yards on the second, lost 22 yards on the third carry, lost 9 yards on the fourth and had no gain or loss on the fifth carry. What was his total amount of yardage for the game?

6) $n + (-8) = 0$   What is the value of $n$ that will make this equation true?

7) If $n$ is equal to -8, what is the value of the expression $n-(n)$?

Use the wind chill chart for questions 8-10

| Wind Speed | Air Temperature | | |
|---|---|---|---|
|  | 10 | 0 | -10 |
| 10 | -9 | -22 | -34 |
| 20 | -24 | -39 | -53 |
| 30 | -33 | -49 | -64 |

8) If the temperature is -10°F and the wind is blowing at 30 mph you would feel much colder than if there was no wind. How many degrees colder would you feel?

9) How much colder does it feel when the air temperature is 10°F and the wind is 30 mph compared to an air temperature of 10°F and a 10 mph wind?

10) Scott went outside when the wind was blowing at 10 mph and the temperature was 10°F. Ryan was playing outside when there was no wind, but the temperature was -10° F. Who felt colder?

## Negative Numbers                                      Level 2

1) Stephanie's watch loses .025 minutes per hour. She set her watch to the correct time at noon on May 1st 1996. What will her watch read exactly one year later? (365 days)

2) $-4n \times -4n =$

3) $-4n \times n =$

4) $-20 \div 5 + 3(-7) + 125 \div 5 =$

5) What is the value of $n^3$ when $n = -4$?

6) What is the value of $n^8$ when $n = -1$?

7) If $n$ is a negative number, is the value of $n^{93}$ a positive or negative number?

8) Circle the correct answer:  **-n is**

    a) always positive
    b) always negative
    c) not enough information

9) $\dfrac{1001}{-13} = \dfrac{77}{n}$  What must $n$ be equal to?

10) Erin's family consists of Erin, her 5 sisters, her mom and her dad. Everyone in the family started with $100. Unfortunately, Erin lost her $100. Because her family felt badly for her loss, they decided that all eight members of the family would share the loss equally. How much money does each member of Erin's family have now?

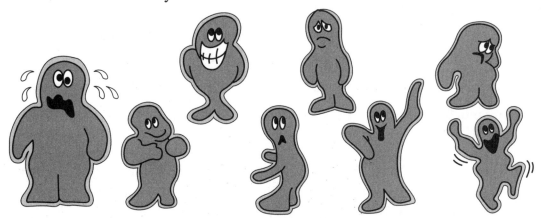

**Negative Numbers**                                    **Einstein Level**

1) A firefighter is standing in front of a 24 step ladder. Every minute he climbs 4 steps and then the next minute he climbs down 3 steps. If he starts at 9:00, what time will he first step on the top rung of the ladder?

2) $\dfrac{n^3}{n^3} \times n^3 =$        Solve when $n = -1$

3) $20 \div -10 \div 20 \div -10 \div -20 =$

4) $100-99+98-97+96\ldots\ldots\ldots+4-3+2-1=$

5) $-1 - \dfrac{9}{10} \times \dfrac{10}{-9} =$

6) What is the cube root of -343? (Asking for a cube root is the same as asking what is the value of $n$ if $n \times n \times n = -343$.)

7) $8 + 2(5-2) \div (-3) + 4 =$

8) The highest point on earth is the top of Mt. Everest with a height of 29,141 feet. The lowest point is a place in the Pacific Ocean called the Mariana Trench with a depth of 36,198 feet below sea level. What is the difference in elevation between the highest and lowest points on earth expressed in meters? (A meter is equal to 39.372 inches.)

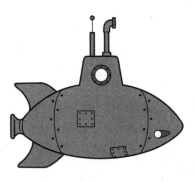

9) For what values of $n$ is $n^2$ greater than $n$?

10) $n^5 - n^4 - n^3 - n^2 - n$        Solve when $n = -5$

I know that the coldest temperature possible is -459.6° F because that is when molecular movement stops. Is there a limit to how high temperatures can go?

When we talk about temperatures increasing, we are talking about atoms and molecules moving faster. For example, the nitrogen molecules in the air that is in an oven set at 350° F are moving at a speed of 1400 mph.

Because we know that nothing in the universe can ever go faster than the speed of light, molecules cannot move faster than 670 million miles per hour. (The speed of light) Because of this, scientists estimate that the highest temperature possible is 140,000,000,000,000,000,000,000,000,000,000° F.

# The Distributive Property

There once was a student who did not like parentheses in math problems. Every time he saw a problem with parentheses, he would immediately do the work inside them so he could take the parentheses away.

$$5(9 + 6)$$
$$5 \times 15 = 75$$

As the school year went on, he became more and more agitated when he saw parentheses and made a goal to quickly do the work inside them so he could remove the parentheses. Eventually he became so obsessed with removing parentheses that he could not sit quietly in his chair while they remained. He would fidget and squirm until he could work out what was inside the parentheses so he could take them away.

As you might imagine, his classmates found his behavior quite amusing and would make harder and harder problems inside the parentheses just to tease him. But the boy who didn't like parentheses would always quickly solve what was in the parentheses and then remove them.

$$6(987 - 421)$$
$$6(566) = 3{,}396$$

$$5(n + 8)$$

Then one day the class came up with a problem where the boy couldn't remove the parentheses. Try as he might, he could not remove the parentheses because he didn't know the value of $n$. At first the children were overjoyed that they had thought of such a difficult problem, but eventually they started feeling bad because the boy became very upset.

That night they all went home and studied as many math books as they could find to try and find a way to remove the parentheses from the problem they wrote. When they returned to school the next day, one of the students announced that he found the solution. He read a section of an algebra book that talked about the distributive property.

Each thing inside the parentheses can be multiplied by the number outside the parentheses. Then you simply take the parentheses away.

After a few minutes of thinking, a smile slowly came across the face of the boy who didn't like parentheses. He quickly ran to the board and used the distributive property to remove the parentheses.

$5(n + 8)$
Step 1: $5n + 5 \times 8$
Step 2: $5n + 40$

The class was now happy because they were relieved that an upset classmate was happy again. They were also happy because they learned a new math skill that would help them solve problems.

When I am doing algebra problems, I often see something like this: 5(*n*+8)

Don't let the parentheses scare you. All this is saying is that you must multiply each thing inside the parentheses by the 5 that is outside the parentheses. When you do that, you are using the distributive property.

**5(*n* + 8)** Is the same as **5*n* + 5 x 8**

What if there was a minus sign inside the parentheses?

Just remember the rules that you use when you multiply with negative numbers. Look at the two examples below.

It is a -36 because (6) x (-6) is multiplying a positive number by a negative number, which is always negative.

**6(2*n* – 6)**  **12*n* – 36**

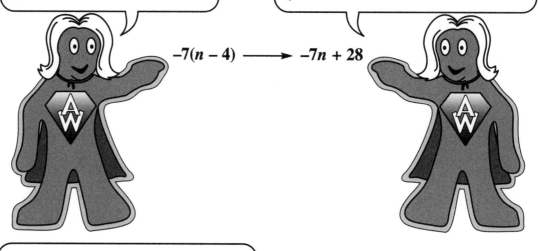

-7 x *n* is negative because we are multiplying a negative number times a positive number.

If you remember your rules, when we multiply a negative number by a negative, we end up with a positive number. -7 x -4 = 28

$$-7(n - 4) \longrightarrow -7n + 28$$

That doesn't seem too hard to remember. Sometimes I forget that when you multiply two negative numbers your answer is positive. Do you think it will impress my friends that I know how to use the distributive property.

I doubt if they will be impressed, but I will be if you can get the correct answers to the problems on the next page.

Remember, when you multiply a negative number by a positive number, your answer will be negative. If you multiply a negative number by a negative number, your answer will always be positive.

**Try the following problems.**

1)  $6(4n - 2) = 12$

2)  $16(2n + 4) = -32$

3)  $-10(n - 5) = -100$

4)  $-2(-n - 8) = 17$

5)  $2(2n - 4) = 20$

6)  $-5(n - 10) = 30$

7)  $7(3n - 1) = 98$

8)  $3(2n - 4) = 36$

9)  $-8(n + 4) = -32$

10)  $19(3n + 2) = 665$

### Cross-Multiplying to Make Equations Easier to Solve

I'm glad you taught me the distributive property. Could you also teach me an easier way to solve equations with fractions in them?

Equations that contain fractions are much easier to solve if you cross-multiply. Look at the equation below.

$$\frac{1}{5} = \frac{n}{12} \longrightarrow \frac{1}{5} \text{ X } \frac{n}{12}$$

changes to **5n = 12**

I turned it into a kind of equation that is much easier to solve. Now I need to divide both sides by 5. n is equal to $\frac{12}{5}$ or $2\frac{2}{5}$ .

Cross-multiplying made that equation much easier to solve. How can I cross-multiply if I have an equation like $\frac{7}{8}n = 42$?

A very important thing to remember is that $\frac{7}{8}n$ is the same as $\frac{7n}{8}$ . And of course 42 is the same as $\frac{42}{1}$. Now you can cross-multiply to solve the equation.

$$\frac{7}{8}n = 42 \longrightarrow \frac{7n}{8} \times \frac{42}{1} \longrightarrow 7n = 336 \longrightarrow n = 48$$

Wow, that was amazing. I have one more question about cross-multiplying. How would you solve an equation like $\frac{n+7}{3} = 4\frac{1}{3}$ ?

Because you know about the distributive property, this question is easy. You simply cross-multiply. Remember, $4\frac{1}{3}$ is the same as $\frac{13}{3}$ .

$$\frac{n+7}{3} = 4\frac{1}{3}$$

| | |
|---|---|
| Step 1:  Make $4\frac{1}{3}$ an improper fraction | $\frac{n+7}{3} = \frac{13}{3}$ |
| Step 2: Cross-multiply | $3(n+7) = 3 \times 13$ |
| Step 3: Use the distributive property | $3n + 21 = 39$ |
| Step 4: Solve the equation | $n=6$ |

*Remember, when you want to use cross-multiplying to make an equation easier, you must have a fraction on both sides of the equation. That means you must change the form of some numbers so they will be fractions. Look at the examples below to see how easy it is to change numbers into fractions.*

1)  $3\frac{1}{2} \longrightarrow \frac{7}{2}$     2)  $29 \longrightarrow \frac{29}{1}$     3)  $3n \longrightarrow \frac{3n}{1}$

4)  $6.3 \longrightarrow \frac{6.3}{1}$     5)  $n-6 \longrightarrow \frac{n-6}{1}$     6)  $2n+14 \longrightarrow \frac{2n+14}{1}$

7)  $.326 \longrightarrow \frac{.326}{1}$     8)  $1046 \longrightarrow \frac{1046}{1}$

*As you can see, putting anything over 1 changes it into fraction form but doesn't change the value.*

Solve the following problems using cross-multiplication. It is important to remember that numbers like $\frac{5}{6}n$ are the same as $\frac{5n}{6}$.

1) $\frac{3}{16} = \frac{n}{10}$

6) $\frac{2}{5} = \frac{5}{n+8}$

2) $\frac{3}{4} = \frac{n}{6}$

7) $\frac{7}{8} = \frac{n-6}{20}$

3) $\frac{n+2}{5} = \frac{n-3}{7}$

8) $\frac{3}{4}n = \frac{9}{10}$

4) $\frac{1}{8}n = \frac{2}{7}$   Remember: $\frac{1}{8}n = \frac{n}{8}$

9) $\frac{1}{2}n = \frac{7}{8}$

5) $\frac{n}{9} = \frac{9}{40}$

10) $\frac{4}{6}n = 4 - n$

Don't worry if #10 gives you trouble. I always have to think a little about that one too. Just remember that 4-n needs to be turned into a fraction by putting it over 1. Then you can cross-multiply.

# Algebra and Proportions

Janelle loved her pet flea. She taught it to do tricks like pulling a marble with a silk thread around its neck. Her flea was an amazing insect that could pull objects hundreds of times heavier than its own weight and jump many times higher than its height. As sometimes happens when children are proud of their pets, she started bragging at school.

Janelle told all her friends that if people could jump like fleas, they could jump 500 feet high. Now this was an amazing story that no one really believed, but everyone knew how proud Janelle was of her pet so they didn't tell her they didn't believe her.

Then one day in algebra class, Janelle's math teacher asked the class if anyone believed the story about how high people could jump if they had legs like fleas. Instead of answering, all the children started laughing. "Of course not, that is a silly story," one of the children finally said.

Janelle asked the teacher if she could prove that what she said was true. Janelle then went to the blackboard and set up two ratios.

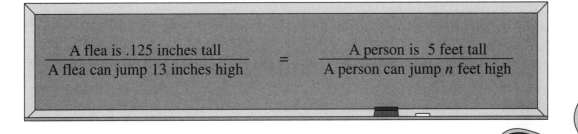

$$\frac{\text{A flea is .125 inches tall}}{\text{A flea can jump 13 inches high}} = \frac{\text{A person is 5 feet tall}}{\text{A person can jump } n \text{ feet high}}$$

Janelle put in the *n* because she was trying to find out how high a person could jump. Janelle knew that when you have a fraction on each side of the equation, you can cross-multiply to make the equation easier to solve.

$$\frac{.125}{13} \; \mathbf{X} \; \frac{5}{n} \qquad\qquad .125n = 65 \longrightarrow n = 520$$

A smile came over Janelle's face when she realized that she was right. She had proven that if humans could jump like fleas they could jump over 500 feet high. The rest of the class was shocked, but Janelle had used a powerful part of math to prove her point. She had used algebra with ratios and proportions.

It looks like using ratios and proportions is a very powerful problem-solving tool.

When you combine what you know about algebra with ratios and proportions, you can easily solve some very difficult problems. Look at the problem below.

A family gives an allowance based on the ages of their children. Their 6-year old has an allowance of $8 while their 9-year old has an allowance of $12. They are planning to adopt a 4-year old child. What allowance should they give her?

| | |
|---|---|
| Step 1:  To solve this problem we set up two ratios. | $\dfrac{\text{(age)} \quad 6}{\text{(money)} \quad 8} = \dfrac{4 \text{ (age)}}{n \text{ (money)}}$ |
| Step 2: Cross-multiply to make an easier equation. | $6n = 32$ |
| Step 3: Solve the equation | $n = \$5.33$ |

*When we set up the two ratios, we put the ages on the top and the money on the bottom. We could have solved this problem by putting the ages on the bottom and the money on the top. If we did our problem that way, we would have come out with the exact same answer. You can put things such as money or age on the top or the bottom, but the same thing must be on the top or bottom of the ratio.*

Use the three steps to solve the following ratio and proportion algebra problems.

1) Luke had $84 in the bank while Jordan had $48. Luke wanted to always have the same ratio of money with Jordan. If Jordan works all summer and has his savings increase to $828, how much money must Luke have in his savings account to keep the same $\frac{84}{48}$ ratio?

2) The age to allowance ratio in a certain family is 4:5. How much allowance would a 9 year old receive?

3) The ratio of sugar to flour in a certain cookie recipe is 6:7. If there is 8.5 cups of sugar that is to be used, how much flour must be used? (Round to the nearest tenth of a cup.)

4) A 10-foot stick casts a 17 foot shadow at the same time a tree casts a 229.5 foot shadow. How tall is the tree?

5) A 5 foot stick casts a shadow of 4 feet at the same time Elin casts a shadow of 4 feet 6 inches. How tall is Elin?

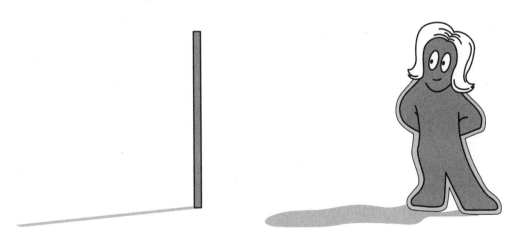

Are there any other kinds of problems that can be solved by using algebra and proportions?

There are many other types of problems that can be solved in this way. Look at how problems with scale and distance can be solved.

Lyn was going to travel from Chicago to Boston. She noticed that the distance between the cities was 7.25 inches on the map and the scale on the map said that 1/4" = 32 miles. How far is it between Chicago and Boston?

Step 1: Set up two ratios. ⟶ $\dfrac{(\text{map})}{(\text{real miles})} \dfrac{1/4}{32} = \dfrac{7.25\ (\text{map})}{n\ (\text{real miles})}$

Step 2: Cross-multiply to make the equation easier. ⟶ $\dfrac{1}{4}n = 232$

Step 3: Solve the equation. ⟶ $n = 928$ miles

You can even use this problem-solving method when you look at models of things such as pyramids.

Mark was at a museum and saw a model of a famous Egyptian pyramid. The model was 26" high and the sign said 1.2 inches equals 8 feet. What is the height of the real pyramid?

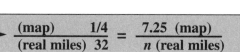

Step 1: $\dfrac{(\text{model})}{(\text{real})} \dfrac{1.2}{8} = \dfrac{26\ (\text{model})}{n\ (\text{real})}$

Step 2: $1.2n = 208$

Step 3: $n = 173\dfrac{1}{3}$ feet tall

Use the three steps to solve the following ratio and proportion problems that have to do with scale.

1) The scale on the map of a bike trail said that 1 inch = 3.25 miles. If the distance on the map that a group of cyclists would like to cover is 4.75 inches, how many miles will they travel?

2) A model of a town was 28 inches across. If the scale was 1.2 inches equals 300 feet, how many feet wide is the town?

3) If Los Angeles and Boston are 3000 miles apart and the scale of a map is 1 inch equals 245 miles, how many inches apart are Boston and Los Angeles on the map?

4) Nancy was trying to guess how tall her friend was. Her friend said that her height (in feet) to allowance ratio was 5:6. If her allowance is $8, how tall is Nancy's friend?

5) The sign on a 16 inch model race car said that 1.2 inches = 1 foot. How long was the real race car?

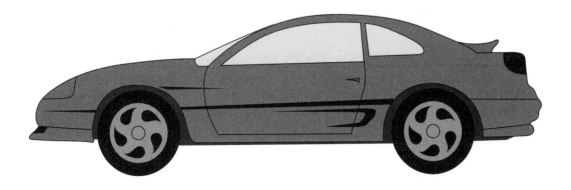

There are problems that drive me crazy. Look at this problem and tell me if this new problem-solving method will help.

A statue is made up of copper and nickel. The ratio of the weights of the two metals is 5:8. If the statue weighs 5,525 pounds, what is the weight of the copper in the statue?

You can solve this problem by using algebra and ratios, but you have to be a little bit clever. Because the total weight of the statue is given, we want to know the ratio of copper to the whole statue. Because the copper: nickel ratio is 5:8, we know that the statue has 13 total parts. So the copper to whole statue ratio is 5:13.

Step 1: $\dfrac{\text{(copper) } 5}{\text{(statue) } 13} = \dfrac{n \text{ (copper)}}{5525 \text{ (statue)}}$

Step 2: $13n = 27{,}625$

Step 3: $n = 2{,}125$    **The weight of the copper is 2,125 pounds**

Use the three steps to solve the following ratio and proportion problems.

1) The ratio of boys to girls in a school is 7:9. If there are 176 children in the school, how many are boys?

2) The ratio of boys to girls in a school is 8:9. If there are 378 girls, how many boys are there?

3) The weight of gold and silver in a statue is in a ratio of 9:14. If the weight of the statue is 1909 pounds, what is the weight of the gold?

4) If the ratio of cats to dogs in a country is 3:7, how many cats are there if the total number of cats and dogs is 89,710?

5) A favorite drink is made with 7 parts lemonade and 13 parts orange juice. If Debra wants to fill an 85 cup bowl with the drink, how much lemonade should she put in?

You can even use the algebra and ratios problem-solving method to convert from our unit of measure to the metric system or from the metric system to ours. All you need is the conversion ratio chart. Watch how I use the chart for this problem.

Angie saw a sign that said the distance to Toronto was 450 kilometers. How many miles would it be to Toronto?

**Conversion Ratio Chart**

$$\frac{(miles)\ .621}{(kilometers)\ 1}$$

$$\frac{(pounds)\ 2.2}{(kilograms)\ 1}$$

$$\frac{(quarts)\ 1.057}{(liters)\ 1}$$

$$\frac{(inches)\ 39.372}{(meters)\ 1}$$

Step 1: ⟶ Set up ratios $\dfrac{(miles)\ .621}{(kilometers)\ 1} = \dfrac{n\ (miles)}{450\ (kilometers)}$

Step 2: ⟶ Cross-multiply to make an easier equation $n = 279.45$

Step 3: ⟶ Solve the equation (Already solved) **279.45 miles**

Most people think that mass and weight are the same thing. This is not true. Weight refers to the force the earth exerts on you (Gravity). Mass is the amount of stuff in you. I know that doesn't have anything to do with algebra and ratios, but I thought you'd like to know the difference between weight and mass.

So my weight would change if I traveled to the moon because the moon has less gravity than the earth. And because the amount of stuff I am made of wouldn't change, my mass would be the same whether I am on the moon or the earth.

Use the three steps of ratios and algebra to do the conversions in the following problems.

1) 32 people went on a hike into the Grand Canyon. Rangers strongly suggest that each person carry $1\frac{1}{2}$ gallons of water on the hike. Because the hikers were from Europe, all they had were liter containers. How many liters of water will the entire group need? (Round to the nearest liter.)

2) While driving in Canada, Mike saw a sign that said the speed limit was 88 kilometers per hour. How many miles per hour would this be? (Round to the nearest mile per hour.)

3) Rachel weighed herself on a scale in Germany which said that she weighed 45 kilograms. How many pounds does Rachel weigh?

4) On a baseball field, the distance from home to first base is 90 feet. How many meters is it between home and first base? (Round to the nearest tenth.)

5) A bridge had a weight limit sign as shown below. Can a 32,000 pound truck safely cross the bridge?

**Weight-Limit
14,750 Kilograms**

Sometimes I am forced to change a certain number of minutes into hours. When it is 15 minutes or 30 minutes, I can easily do those in my head. 15 minutes is .25 hours or 1/4 hour. 30 minutes is 1/2 hour. What really throws me is when I have to change times such as 3 minutes into hours.

Those kinds of problems are easy if you use ratios and algebra. All you need to know is the minutes to hours ratio, which of course is 60 minutes: 1 hour.

| | |
|---|---|
| Step 1: Set up two ratios | $\dfrac{\text{(minutes) } 3}{\text{(hours) } n} = \dfrac{60 \text{ (minutes)}}{1 \text{ (hour)}}$ |
| Step 2: Cross-multiply | $60n = 3$ |
| Step 3: Solve | $n = .05$ hours |

There are hundreds of ratios that will help you solve problems. As you solve the problems on the next page, use the ratios that are shown here or use others that you know.

**Common Ratios**

$$\frac{24 \text{ hours}}{1 \text{ day}} \qquad \frac{4 \text{ quarts}}{1 \text{ gallon}} \qquad \frac{16 \text{ ounces}}{1 \text{ pound}}$$

$$\frac{365 \text{ days}}{1 \text{ year}} \qquad \frac{5280 \text{ feet}}{1 \text{ mile}} \qquad \frac{36 \text{ inches}}{1 \text{ yard}}$$

$$\frac{3600 \text{ seconds}}{1 \text{ hour}} \qquad \frac{3.26 \text{ light-years}}{1 \text{ parsec}}$$

Use ratios and algebra to solve the following problems. If the answer does not come out as a whole number, round to the nearest hundredth.

1) If Bill ran 1000 feet, how many miles did he run?

2) How many hours are in 2,160 seconds?

3) How many parsecs are in one light-year?

4) How many yards are in 38 inches?

5) If Mandy drank 2.25 quarts of water, how many gallons did she drink?

6) A typical candy bar might weigh 1.5 ounces. What is the weight of a typical candy bar expressed in pounds?

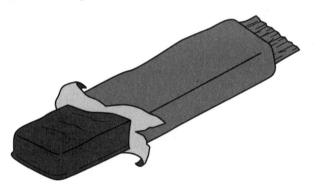

7) Mike was filling out a time-card at work. He was asked to write in how many hours that he worked. Because he wasn't feeling well that day, Mike only worked 9 minutes. How many hours did Mike work?

8) Two children were bored on a family vacation so they decided to try and find out how many miles per second they were traveling. They looked at the speedometer of their car and it indicated that they were traveling at a speed of 60 mph. How many miles were they traveling each second?

9) How many years are there in a week? (7 days)

10) Molly was mad at the receptionist in the doctor's office, so when she filled out her medical card, she decided to express her height in miles instead of feet and inches. If Molly is 5' 6", what did she write on her card?

## Ratios, Proportions and Algebra       Level 1

1) The ratio of boys to girls on a soccer team is 3:4. If there are 49 players on the team, how many are girls?

2) A map has a scale of 1/8 inch equals 12 miles. How many inches would represent 108 miles?

3) What is the height of a 6-foot tall person expressed in meters?

4) Aquaman was taking his pulse while he was jogging. He found that his heart beat 21 times in 13 seconds. Aquaman is trying to keep his heart rate below 135 beats per minute. What is Aquaman's heart rate expressed in beats per minute?

5) How many yards are in 7 inches?

6) If a 10-foot stick casts a shadow of 8 feet, how tall is a tree that casts an 82 foot shadow?

7) A car that had traveled 100,000 miles was being sold to someone in Europe. She wanted to know the number of kilometers that the car had traveled because she didn't understand what miles were. How many kilometers had this car traveled?

8) A flea that is 1/8 inch tall can jump $9\frac{1}{8}$ inches high. If a person who is six feet tall had the ability to jump like a flea, how high could she jump?

9) If Kirsten can run 42 feet in 7 seconds, how long does it take her to run 60 feet?

10) A metal cube is made of gold and silver. The weights of the gold and silver are in a ratio of 8:7. If the weight of the gold is 960 pounds, what is the weight of the silver?

## Ratios, Proportions and Algebra                    Level 2

1) 2 out of 9 students at Einstein Elementary School are home with the flu. If there are 477 students at the school, how many have the flu?

2) The yearly birth rate in the United States is 9 births per 1000 people. How many births would you expect in one year in New York City? (Population 14,642,000)

3) A well-known formula in physics is Distance = Rate x Time. When this formula is used, the time is usually expressed in hours. Phil wants to use this formula to find his speed after he ran 200 yards in 20 seconds. Find out how many hours are in 20 seconds.

4) The circumference of the earth is 25,000 miles. A desk-top globe has a circumference of 32 inches. The scale of this globe is 1/5 inch = _____miles.

5) The ratio of smokers to non-smokers in lung cancer patients is 85:15. In a group of 47,000 lung cancer patients, how many smokers would you expect to find?

6) An odometer in a car is broken and only registers 6 miles when the car has traveled 7 miles. If the odometer registers 1137 miles, how far did the car really travel?

7) A broken clock loses 4 minutes every hour. If the broken clock and a normal clock are both set at noon, what time will the normal clock say when the broken clock reads 2:20 P.M.?

8) Due to a malfunction in his time machine, Derek ended up face to face with a Tyrannosaurus Rex. If the dinosaur runs 60 feet per second and Derek runs 8 feet per second, how long until the dinosaur catches Derek if it starts 988 feet behind Derek?

9) Two similar triangles have sides as shown. What is the length of side *n*?

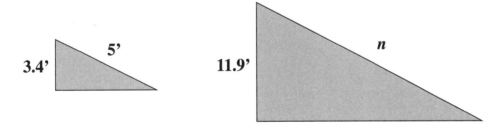

10) The amount of a certain medicine that a patient needs is dependent on the weight of the patient. If a 140 pound person takes 28 mg of the medicine, what would the proper dosage be for a 200 pound patient?

1) Anna beat Kirsten by 10 yards in a 60-yard race. If they both run at the same pace, how many yards behind would Kirsten be in a 100-yard race?

2) In a recent running of a 100-yard dash, the winning time was 9.95 seconds. If the second place finisher had a time of 10.04 seconds, how far behind the winner was the second place finisher when the winner crossed the finish line? (Round to the nearest inch.)

3) A broken clock loses 7 minutes each hour. If a normal clock and the broken clock are both set to 12:00 noon, what time will the normal clock read when the broken clock reads 5:18 P.M.?

4) A cubic meter is equal to how many cubic yards? (Round to the nearest tenth of a cubic yard.)

5) When Eric bought an odometer for his bike, it required 24" diameter wheels. Because Eric's wheels are 22" wide, the odometer registers an incorrect reading. When the odometer says Eric traveled 10 miles, how far has he really gone? (Round to the nearest tenth.)

6) If a dollar of Canadian money is equal to 74 cents of United States money, how much Canadian money would you receive for a dollar of United States money?

7) Warren thought the discount on a lawn mower was 40% when it should have been 35%. If Warren calculated the incorrect 40% discount as $51.40, what was the amount of the correct discount?

8) 9.9 feet equals 9 feet and how many inches? 14.6 pounds equals 14 pounds and how many ounces? 16.7 minutes equals 16 minutes and how many seconds?

9) Meagan needs to find out how tall a tree is. She knows her shadow is 10 feet $7\frac{1}{2}$ inches long and she knows she is 5 inches shorter than Mark. If Mark has an 11 foot 8 inch shadow and the tree has a shadow of 110 feet, how tall is the tree?

10) A metal ring is made of gold and silver. The weights of the metals are in a ratio of 8:9. If the weight of the ring is 1/8 pound, what is the weight of the gold in the ring?

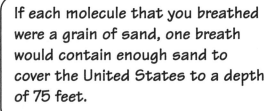

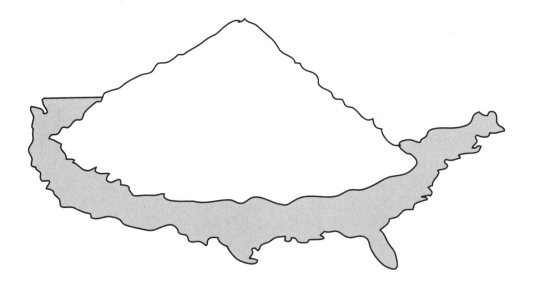

# Algebra and Percents

Dan loved to play soccer and he loved to buy soccer equipment, so it was no surprise that the day the new soccer store opened, Dan spent two hours shopping. When Dan arrived home, his sister Rachel was there to question him about how much money he spent on soccer equipment. Dan, who knew that he would be in trouble for spending so much, immediately tore up the receipt and threw the pieces into the fire that was burning in their woodstove. As he did this though, a small sliver of paper fell to the floor.

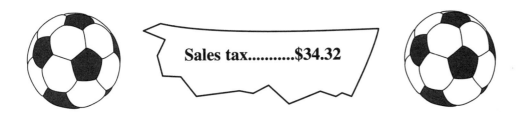

Rachel, who was studying algebra and knew that the sales tax rate was 6%, immediately wrote out the following equation:

$$.06n = \$34.32$$

After spending a couple minutes solving the equation, Rachel yelled upstairs to her brother. "You're going to be in trouble when Mom and Dad get home. They're going to ground you when they find out that you spent $572 on soccer equipment."

Dan's face turned white. He knew that Rachel was always figuring out things by using math, but he was very perplexed this time. He didn't know how she found out how much he spent, but he knew he was in a lot of trouble.

Before you learn about algebra and percents, you need to review some basic information about percents. When you write a number as a percent, or a fraction, or a decimal, it is just three different ways of saying the same thing.

The fish ate 1/2 my worm.

The fish ate 50% of my worm.

The fish ate .5 of my worm.

A skill you will need to have is the ability to change percents into decimals.

I see what you are doing. To change from a percent to a decimal, you simply move the decimal two places to the left.

50% ⟶ .5

5% ⟶ .05

2% ⟶ .02

160% ⟶ 1.6

.7% ⟶ .007

Change the following percents into decimals. Remember that when you write a percent like 82%, there is a decimal after the 2 but it usually isn't written.

**82.%**

1) 75%

2) 7%

3) 100%

4) .5%

5) 250%

6) 5%

7) 12%

8) .008%

9) 1000%

10) 95%

The next thing you need to know how to do is change decimals into percents. I guess you won't be shocked when I tell you that it is the reverse of what you just did.

*When you change a decimal to a percent. The point to the right is sent.*

I remember how to change a decimal to a percent by using this poem.

I would suggest sticking to math and leaving the poetry to the poets. Try changing these decimals into percents.

1) .07

2) .7

3) 7

4) .12

5) .012

6) .0001

7) 45

8) .03

9) 1

10) 9.2

You will also need to know how to change fractions into percents. It is fortunate that you just learned how to do algebra and ratios because this will make it very easy to change fractions into percents. Watch how I change 1/8 into a percent.

| Step 1: Set up ratio | $\frac{1}{8} = \frac{n}{100}$ |
| Step 2: Cross-multiply | $8n = 100$ |
| Step 3: Solve | $n = 12.5\%$ |

That was very clever. Because percents are always talking about 100 parts, you wrote n/100. That will make changing fractions into percents very easy. Watch how I turn 1/4 into a percent.

| Step: 1 | $\frac{1}{4} = \frac{n}{100}$ |
| Step 2: | $4n = 100$ |
| Step 3: | $n = 25$ |
| Step 4: | $25\%$ |

Change the following fractions into percents. Remember that when you have a mixed number, you must first change it into an improper fraction.

1) $\frac{3}{8}$

2) $\frac{3}{4}$

3) $\frac{1}{16}$

4) $\frac{1}{5}$

5) $\frac{1}{3}$

6) $2\frac{1}{2}$

7) $3\frac{5}{8}$

8) $\frac{5}{6}$

9) 1

10) $\frac{4}{5}$

Changing percents into fractions is so easy that I hate to waste your time having you do problems, but go ahead and try the problems below.

$$60\% = \frac{60}{100} = \frac{6}{10} = \frac{3}{5}$$

$$4\% = \frac{4}{100} = \frac{1}{25}$$

$$.5\% = \frac{.5}{100} \text{ x } \frac{2}{2} = \frac{1}{200}$$

1) 5%

2) 40%

3) 75%

4) 2%

5) 14%

6) .8%

7) 100%

8) 225%

9) 90%

10) 1%

The next skill you will need to know is how to find a percent of a number. To find the percent of a number, you simply turn the percent into a decimal and multiply.

What is the sales tax on a $48 skateboard in a state with a tax rate of 6%?

| Step 1: Change percent to a decimal | .06 |
| Step 2: Multiply | .06 x 48 = 2.88 |

**The sales tax is $2.88**

Try the following problems.

1) A helmet was discounted 30%. If the regular price of the helmet is $80, what is the new price? Hint: You are looking for the new price, not the amount of discount.

2) It is customary to leave a 15% tip at most restaurants. What would be the recommended tip for a $65.00 meal?

3) If a bank pays 4% yearly interest on money in savings accounts, how much interest would you earn if you deposited $960 for a year?

4) Teachers at Einstein Elementary School are going to be given a 5.1% raise in their salary. If Algebra Woman is currently earning $36,000 in salary, what will her new salary be after she is given a raise?

5) Store A was offering a 40% discount on a $250 lawnmower. Store B was offering a 15% discount on the same lawnmower which they regularly sell for $175. Which store has the better deal? Make sure you explain why.

6) A report in a school newspaper said that 18% of the school's 568 students were home with the flu. How many students were home with the flu? (Round to the nearest student.)

7) Donna can buy a new riding mower at a store in Illinois or at a store in Iowa. Both stores are selling the mower for $1295, but Iowa's sales tax is 6% while Illinois's sales tax is 7%. How much money will Donna save if she buys the riding mower in Iowa?

8) Keith bought a group of stocks in 1999 for $22,500. Since that time, his stock has lost 42% of its value. What is Keith's stock worth now?

9) Luke is using a credit card that charges a 22.9% yearly interest. If he buys a computer for $1250, what will be his interest charge for the first year?

10) Jay decided to give Steve .5% of the $80 he found. How much money will Jay be giving to Steve?

The second type of percent problem you should know has to do with comparing. When you compare numbers, all you do is make a fraction.

Denzel's allowance is $5 and Brian's is $8. Compare Denzel's allowance to Brian's using percent.

$$\frac{5 \text{ (Denzel)}}{8 \text{ (Brian)}}$$

$$\frac{5}{8} = \frac{n}{100}$$

$$8n = 500$$

$$n = 62.5\%$$

Once I have the fraction, it is easy to change to a percent. I just learned how to do that a few pages ago.

**Denzel's allowance is 62.5% of Brian's allowance.**

Be careful when you are doing percent problems that compare. That problem asked you to compare Denzel's allowance to Brian's allowance. If the problem asked you to compare Brian's allowance to Denzel's, then the fraction would be reversed.

$$\frac{8 \text{ (Brian)}}{5 \text{ (Denzel)}}$$

$$\frac{8}{5} = \frac{n}{100}$$

$$5n = 800$$

$$n = 160\%$$

**Brian's allowance is 160% of Denzel's allowance.**

Try these percent problems that have to do with comparing.

1) Compare $2 to $16 using percent.

2) Compare a foot to a yard using percent.

3) Larry's yearly salary is $28,000. His sister Nancy earns a salary of $42,000. Compare Larry's salary to Nancy's salary using percent.

4) Compare a yard to a foot using percent.

5) Scott and Dan were arguing over the size of their bedrooms and how to compare them using percents.

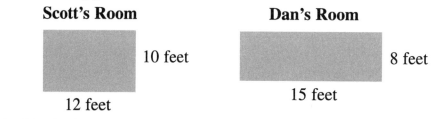

**Scott's Room**                    **Dan's Room**

10 feet                                        8 feet

12 feet                          15 feet

Fill in the blank: Dan's room is _____percent of Scott's room.

6) The top speed of a human is approximately 25 mph while a cheetah can travel at a speed of 70 mph. Compare the top speed of a human to a cheetah's top speed using percents. (Round to the nearest whole percent.)

7) The Madam Curie State Bank will only allow you to spend a certain percentage of your monthly income on a house payment. Your monthly income is $1800 and the most they will allow you to spend on a mortgage is $540 per month. What is the Madam Curie State Bank's highest percentage of income that they allow for a monthly house payment?

8) Compare a quart to a gallon using percent.

9) Compare a centimeter to a meter using percent.

10) Compare a meter to a kilometer using percent.

When a number gets larger or smaller, you can determine the percent of change by making a very simple fraction:

amount of increase or decrease
original

I'm not sure what you're talking about. Could you give me an example.

What if the price of gas went from $1.25 to $1.50, what was the percent of increase? Watch how I go through two steps to solve the problem.

| Step 1: Make fraction | $\dfrac{.25 \text{ (amount of increase)}}{1.25 \text{ (original price)}}$ |
|---|---|
| Step 2: Turn fraction into a percent | $\dfrac{.25}{1.25} = \dfrac{n}{100}$ |
| | $1.25n = 25$ |
| | $n = 20$ |

**The price of gas increased by 20%**

Try the following percent problems that have to do with an increase or a decrease.

1) Collin's allowance went from $8 to $10. What was the percent of increase?

2) The weight of one astronaut went from 180 pounds on the earth to only 30 pounds on the moon. What percent did his weight decrease?

3) After a long rain, the river went from a depth of 15 feet to a depth of 18 feet. What percent did the river level increase?

4) Calculators used to be very expensive when they were first invented. A calculator that can be purchased for $10 today, would have cost $300 thirty-five years ago. What is the percent of decrease in the price of calculators?

5) When people exercise, their heart rate can jump significantly. When Jacob is sitting, his heart beats at a rate of 50 beats per minute. When he runs, his heart rate jumps to 160 beats per minute. What is the percent of increase in Jacob's heartbeat when he runs?

6) Sharon was a softball pitcher who was very good at striking out batters. In one year she struck out 68 batters. The next year she struck out 92. What was the percent of increase in her strikeout total?

7) The original price for a snowboard was $125. Because they weren't selling well, they were discounted to $75. What percent discount is the store offering?

8) A painting was bought at a garage sale for $5. Two years later it sold for $50,000. What was the percent of increase of the painting?

9) On December 24th, a Christmas tree cost $30. The next day its price dropped to 25 cents. What is the percent of decrease?

10) A sprinter ran a 100-yard dash in 10 seconds. The next time he ran, his time was 9.9 seconds. What was the percent of decrease in his time?

Now you are ready to do some difficult percent and algebra problems. Let's start by looking at how Rachel was able to find out how much money her brother spent in the story at the beginning of the chapter. Rachel knew that 6% of some number was equal to $34.32. She remembered that to find a percent of a number, you need to change the percent to a decimal and then multiply.

**6% of some number = $34.32**

$$.06n = 34.32$$

$$\frac{.06n}{.06} = \frac{34.32}{.06}$$

$$n = \$572$$

**9% of some number = $23.22**

$$.09n = 23.22$$

$$\frac{.09n}{.09} = \frac{23.22}{.09}$$

$$n = \$258$$

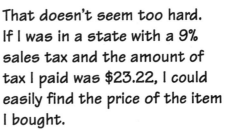

That doesn't seem too hard. If I was in a state with a 9% sales tax and the amount of tax I paid was $23.22, I could easily find the price of the item I bought.

Remember to think in the language of algebra. That will help you set up the right kind of equation.

Solve the following problems by changing them into the math language of algebra. The first one is done for you.

1) Holly put her saving into a bank that paid 4% annual interest. After a year, Holly had earned $21.12 interest. How much money did Holly start with?

**4% of some amount of money equals $21.12**

**.04n = 21.12**

$$\frac{.04n}{.04} = \frac{21.12}{.04}$$

**n = $528**

2) 15% of some number equals 123.75.

3) Ryan's weight is 42% of his father's weight. If Ryan weighs 73.5 pounds, how much does his father weigh?

4) A pair of socks cost 22% of what shoes cost. If the total price of the socks and shoes is $54.90, what is the cost of the socks? (Hint: Call the shoes *n* and the socks .22*n*)

5) The sales tax on a painting is $15.40. If the tax rate is 7%, what is the price of the painting?

I bought a computer for $593.60, including a 6% sales tax. How do I find the cost of the computer without sales tax?

The best way to solve this problem is to change the problem into the math language of algebra.

Cost of the computer      *n*

Sales tax      **.06*n***    **(Just like in the earlier problems)**

Computer plus tax      ***n* + .06*n* = $593.60**

$$1.06n = 593.60$$

$$\frac{1.06n}{1.06} = \frac{593.6}{1.06}$$

***n* = $560**

Solve the following problems by changing them into the math language of algebra. The first one is done for you.

1) A shirt cost $30.60 after a 15% discount. What is the regular price for the shirt?

Regular Price      *n*

Amount of discount      **.15*n***

Regular price minus the 15% discount      ***n* - .15*n* = 30.60**

**n - .15n is .85n**     **so:**

$$.85n = 30.60$$

$$\frac{.85n}{.85} = \frac{30.60}{.85}$$

***n* = 36**

2) A Christmas tree farm had a 95% off sale on all Christmas trees on December 26th. If the sale price was $1.46, what was the regular price of the trees?

3) After a year in the bank at 7% interest, Molly's money grew to $982.26. How much money did Molly put in the bank a year ago?

4) The total cost of a car, including a 5% tax, is $28,350. What is the cost of the car before tax?

5) Mike's new salary after a 22% raise is $34,770. What was his original salary?

I bought a bike in 1990 for $180. My brother said that the $180 price was a 125% increase over the price he paid in 1980. How can I find out what my brother paid?

This problem can be solved if you remember that the percent of increase is equal to the amount of increase divided by the original price. Let's turn this problem into the language of algebra.

## Language of Algebra

New price            **$180**

Original price       **$n$**

Amount of increase   **180 - $n$**   (Think about this carefully.)

Percent of increase  **125%**

$$\frac{\text{(amount of increase) } 180 - n}{\text{(original) } n} \quad \text{Make equation:} \quad \frac{180 - n}{n} = \frac{125}{100}$$

Cross multiply       **$125n = 18{,}000 - 100n$**

Solve
$$125n = 18{,}000 - 100n$$
$$+100n \qquad\qquad +100n$$

$$225n = 18{,}000$$

$$\frac{225n}{225} = \frac{18{,}000}{225}$$

$$n = \$80$$

Solve the following problems by changing them into the math language of algebra. The first one is done for you.

1) Ed's new allowance of $10.40 is a 30% increase over his previous allowance. What was his previous allowance?

Old allowance           $n$

New allowance         **$10.40**

Amount of increase     **$10.40 - $n**    (This is a little hard to understand.)

$$\frac{\textbf{amount of increase}}{\textbf{original}} = \textbf{percent of increase} \qquad \frac{10.40 - n}{n} = \frac{30}{100}$$

Cross-multiply:         $\mathbf{1040 - 100n = 30n}$

                            $\mathbf{+100n \;\; +100n}$

Solve:               $\mathbf{1040 = 130n}$

                   $\mathbf{n = 8}$

2) The area of a square was enlarged 125% to 144 square feet. What were the dimensions of the original square?

3) Monthly electric rates increased by 72% to $117.82. What were the old electric rates?

4) The area of a picture was enlarged 225% to 234 square inches. What was the area of the original picture?

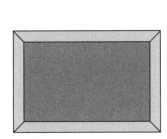
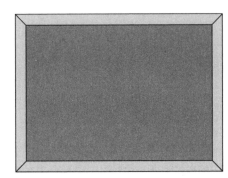

5) Over the last 30 years, the volume of a computer has dropped from 200 cubic feet to 1 cubic foot. What percent decrease is this?

## Percents and Algebra                                    Level 1

1) Pedro paid $11.10 tax when he bought a bike. The tax rate in Pedro's community is 6%. What was the cost of the bike without tax?

2) Nancy wanted to buy a chainsaw that usually sold for $245. The store was having a 15% off sale on Saturday for all items in the store. The store was also having a special chainsaw sale on Friday only when all chainsaws would be discounted $35. What day should Nancy buy the chainsaw and why?

3) Marissa earned $20.16 interest during the year she kept her college savings account at Hoover Bank. If Hoover Bank pays 3% annual interest, how much money was in Marissa's college savings account at the beginning of the year?

4) 17.6% of some number equals 164.032. What is that number?

5) Rick always wanted to have 82% of Ed's money. If Rick has $78.72, how much money should Ed have?

6) Sara's May electric bill is only 32% of her April bill. If her May bill is $45.44, what is the amount of her April bill?

7) Nathan weighs only 50% of his dad's weight. If their total weight is 243 pounds, how much does Nathan weigh?

8) In a weightlifting class, Tom found that he could lift 85% of the weight Brad could lift. If Tom can lift $161\frac{1}{2}$ pounds, how much can Brad lift?

9) Larry wouldn't let anyone know his new salary, but he gave this clue: I just received a $1650 raise, which was 15% of my old salary. What was Larry's new salary?

10) Jay was trying to find out how much money Janie spent at the hardware store. When he tried to look at the receipt, Janie grabbed it out of his hand and ripped it. All Jay had left in his hand was a part of the receipt that showed that Janie had paid $80.55 in tax. The community where Janie and Jay live charges a 9% sales tax. How much money did Janie spend at the hardware store?

## Percents and Algebra                    Level 2

1) A lawn mower cost $396.90 with tax included. If the tax rate is 5%, what is the cost of the lawn mower before tax was added?

2) After a 35% discount, a leather coat cost $180.70. What was the original price of the coat?

3) Brand B snowblower has a 7 horsepower engine that is being advertised as a 40% larger engine than Brand A. How many horsepower does Brand A have?

4) If a 5' 10" man is 350% of his length as a newborn baby, how many inches long was he when he was born?

5) The Iowa Room and the Mississippi Room are both square rooms. The area of the Iowa Room is $56\frac{1}{4}$% of the area of the Mississippi Room. If the Iowa Room is a 12' by 12' room, what is the area of the Mississippi Room?

6) Brianna wanted to buy a microscope that cost $35.43. She had $1181 that she planned to put in a bank to earn enough interest to buy the microscope. If she kept her money in the bank for a year, what interest rate must the bank pay so Brianna will earn exactly $35.43?

7) If the yearly interest charge for a $27,000 loan is $6183, what is the interest rate that is being paid?

8) How many correct answers must Diane get on a 138 question test if she wants a grade of 82%? (Round to the nearest whole number.)

9) The width of a rectangle is only 15% of its length. If the perimeter of the rectangle is 207 inches, what is its length?

10) The price of a saddle is 15% of the cost of a horse. If the total cost of the horse and the saddle is $1437.50, what is the cost of the saddle?

| Percents and Algebra | Einstein Level |

1) Mark charged a 5% tax on his first day working at a music store. The amount of money Mark collected, including tax, was $1958.25. Mark's boss was very upset because Mark was supposed to charge a 7% sales tax. Mark wanted to keep his job so he offered to pay the money he should have collected but didn't. How much money should Mark pay?

2) Dan bought a computer during a 45% off sale for $772.20, including an 8% sales tax. What was the original price of the computer before the sale and without tax?

3) Two workers were required to paint a bridge. They decided to split the bridge in half so each had his own area to paint. After one week, Andy was 85% done with his section while Todd was 45% done with his part. What percent of the bridge remains to be painted?

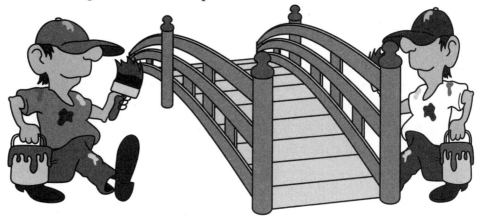

4) Dave is 80% of Donna's height, who is 93.75% of Sue's height. If Dave is 54 inches tall, how tall is Sue?

5) A quart of milk today cost $1.20. This is a 380% increase over the price that was charged in 1965. How much did milk sell for in 1965? (Hint: Remember that the percent of increase is equal to $\frac{\text{amount of increase}}{\text{original}}$. )

6) Rachel has taken 6 tests so far and has received scores of 83%, 92%, 79%, 98%, 89%, and 95%. What must Rachel receive on her 7th test to have an average score of 90%?

7) Angle B is 45% of angle A. Angle C is 35% of angle A. What is the measurement of angle A?

8) The width of a rectangle is 20% of its length. If the area of this rectangle is 720 square inches, what is its length?

9) The number of cows on a farm is 30% of the number of pigs, while the number of horses is 12.5% of the number of pigs. The number of sheep is 12.5% of the number of cows. If the total number of the four animals is 234, how many pigs are there on the farm?

10) Four friends needed to unload 4 trucks full of bricks. Because the trucks were the same size, they each were given one to unload. At the end of the day, Mark was 64% finished, Mike was 56% finished, Janelle was 80% finished and Debra was 72% done unloading her truck. What percent of the entire job remains to be completed?

When we are in the same room, do I breathe the same molecules after you have already breathed them?

Yes you do! As a matter of fact, each breath you take almost certainly contains molecules from the breath of every person who ever lived-----up to about 100 years ago. (Time is needed to mix the air molecules that people breathe with the rest of the air in the atmosphere.)

That means that every breath I take includes molecules that my hero Isaac Newton breathed!

# Exponents, Radicals and Scientific Notation

Stuart had a problem. His consequence for inappropriate talking in class was to write the number googol a hundred times on the blackboard after school. Now this punishment wouldn't be too bad except for the fact that the number googol has 100 zeros and Stuart had an important soccer game to play 15 minutes after school ended. His only hope was to see if Algebra Woman could give him advice on writing large numbers more quickly.

There is an easy way to write large numbers very quickly. You can do this by using exponents. Watch how I turn these numbers into exponent form.

$100 = 10 \times 10$   Which is $10^2$ in exponent form.

$1000 = 10 \times 10 \times 10 \longrightarrow 10^3$

$1,000,000 = 10 \times 10 \times 10 \times 10 \times 10 \times 10 \longrightarrow 10^6$

Stuart had the solution to his problem. He knew that a googol was equal to $10^{100}$ because it had one hundred zeros. After school he went up to the blackboard and wrote $10^{100}$ one hundred times and quickly left for his soccer game. The next day his teacher was not very pleased. While she was happy that Stuart was creative and learned about exponents, she felt he still didn't have enough of a consequence for his classroom behavior the previous day. The teacher decided that Stuart would still need to write a long list of numbers on the board, so she asked him to stay after school and write the distance from the earth to the sun 100 times. Because this distance was 93,000,000 miles, Stuart's teacher knew he couldn't turn it into just exponents.

Stuart was worried. This task, though easier than writing a googol 100 times, would certainly take more than 15 minutes. Stuart had another soccer game to go to, so he hoped Algebra Woman would be able to come up with some way to shorten this punishment.

There is a way to write large numbers very quickly, even when they don't come out even like a hundred or a thousand. Scientists use this method, so we will call this shortcut putting numbers into scientific notation. Look at the examples I've written. As you can see, 930 is exactly the same as 9.3 x 100 so we can write it as $9.3 \times 10^2$.

Example 1: **930 = 9.3 x 100 ⟶ $9.3 \times 10^2$**

Example 2: **93,000 = 9.3 x 10,000 ⟶ $9.3 \times 10^4$**

Example 3: **93,000,000 = ⟶ $9.3 \times 10^7$**

Stuart's teacher was not amused when she saw what Stuart had written on the blackboard. She had to give him credit though for being tenacious in coming up with ideas to try and lessen the amount of writing he did. She decided to give him one more assignment. A certain virus was found to be .00000023 meters wide. Stuart was asked to write this number on the blackboard 100 times.

Stuart again turned to Algebra Woman for help. He wondered if there was any shortcut when very small numbers are written.

I hope there is some different way to write these numbers. I really don't want to write .00000023 one hundred times.

Scientific notation can be used for very small numbers also. Look at the two examples I've given you. As you can see .0023 can be written as 2.3 x .001. .001 can also be written as $10^{-3}$. Don't worry if this is confusing. You will learn about negative exponents in this chapter.

$$.0023 = 2.3 \times .001 \longrightarrow 2.3 \times 10^{-3}$$

$$.00000023 = 2.3 \times .0000001 \longrightarrow 2.3 \times 10^{-7}$$

*When you are using scientific notation, there are a few things that you must remember. The most important rule is that the first number must be at least one and also less than ten. If we were changing 85,000 to scientific notation, we would not be able to write 85 x 1000. We would have to write 8.5 x 10,000.* **The first number must always be at least one and less than ten.**

When I changed .00000023 into scientific notation, I needed to have the first number 2.3. I couldn't have it .23 or 23 because those numbers don't follow Einstein's rule: The first number must always be at least one and less than ten.

## Exponents

Exponents are a very easy way of saving time and space. Instead of writing $5 \times 5 \times 5 \times 5 \times 5 \times 5$, You can write it as $5^6$. If you were given the problem 4x4, you could write it as $4^2$.

I wrote a report once about the age of the universe. I had to write about how some scientists think the universe is 10,000,000,000 years old. The report had the number 10 billion in it about 20 times. If I wanted some variety, could I have put the number in exponent form and called it $10^{10}$?

Scientists do that all the time. They deal with very large numbers that are used so little that even the scientists don't remember the names of the numbers. Some scientists estimate that there are $10^{87}$ atoms in the entire universe. Even I don't know the name of that number!

I know about millions, billions, and trillions, but after that I just say a kazillion. What are the real names of the numbers after trillions?

A Kazillion is not a real number. I've made a list for you of several large numbers. The last number is an interesting one. Googolplex is such a large number with so many zeros in it that there isn't enough ink in the world to write it out.

| | |
|---|---|
| Billion | 9 zeros |
| Trillion | 12 zeros |
| Quadrillion | 15 zeros |
| Quintillion | 18 zeros |
| Sextillion | 21 zeros |
| Septillion | 24 zeros |
| Octillion | 27 zeros |
| Nonillion | 30 zeros |
| Decillion | 33 zeros |
| Undecillion | 36 zeros |
| Duodecillion | 39 zeros |
| Tredecillion | 42 zeros |
| Quattuordecillion | 45 zeros |
| Quindecillion | 48 zeros |
| Sexdecillion | 51 zeros |
| Septendecillion | 54 zeros |
| Octodecillion | 57 zeros |
| Novemdecillion | 60 zeros |
| Vigintillion | 63 zeros |
| Googol | 100 zeros |
| Googolplex | a googol of zeros |

Try the following exponent problems.

1) Write 6 x 6 x 6 in exponent form.

2) What number is $2^5$?

3) Write one million in exponent form.

4) If $n = 8$, what is $n^3$?

5) $5^3 = ?$

6) Write 100,000 in exponent form.

7) What number is $1^7$? (Don't be fooled.)

8) What is the next number in the following sequence? 4, 16, 64, 256...

9) Which is larger $3^2$ or $2^3$?

10) What is the next number in the following sequence? 1, 4, 9, 16, 25...

## Negative Exponents

I've seen some very strange exponents in a science book. What does it mean when you see a number such as $10^{-2}$?

A lot of people think that numbers with negative exponents are negative numbers. They are not! $10^{-2}$ is just another way of writing $\frac{1}{10^2}$ or $\frac{1}{100}$. A negative exponent simply means that you put a 1 over the number. I know that sounds confusing, so look at these examples.

$$10^{-3} = \frac{1}{10^3} = \frac{1}{1000}$$

$$5^{-2} = \frac{1}{5^2} = \frac{1}{25}$$

$$10^{-7} = \frac{1}{10^7} = \frac{1}{10,000,000}$$

That's simple! I can't believe I was so scared of negative exponents. I can even turn negative exponents into decimals. Look at how easy it is.

$$10^{-2} = \frac{1}{100} = .01$$

$$10^{-3} = \frac{1}{1000} = .001$$

$$10^{-1} = \frac{1}{10} = .1$$

*Changing a negative exponent into a positive exponent is an easy process, especially if you know about reciprocals. $6^{-3}$ can be changed into a number with a positive exponent by taking the reciprocal of 6, which is $\frac{1}{6}$*

$$6^{-3} = \frac{1}{6^3} \text{ or } \frac{1}{216}$$

Try the following problems that deal with negative exponents.

1) Write $10^{-4}$ as a fraction.

2) Write $10^{-1}$ as a decimal.

3) Write .0001 using negative exponents.

4) Write $8^{-2}$ as a fraction.

5) Write $n^{-x}$ as a fraction with a positive exponent.

6) Which is larger $10^2$ or $10^{-4}$?

7) Write $\frac{1}{100}$ using negative exponents.

8) Write $\frac{1}{4}$ using negative exponents.

9) Write .0000001 using negative exponents.

10) Write $\frac{1}{25}$ using negative exponents.

Remember that negative exponents do not make the number negative. Many students get confused about this.

I know now that negative exponents don't make a number negative, but I found an example of a number with a negative exponent that just so happens to be negative. $(-5)^{-3} = \frac{1}{(-5)^3} = \frac{1}{-125}$

## Radicals

$$\sqrt{64} = ?$$

I see this kind of problem in my math book all the time. It looks complicated, so I was hoping you could show me what it means.

That symbol is called a radical sign. All it is asking is what number multiplied by itself equals 64? It is then pretty obvious that the answer is 8. Look at the examples I've given you below and see if you can understand how I got the answers.

$$\sqrt{81} = 9$$

$$\sqrt{144} = 12$$

$$\sqrt{10,000} = 100$$

What you are doing is called taking the square root of a number. The square root of 81 is 9. The square root of 144 is 12. The square root of 10,000 is 100.

*Not only can you have square roots of numbers, you can also have cube roots of numbers. Look at $\sqrt[3]{8}$. This is asking for the number, when multiplied by itself three times, is equal to 8. The answer of course is 2 because $2 \times 2 \times 2 = 8$. You can even have questions like $\sqrt[4]{625}$. This is asking for the number, when multiplied by itself four times, is equal to 625. After a little thinking, it is easy to see that $5 \times 5 \times 5 \times 5 = 625$.*

Try the following problems.

1) $\sqrt{100}$

2) $\sqrt{25}$

3) $\sqrt{1}$

4) $\sqrt[3]{27}$

5) $\sqrt{1,000,000}$

6) $\sqrt[4]{16}$

7) $\sqrt{169}$

8) $\sqrt[3]{1}$

9) $\sqrt[3]{1000}$

10) $\sqrt[n]{64} = 2$  What does $n$ equal?

11) The area of a square room is 225 square feet. What is the length of each side of the room?

12) Alonzo said that if you cube his age, you will end up with 3375. How old is Alonzo?

13) A cubic block has a volume of 27 cubic inches. What is the length of each side of the block?

14) A cube has a volume of 1 cubic inch. What is the length of each side of the cube?

15) The area of a square is $\frac{1}{4}$ square inches. What is the length of each side of the square?

# Scientific Notation: Large Numbers

Scientists use scientific notation as an easy way to write large numbers. Look at the examples I've given you. Remember the rule from earlier in the chapter: The first number must be at least one and less than ten.

Circumference of the earth is 25,000 miles.
**2.5 x 10⁴**

The distance to the moon is 250,000 miles.
**2.5 x 10⁵**

The volume of the earth is 259,880,000,000 cubic miles
**2.59880 x 10¹¹**

The mass of the earth is 5,980,000,000,000,000,000,000 metric tons **5.98 x 10²¹**

*When we changed 25,000 miles to scientific notation, we moved the decimal four places to the left to get the 2.5. That is the same as dividing by 10,000. We need to bring it back to the original large number again so we multiply by 10,000* ⟶ **2.5 x 10⁴**

Turn the following numbers into scientific notation.

1) The diameter of Jupiter is 88,770. Write this in scientific notation.

2) Pluto's diameter is 3600 miles. Write this in scientific notation.

3) Light travels 669,600,000 miles in an hour. Write this in scientific notation.

4) Sound travels 720 miles in an hour. Write this in scientific notation.

5) The sun has a diameter of 800,000 miles. Write this in scientific notation.

## Scientific Notation: Small Numbers

Scientists use scientific notation to make large numbers easier to write. They also use scientific notation to write very small numbers. Look at the examples I've given you. Remember the rule from earlier in the chapter: The first number must be at least one and less than ten.

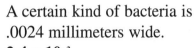

A certain kind of bacteria is .0024 millimeters wide. **$2.4 \times 10^{-3}$**

A nanometer is .000000001 of a meter. **$1.0 \times 10^{-9}$**

A cup is .0625 of a gallon. **$6.25 \times 10^{-2}$**

*When we changed .0024 millimeters to scientific notation, we moved the decimal three places to the right to get the 2.4. That is the same as multiplying by 1,000. We need to bring it back to the original small number again so we multiply by .001.* **$2.4 \times 10^{-3}$**

Turn the following numbers into scientific notation.

1) A quart is .946 liters. Write this in scientific notation.

2) A microsecond is .000001 of a second. Write this using scientific notation.

3) A one pound ball would weigh .06 pounds on Pluto. Write this in scientific notation.

4) A hydrogen atom has a diameter of $1 \times 10^{-8}$ cm. Write this as a normal decimal.

5) A hydrogen atom weighs .000,000,000,000,000,000,000,0017 grams. Write this in scientific notation.

## Exponents, Radicals and Scientific Notation                          Level 1

1) The sun is approximately 93,000,000 miles from earth. Write this distance in scientific notation.

2) A square room has an area of 10,000 square decimeters. What is the length of one side of the room?

3) If the length of one side of a cube is $n$, what is the volume of that cube?

4)  The diameter of the sun is approximately 800,000 miles. Write this in scientific notation.

5) If $n^3 = 64$, what is the value of $n$?

6) Write one million using exponents.

7) $\sqrt{121} =$

8) The most common wrong answer to $5^2$ is 10. Why do many students chose this wrong answer?

9) What is the 8th term in the following sequence?  3, 9, 27, 81, 243...............

10) Which is  heavier, a rock that weighs $1^1$ pounds or a rock that weighs $1^{1,000,000}$ pounds?

| Exponents, Radicals and Scientific Notation | Level 2 |
|---|---|

1) A cube has a volume of 4913 cubic inches. What is the length of one side?

2) $5^x = 625$   What is the value of x?

3) The area of a circle is found by using the formula *Area* $= \pi r^2$. What is the radius of a circle that has an area of 153.86 square inches?

4) Most viruses are so small that they can be seen only with an electron microscope. A typical virus might be $\frac{1}{10,000}$ of a millimeter in size. Express this size using negative exponents.

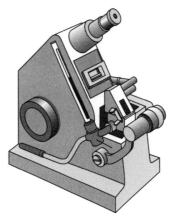

5) What is the square root of $\frac{1}{4}$?   $\sqrt{\frac{1}{4}}$

6) The thickness of a piece of paper is .004 inches. Write this in scientific notation.

7) $10^6 \times 10^5 = 10^{11}$   and   $5^7 \times 5^6 = 5^{13}$   What do you see in these problems that may allow you to come up with a rule for multiplying with exponents?

8) The earth has a diameter of 8000 miles and a circumference of 25,000 miles. Write these two numbers using scientific notation.

9) It has been estimated that 1000 tons of meteorites hit the surface of the earth each day. How many pounds of meteorites hit the earth in a year? Express your answer using scientific notation.

10) $\sqrt[4]{10,000}$

1) The speed of light is 186,000 miles per second and there are 31,536,000 seconds in a year. If you multiply these numbers to determine how far light travels in a year, most calculators will show an error message because they run out of space. Show how scientific notation allows you to quickly get the answer to this problem on a standard calculator.

2) The number of bacteria in a dish doubled every hour. At the 30th hour, the dish reached its capacity. At what hour was the dish half filled?

3) Using what you learned in problem number 1, find out how many miles there are across the Milky Way. (The Milky Way is 100,000 light years across.)

4) The number of grains of sand in a one cubic centimeter sample was $9.37 \times 10^3$. Using this information, predict how many grains of sand would be in a cubic meter of sand.

5) Because $4^2 = 2^4$, Eric decided to make a rule that $n^x = x^n$. Is Eric right? Why or why not?

6) Some scientists estimate that there are $10^{87}$ atoms in the entire universe. If this is true, how many atoms would there be in $\frac{1}{10}$ of the universe?

7) $5^{n-2} = 3125$  What is the value of $n$?

8) If the volume of a small cube of gold is $\frac{1}{64}$ cubic inches, what is the length of each side of the cube?

9) On August 1st, 2001, ten people were given gifts of kindness. The next day these ten people each gave the gift of kindness to ten other people. Then the following day these 100 people each gave a gift of kindness to ten different people. If this was carried forward, on what day in August would the gift of kindness reach all 6 billion people in the world?

10) $n^3 = 15.625$  What is $n$ equal to?

# Pythagorean Theorem

The firefighter was perplexed. Lined up against the wall were over 50 ladders of different lengths. The decision of what length of ladder to buy was a very important one because the ladder had to reach the top of the tallest building in his town. The firefighter knew that the tallest building in town was 72 feet tall and he also knew that when he placed a ladder against the top of the building, the bottom of the ladder was 30 feet from the building.

He knew the ladder he needed to buy had to be more than 72 feet long, but he didn't know how much longer. He drew a picture of the ladder leaning against a building and asked the clerk if she could help him decide how long a ladder he needed.

30 feet

72 feet tall

The firefighter was very lucky that day because the clerk who was working just happened to be someone who was very good at this type of problem. In addition to her job as a super hero, Algebra Woman worked part time in the local ladder store. She took one look at the drawing, took out a piece of paper and a calculator, and then told the firefighter that he needed a 78 foot ladder.

"How in the world did you figure that out?" said the firefighter.

"That kind of problem is easy if you know the Pythagorean Theorem," said Algebra Woman.

The firefighter was very excited about being able to use math to solve difficult problems. "Wow! If the Pythagorean Theorem can help figure out things like that, I'm going to learn about it today."

How was it possible to find out the length of the ladder the firefighter needed? Did you use a formula?

We use formulas for all kinds of things such as finding the areas and circumferences of circles. To find the length of the ladder, I used a very special formula called the Pythagorean Theorem. It helps us find the lengths of different sides of right triangles.

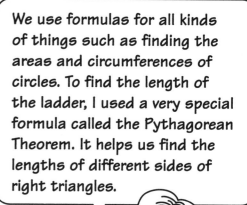

Because the ladder leaning against the building made a right triangle, I was able to find the length.

How do you use the Pythagorean Theorem? I really want to learn how to solve those kinds of problems.

Before you learn how to use the Pythagorean Theorem, you need to know the different parts of a right triangle.

acute angle

side a

hypotenuse (side c)

side b

acute angle

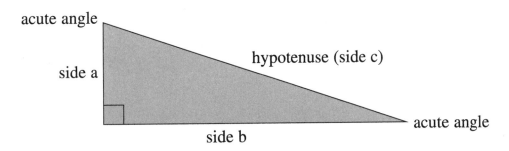

- *The shorter sides of right triangles are called the legs.*
- *The diagonal side, which is the longest, is called the hypotenuse or side c.*
- *The two angles that are under 90° are called the acute angles.*

The Pythagorean Theorem says that if you square the measurement of each leg of a right triangle and then add them together, that number will be equal to the square of the hypotenuse of the triangle.

$$a^2 + b^2 = c^2$$

Maybe it would help if we looked at a problem.

I am very, very confused.

What is the length of the hypotenuse of a right triangle whose legs are 3 feet and 4 feet?

We use the formula   $a^2 + b^2 = c^2$

Step 1:            $3^2 + 4^2 = c^2$

Step 2:            $9 + 16 = c^2$

Step 3:            $25 = c^2$

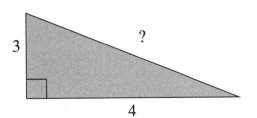

This tells us that some number multiplied by itself equals 25. That's easy!! If you multiply 5 by itself you get 25. The length of the hypotenuse is 5.

I think you are ready to try some on your own. Just remember the formula.

$a^2 + b^2 = c^2$

A triangle has a hypotenuse of 13 inches and side a is 5 inches. What is the length of side b?

We use
the formula        $a^2 + b^2 = c^2$

Step 1:        $5^2 + b^2 = 13^2$

Step 2:        $25 + b^2 = 169$

Step 3:        $b^2 = 144$

Step 4:        $b = 12$

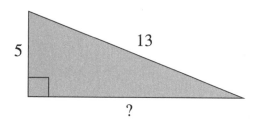

5        13

?

I really like the Pythagorean Theorem.

**Pythagorean Theorem**        Level 1

1) What is the perimeter of the right triangle shown below?

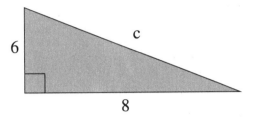

2) Find the length of the hypotenuse. (Round to the nearest tenth.)

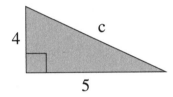

3) Kate needs to travel from point A to point B. How many feet shorter is it if she decides to take the shortcut through the grass instead of staying on the road?

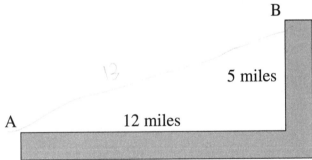

4) Isaac is fencing in a triangular garden. If fencing cost 89 cents per foot, what will it cost to buy fence for his garden?

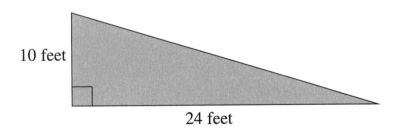

5) A 26-foot ladder is leaning against a building with the top of the ladder touching the exact top of the building. The bottom of the ladder is 10 feet from the building. How tall is the building?

6) What length of ladder will Warren need to buy if his house is 36 feet tall and the base of the ladder will rest 15 feet from his house? (He wants the ladder to reach to the top of his house.)

7) Is a triangle with sides 9', 40', and 41' a right triangle?

8) Tanya drove 15 miles directly north. She then turned and drove east for 20 miles. How far is Tanya from her starting point? (As the crow flies)

9) What is the longest straight line that can be drawn on a 8" by 10" piece of paper? (Round to the nearest tenth.)

10) What is the length of the hypotenuse of the right triangle shown below?

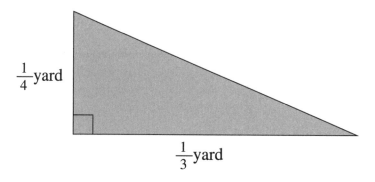

**Pythagorean Theorem**                                   Level 2

1) The triangle has a height of 3 feet. Find the value of *n*.

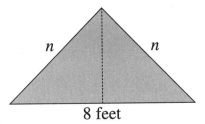

2) A 45 foot ladder is leaning against the top of a building. The bottom of the ladder is 27 feet from the building. How tall is the building?

3) What is the perimeter of this figure?

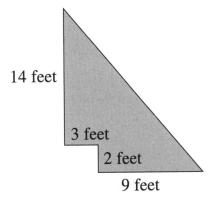

4) Josh needs to buy fencing for his garden. If fencing cost $8.42 per foot, what will be the cost of putting a fence around his garden?

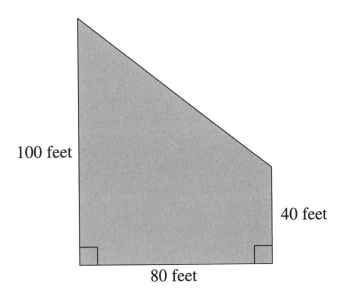

5) The circumference of the circle is 25.12 feet and line AC is the radius of the circle. What is the length of line AB?

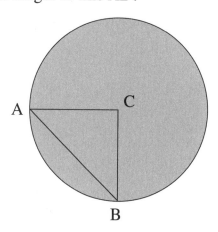

6) Is a triangle with measurements of 15', $\sqrt{31}$, and 16' a right triangle?

7) If Luke hikes 9 miles west and then 40 miles north, how far will he be from his starting point? (As the crow flies)

8) The top of a 16 foot ladder is placed against a tall building at a point 15 feet from the ground. How far is the base of the ladder from the building?

9) A giant redwood tree fell during a storm. The place where it cracked is 28 feet from the ground and the top of the tree is 96 feet from the base. How tall was the redwood tree before it fell?

10) What is the length of a diagonal in a square with an area of 72 square inches?

**Pythagorean Theorem**        Einstein Level

1) A 13 foot ladder is leaning against a 20 foot tall building with the base of the ladder 5 feet from the base of the building. Because the base of the ladder was placed on wet cement, the top of the ladder slipped down the wall until it caught on a nail 5 feet from the ground. How many feet from the building is the base of the ladder now?

2) Find the perimeter of the Isosceles trapezoid which has a height of 4 feet.

10 feet

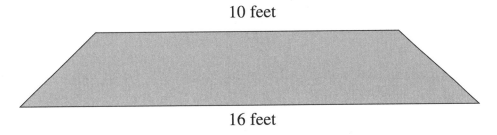

16 feet

3) A firefighter is climbing a ladder that is leaning against the top of a 144 foot building. The base of the ladder is 60 feet from the building. If the fire-fighter climbs at the rate of 9 feet per second, how long until he reaches the top of the building?

4) What is the length of the longest straight line that can be put inside a cube with 5" sides?

5) What is the area of the shaded figure shown below?

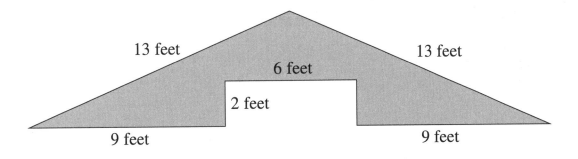

13 feet       13 feet

6 feet

2 feet

9 feet       9 feet

6) What is the area of a square that has a diagonal which is $\sqrt{32}$ inches?

7) If it takes 2 seconds for a throw to go from the catcher to 2nd base, what is the speed of the ball in feet per second? (The distance between each base is 90 feet.)

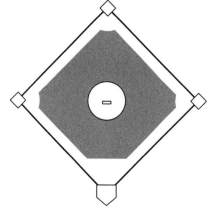

8) Two buildings are 12 feet apart. The first building is 16 feet high and the second building is 25 feet high. A ball is thrown from the top of the 25 foot building. It hits the top of the smaller building and then bounces at a 90° angle and goes directly to the base of the taller building. How far did the ball travel?   (Note: Drawing not to scale.)

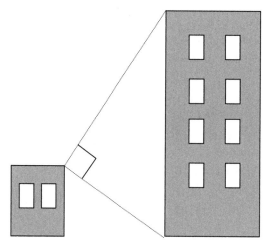

9) What is the area of the figure shown below?

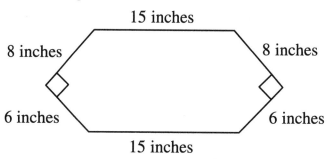

15 inches

8 inches          8 inches

6 inches          6 inches

15 inches

10) A rectangle with a perimeter of 98 feet has a length 31 feet longer than its width. What is the length of a diagonal inside the rectangle?

# Geometry and Algebra

The Einstein Elementary School Math Team was competing against four other teams in the final round of the National Math Bowl. The speed and accuracy with which they answered the final question would determine the winner of the contest. Each team was given a protractor and then a sheet of paper with 5 polygons. The team that determined the sum of the measure of the angles inside each polygon would be the winner.

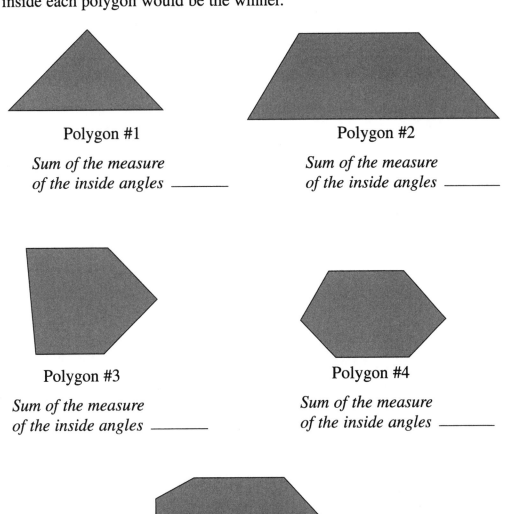

Polygon #1

*Sum of the measure of the inside angles* _____

Polygon #2

*Sum of the measure of the inside angles* _____

Polygon #3

*Sum of the measure of the inside angles* _____

Polygon #4

*Sum of the measure of the inside angles* _____

Polygon #5

*Sum of the measure of the inside angles* _____

The Einstein Math Team was somewhat nervous. They knew that it would take a long time to measure each angle of the polygons and it would also be difficult to measure them accurately. As they prepared to start measuring each angle, one of the team members had a brilliant idea.

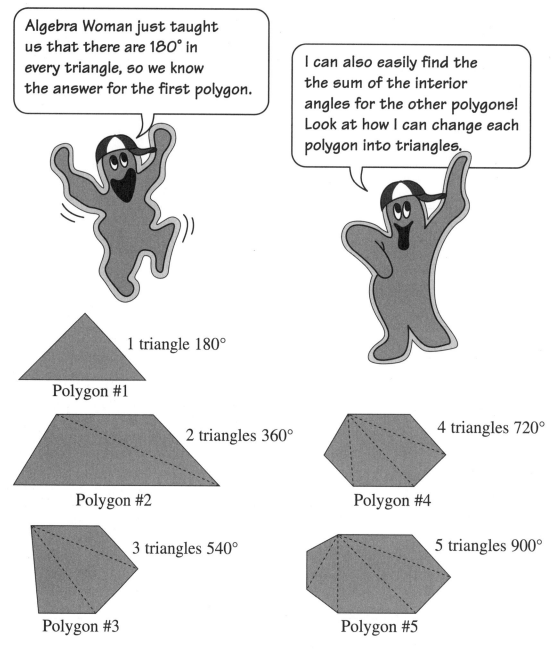

Algebra Woman just taught us that there are 180° in every triangle, so we know the answer for the first polygon.

I can also easily find the the sum of the interior angles for the other polygons! Look at how I can change each polygon into triangles.

1 triangle 180°
Polygon #1

2 triangles 360°
Polygon #2

4 triangles 720°
Polygon #4

3 triangles 540°
Polygon #3

5 triangles 900°
Polygon #5

While all the other teams busily measured each angle, the Einstein Math Team brought their answers to the front of the room. The other teams were not too worried because they didn't think it would be possible for a team to get the correct answer so soon. They were very surprised when it was announced that Einstein Elementary School had won the contest.

You can solve many geometry problems by using algebra. It really helps if you draw a picture. Look at this problem.

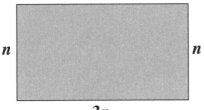

The length of a rectangle is three times its width. The perimeter of the rectangle is 56 inches. What are the dimensions of the rectangle?

Step 1: Language of algebra

Width ⟶ $n$
Length ⟶ $3n$

Step 2: Make equation

$n + n + 3n + 3n = 56$

Step 3: Solve the equation

$8n = 56$    $n = 7$

You can use the same procedure for finding unknown angles in triangles or other polygons. Look at how easy it is to solve this geometry problem by drawing a picture and using algebra.

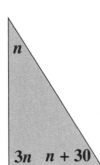

The first angle in a triangle is three times the second. The third angle is 30° larger than the second angle. Find the three angles.

Step 1: Language of algebra

Angle 1 ⟶ $3n$
Angle 2 ⟶ $n$
Angle 3 ⟶ $n + 30$

Step 2: Make equation

$3n + n + n + 30 = 180$

Step 3: Solve the equation

$5n + 30 = 180$    $n = 30$

Try the following geometry problems by drawing a picture and then using algebra to solve them.

1) The largest angle in a triangle is 10° larger than the smallest angle. The remaining angle is 5° larger than the smallest angle. Find the measurements of all three angles.

2) Sara has 484 feet of fence with which to make a square garden. What would be the measurement of each side of the square?

3) The length of a room is 9 feet more than three times its width. If the perimeter of the room is 106 feet, what are the dimensions of the room?

4) A four sided room has two angles that are the same size. One of the remaining angles is 10° larger than each of these two equivalent angles. The fourth angle is 30° less than each of the two equivalent angles. What are the four angle measurements in this room?

5) The largest angle in a triangle is three times the smallest angle while the remaining angle is two times the size of the smallest. Find the three angles.

Finding areas of circles and triangles is fairly easy when you use the proper formula. The problems that I find very difficult are the ones where you are given the area and then you are asked to find the base, height, or radius.

If you use algebra, it makes those backward type problems very easy. Watch how I do the next two problems.

The area of a circle is 254.34 square inches. What is the radius of the circle?

Step 1: Formula $A = \pi r^2$

Step 2: Equation $254.34 = 3.14 r^2$

Step 3: Solve $\dfrac{254.34}{3.14} = r^2$

$81 = r^2$

$r = 9$

The area of a triangle is 27 square inches. If the base of the triangle is 9 inches, what is the height?

Step 1: Formula $A = \dfrac{1}{2}bh$

Step 2: Equation $27 = \dfrac{1}{2} \cdot 9 \cdot h$

Step 3: Solve $27 = 4.5h$

$6 = h$ height is 6"

Use algebra to solve the following "backwards" problems.

1) If the circumference of a round table is 25.12 feet, what is the diameter of the table?

2) The area of a triangle with a 15 inch base is 315 square inches. What is the height of the triangle?

3) Travis spent $282.60 to carpet his circular room. If carpet cost $2.50 per square foot, what is the diameter of Travis's room?

4) The formula for finding the volume of a rectangular room is **Length x Width x Height**. If the volume of a room is 1152 cubic feet and the length and width of the room are both 12 feet; what is the height of the room?

5) The formula for the volume of a cylinder is $V = \pi r^2 h$. If the volume of a 15" tall cylinder is 3014.4 cubic inches, what is the radius of the cylinder?

**Geometry and Algebra**                                    Level 1

1) A square has an area that is equal to its perimeter. How long is each side of the square?

2) A rectangle with a perimeter of 58 inches is 7 inches longer than it is wide. How wide is the rectangle?

3) One of a right triangle's acute angles is 22° larger than the other acute angle. What are the measurements of each acute angle?

4) A square and an equilateral triangle have sides that are equal in length. If the perimeters of both figures are combined, the total would be 98 inches. How long is each side of the square?

5) Zach's school is directly across a circular lake from his home. When Zach walks to school, he travels 3.14 miles. If Zach decides to canoe to school, how far will he travel?

Zach's Home  School

6) Weston needs to know when he has traveled exactly five miles. Unfortunately, the odometer on Weston's bike was broken so he tied a ribbon to the front tire so he could count how many times the tire rotated. If the front tire has a 30" diameter, how many times will it rotate when Weston has traveled 5 miles? (Round to the nearest whole number.)

7) The largest angle in a triangle is 6 times the size of the smallest angle. The remaining angle is twice as large as the smallest angle. What is the size of the smallest angle?

8) The length of a rectangle is 4 times its width. If the area of the rectangle is 256 square inches, what is its width?

9) King Arthur is hiring a carpenter to build a round table for his knights. If there are 45 knights and each knight needs 4 feet of space, what must the diameter of the round table be? (Round to the nearest foot.)

10) One side of a triangle is 3 inches longer than the smallest side. If the smallest side of the triangle is 10 inches shorter than the longest side and the perimeter of the triangle is 46 inches, what is the length of the longest side?

**Geometry and Algebra**                                    **Level 2**

1) Find the measurement of ∠d by using the information given below.

- ∠ a is 10° larger than ∠ b
- ∠ c is equal to ∠ a
- ∠ e is 7° larger  than ∠ b
- ∠ d is half as big as ∠ b

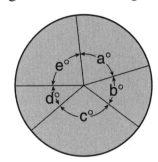

2) When an equilateral triangle is folded along one of its lines of symmetry, its height is 12.99" and its perimeter is 35.49".  What is the length of each side of the equilateral triangle?

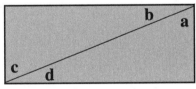

3) In the rectangle shown below, angle a is 15° more than angle b. What is the measurement of angle d?

4) Parallelogram ABCD has obtuse angles that are twice as big as the acute angles. What is the measurement of each acute angle?

5) A school made a circular graph to show how its money is spent. If the diameter of the circle is 10 inches, what is the area of the supplies part of the graph?

Books 20%

Other 30%

Supplies 15%

Teacher's salaries 35%

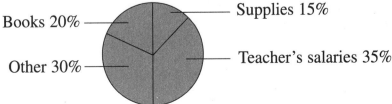

6) The smallest angle in a quadrilateral is 30° less than the next largest angle which is 30° less than the next largest angle which is 30° less than the largest angle. What is the measurement of the smallest angle?

7) A triangle's base and height are the same measurement. The area of the triangle is 288 square feet. What is the height of the triangle?

8) What is the value of x?

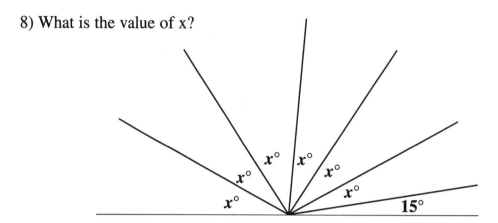

9) The area of the room shown below is 320 square feet. What is the width of the room?

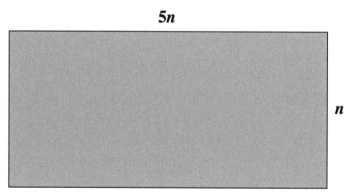

10) The three angles inside a triangle are in a ratio of 1:7:10. What is the measurement of the largest angle?

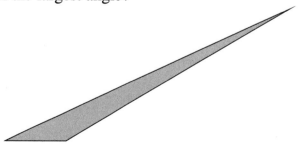

## Geometry and Algebra     Einstein Level

1) When a rectangle, whose length is 15" more than its width, is folded along one of its lines of symmetry, its perimeter is 54 inches. What is the length of the rectangle?

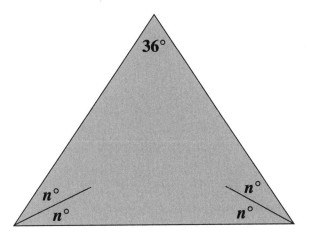

2) Jordan has a photograph whose width is 3 inches shorter than its length. The perimeter of the photograph is 22 inches. Jordan went to a photo shop to have the length and the width of the photo tripled. What is the length of the enlarged photograph?

3) Find the value of *n* in the triangle below.

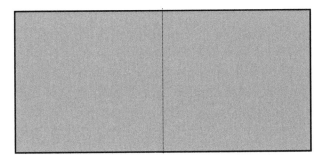

4) Each side of the square is *n* inches in length. Write an expression showing the area of the shaded part of the figure. Remember, the area of a circle is found by using the formula $A = \pi r^2$.

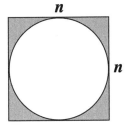

5) Angle a is equal to angle b and angle c is three times the size of angle a. What is the measurement of angle d?

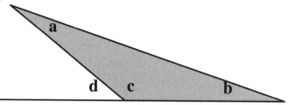

6) Eratosthenes was a Greek mathematician who used math in a clever way to not only prove the earth was round but also find its circumference. Eratosthenes knew that when the sun was directly overhead in Alexandria, it was $7\frac{1}{2}$ degrees off of center in Syene; a city which was 500 miles away. How did Eratosthenes find the circumference of the earth with this information?

7) What is the area of the shaded triangle if the circumference of the circle is 56.52 square inches?

8) Nana had enough batter to make eight 10" diameter pancakes. She had 32 grandchildren to feed that morning so she decided to use algebra to find out what diameter pancakes she should pour to allow each one of her grandchildren to have a whole pancake. What diameter pancakes should Nana make?

9) The amount of light a telescope receives depends on the area of the mirror. The same is true for the human eye. A telescope mirror has a diameter of 200 inches and the pupil of Eric's eye has a diameter of $n$ inches. This telescope receives a million times as much light as Eric's eye. What is the diameter of Eric's eye?

10) A dog is tied up in the center of a lawn. The dog has killed the grass everywhere it can reach. The seed Selena bought covers 235.5 square feet per packet and Selena used exactly 12 packets to reseed her lawn. How long is the chain on Selena's dog?

# Algebra and Levers

It happened so quickly that the children at Einstein Elementary School had very little time to react. A large boulder came crashing down from the hill above their school and rolled through the playground. It was fortunate that the path the boulder took was far away from where the children were playing and when it came to a stop, several children ran over to see the strange sight.

As they gathered around the boulder, they heard a faint sound coming from underneath the rock. After listening carefully, it became apparent that the noise was from one of the neighborhood dogs that had somehow got trapped beneath the boulder. The dog didn't sound hurt, so the children decided it probably crawled in a large gopher hole when it tried to escape from the approaching boulder.

The children tried to push the rock, but because it weighed close to 2000 pounds, they were unsuccessful. They were starting to think that they would never get the dog out when they saw Algebra Woman approach them.

"Can you use your super powers to move the boulder?" they asked.

Algebra Woman was flattered, but she had to tell the group of children that her super powers had nothing to do with being strong. "I do not have that kind of power," she told the group. "I use my brain to accomplish great feats."

Algebra Woman disappeared behind the school and returned with a small rock and a 34-foot long metal bar. She placed the 34-foot long bar under the boulder and then placed the small rock under the bar. Algebra Woman then pulled down on the end of the bar and the boulder magically started to roll.

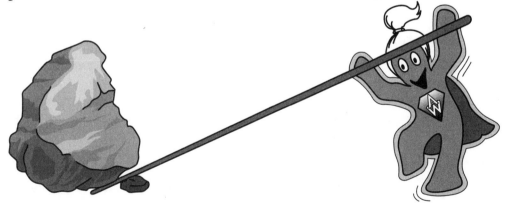

The children were happy to see the dog peek its head out of the ground when the boulder moved. After the dog ran away, they all crowded around Algebra Woman so that they could find out how she was able to move the rock all by herself.

"When you learn about algebra and levers, you will have information that will allow you to do things that seem like magic."

*Weight A  x  Distance from fulcrum = Weight B x Distance from fulcrum*

This formula is a very simple formula. Watch how I use the formula and a chart to solve the following problem.

A 50-pound child is playing on a 10-foot see-saw with her mother. Where should the mother sit to make the see-saw balanced? (The mother weighs 100 pounds.)

Make a box chart and put in everything you know. Because you *do not know* where the mother needs to sit, write an *n* in that box.

| Mother's Weight x Distance from Fulcrum | | | Child's Weight x Distance from Fulcrum | |
|---|---|---|---|---|
| 100 | *n* | = | 50 | 5 |

100n = 250

n = 2.5 feet

**The mother needs to sit 2.5 feet from the fulcrum**

Try this slightly harder problem.

There is a 10-foot board with the fulcrum sitting 4 feet from one end. Sitting on that end is a 75 pound child. A block is resting on the other end of the board 3 feet from the fulcrum. The weight of the block is causing the board to be perfectly balanced. How much does the block weigh?

This problem is pretty easy if I use the formula and a chart. I'll first put in all the information I know and then put an *n* in the box that I don't know.

| Weight<br>x<br>Distance from Fulcrum | | | Weight<br>x<br>Distance from Fulcrum | |
|:---:|:---:|:---:|:---:|:---:|
| *n* | 3 | = | 75 | 4 |

$$3n = 300$$
$$n = 100$$

**The block weighs 100 pounds**

You can even use a similar formula with complicated problems that have two people on each side of a board. Look how easy this problem is to solve even though it sounds complicated.

Two students weighing 150 and 100 pounds are standing on opposite ends of a 16 foot board that has a fulcrum in the middle. A 120 pound child is sitting 4 feet away from the fulcrum on the same side as the 100 pound child. An 80 pound child wants to sit on the same side as the 150 pound child. Where on the board must he sit so it will be perfectly balanced?

Formula:    Weight 1  x  Distance          Weight 3  x  Distance
                          +                =                +
             Weight 2  x  Distance          Weight 4  x  Distance

**150 x 8  +  80 x *n***                    **120 x 4  +  100 x 8**

Equation:    $1200 + 80n = 480 + 800$
$$80n = 80$$
$$n = 1 \text{ foot}$$

| Algebra and Levers | Level 1 |

Note: Ignore weight of lever when solving problems.

1) Venus, who weighs 50 pounds, is going to play on a 20 foot see-saw with her 40 pound sister Serena. If the fulcrum is exactly in the center of the see-saw and Serena will be sitting at the very end of one side, where should Venus sit to balance the see-saw?

2) A 60-pound child is sitting on the end of a 12-foot board, 4 feet away from the fulcrum. How far away from the fulcrum should his 75-pound friend sit to make the board balanced?

3) Jared, who weighs 84 pounds, is sitting on the end of a 14-foot see-saw 4 feet from the fulcrum. There is a box 7 feet from the fulcrum where Jared's friend will sit. How much should the friend weigh so that the see-saw is balanced? (The box weighs 6 pounds.)

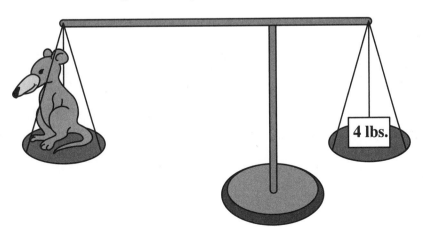

4) Sam, who weighs 48 pounds, is on the end of a 16 foot board that has a fulcrum in the middle. His friend Jordan, who weighs 72 pounds, wants to sit on the other side of the board. Where should he sit so the board is balanced?

5) Kyle has a scale as shown below. The side with the 4 pound weight is 6 inches from the fulcrum while the side with his pet rat is 18 inches from the fulcrum. Because the scale is perfectly balanced, Kyle can tell the weight of his rat. What is the weight of his pet rat?

6) Eric is sitting on the far right end of an 18 foot board which has a fulcrum in the middle. Mike is sitting 6 feet from the fulcrum on the left side of the board. If Eric weighs 80 pounds and Mike weighs 115 pounds, what side of the board will move down?

7) Fritz couldn't find someone to play on the see-saw with so he tied his 110 pound weight set to the end of the 16 foot see-saw. If the fulcrum was exactly in the center at the 8 foot mark and Fritz weighed 120 pounds, how far from the fulcrum should Fritz sit so the see-saw would be perfectly balanced?

8) A 2000 pound weight is sitting 3 feet from the fulcrum on one end of a lever. If the length of the lever is 15 feet, how much weight must be applied to the other end to lift the 2000 pound weight?

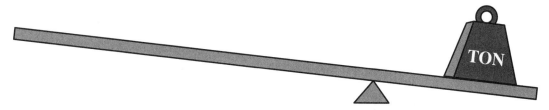

9) Two girls place a 20-foot board on a rock to make a teeter-totter. If the 50-pound girl sits all the way on the end of one side, how far from the fulcrum would her 80-pound friend have to sit in order to make the teeter-totter balanced?

10) Is it possible for a small child to lift 200,000 pounds by using a lever? Explain your answer.

1) A 50-pound child is playing on a 12-foot see-saw with her 100 pound mother. Where should they place the fulcrum to be in perfect balance if they each sit on the ends of the see-saw?

2) Kirsten weighed 60 pounds and stood on one end of a 16 foot board which had a fulcrum exactly in the center. Claire, who weighed 80 pounds, wanted to sit on the other side of the board so the two would be perfectly balanced. How far from the fulcrum should Claire sit?

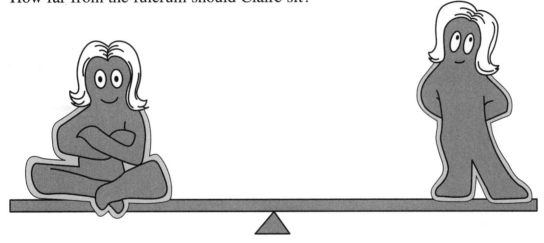

3) Anna, who weighs 50 pounds, is sitting on the end of a 10-foot board with a fulcrum placed 4 feet from where she is sitting. Anna wants to ask a friend to use the see-saw with her. What should the weight of the friend be if the friend will be sitting on the far end of the board?

4) Mark, who weighs 80 pounds, sits on the end of a 16 foot board. If the center of the board is resting on a rock, where should Mark's 120 pound friend sit so they will be balanced?

5) Susan wants to see how much her cat weighs, but all she has available is a 12-foot board, a fulcrum, and a 60 pound weight. She put the weight two feet from the fulcrum and kept moving her cat further and further out on the board until the board balanced perfectly. When the cat was 10 feet from the fulcrum, the board balanced perfectly. How much does her cat weigh?

6) A rancher is trying to lift up one side of a stump by using a bar as a lever. If it will take 1000 pounds of lift to raise that part of the stump, how much downward force at the end of the bar must he use to lift up the end of the stump? The bar is 17 feet long and the fulcrum is placed one foot from the end of the bar.

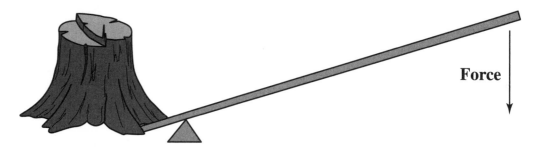

7) A tire from a 4000 pound car is resting on someone's foot. The amount of weight resting on the foot is 1250 pounds. If rescuers place a 13 foot bar under the tire with a fulcrum 6 inches from the end, how much downward force do they need to apply to the other end of the bar to raise the car off the victim's foot?

8) A 100 foot long board has a fulcrum placed exactly in the center. If a 50 gram weight is placed at the end of one side, where would you place a one kilogram weight to balance the board?

9) A car with its engine running is perfectly balanced on a fulcrum. After an hour, without anyone touching the car, it tips to one side. Which side would it tip to and why?

10) A 72 pound 4 ounce girl is sitting at the end of a 12 foot see-saw. How far from the fulcrum should her 120 pound 6 ounce mother sit to balance the see-saw? (The fulcrum is exactly in the center.) Round to the nearest tenth of a foot.

**Algebra and Levers**                                          **Einstein Level**

1) Kate is trying to remove a rock from her yard. She placed a 10 foot metal bar under the rock and she put a cylinder under the metal bar to use as a fulcrum. If the cylinder is 2 feet from the edge of the bar and the rock weighs 500 pounds, how much force will Kate need to use on the other end of the bar to lift the rock?

2) A 200 pound block is sitting on the end of a 40 foot board, 12 feet from the fulcrum. A rock is keeping the board from hitting the ground. Eric, who weighs 90 pounds, starts walking toward the other end of the board. How far from the fulcrum will Eric be when his weight causes the board to fall on the apple sitting under the end of the board?

3) Two students weighing 150 and 100 pounds are standing on opposite ends of a 16 foot board that has a fulcrum in the middle. A 120 pound child is standing 4 feet from the fulcrum on the same side of the board as the 100 pound child. A fourth child, who weighs 80 pounds, joins the group and wants to stand on the same side as the 150 pound child. How far from the fulcrum should she stand to balance the board?

**Hint:** When you are dealing with more than one weight on each side of a board, use the following formula:

(Weight 1  x  Distance)                  (Weight 3  x  Distance)
            +                      =                  +
(Weight 2  x  Distance)                  (Weight 4  x  Distance)

4) A hundred pound weight and a 150 pound weight are sitting on opposite ends of a 10 foot board that has a fulcrum placed in the middle. An 80 pound weight is going to be added so that the board balances perfectly. Where should the 80 pound weight be placed?

5) A 40 foot metal bar is being used to try to lift a 500 pound rock. Another rock was placed 2 feet from the end of the metal bar to serve as a fulcrum. How much force (weight) should be applied to the end of the bar in order to lift the rock?

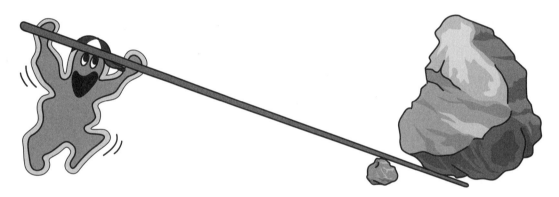

6) How much downward force will it take to lift the 2000 pound weight? The rope is attached to the ceiling of a room.

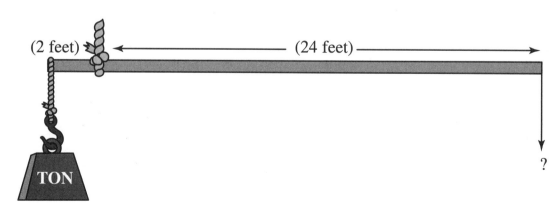

7) Kristin was unable to loosen a nut with the wrench she had. Explain what she could do to apply more force to the nut with the same wrench shown below. If she decided to buy a different wrench, explain what characteristics it should have to allow her to provide more force. (She will not be buying a power wrench.)

8) Proper use of a screwdriver allows an individual to apply a large amount of force. Screwdrivers can even be used to pry nails out of boards. A 150-pound person places the tip of a 12 inch screwdriver under the head of a nail and places a fulcrum one inch from the tip of the screwdriver. How much upward force will she be able to apply to the nail if she puts her entire weight on the far end of the screwdriver?

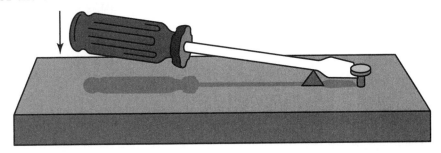

9) Sara was unable to move a 500 pound rock that was partially buried in her garden. When she used a shovel though, she was able to lift one end of the rock. Explain how this could happen. When she places the shovel into the ground and lifts the rock, what is being used as the fulcrum?

10) A diving board should be very strong because of the forces it must carry. If you had a 10-foot diving board with the fulcrum 1.5 feet from the end, how much upward force is there at point A if a 200-pound man is standing at the far end of the board?

**Point A**

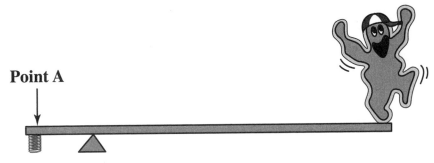

I know water evaporates, but someone told me that iron also evaporates. That just doesn't seem possible.

Believe it or not, iron does "evaporate". Before you start worrying about cars and other things disappearing, you must know that the tendency of water to evaporate is 500,000,000,000,000,000,000,000,000 000,000,000,000,000,000,000,000,000, 000,000,000 times higher than iron.

I guess that means that an occasional iron atom will break off from a piece of iron, but not enough for anyone to notice.

# Algebra and Money

Just as the Amoeba family sat down for dinner, it happened again. The phone rang with another offer for a great deal on long-distance service. This was the fifth call they took that month and being more polite than they probably should have been, they listened carefully to the offer and wrote it down with all the previous offers they received.

| | |
|---|---|
| Offer A: | $5 per month plus $.08 per minute |
| Offer B: | No monthly fee and $.10 per minute |
| Offer C: | $45 per month and all calls free |
| Offer D: | $10 per month plus $.05 per minute |
| Offer E: | $12 per month plus $.04 per minute |

The Amoeba Family was very confused about two things. One, how could they decide what was the best deal among all these offers? Two, how did the sales people know just when they were sitting down for dinner?

They decided that they would probably never find out the answer to their second question, but they knew Algebra Woman could probably help them find the best long-distance plan.

Study the chapter on money and algebra and you will be able to determine the best long-distance plan for you.

Many businesses use algebra when they are deciding how much to charge a customer. Look at the equation in this problem and notice how easy it is to figure out what to charge someone who rents a car.

The Mavis Car Company charges $15 per day plus $.18 a mile when they rent cars. What is the charge for a one day rental that is driven 93 miles?

Charge = **$15 + (93 x $.18)**

**$15 + $16.74**

Charge = **$31.74**

I see how easy it is. The equation to determine any charge for a car rental at this company would be: Price = 15d + .18m. d would stand for the number of days the car was rented and m would stand for the miles driven. Watch how fast I can do this problem using the equation.

Jonathan rented a car for 6 days and drove it 692 miles. What would he end up paying the Mavis Car Rental Company?

Equation: **Charge = 15d + .18m**

**Charge = (15 x 6) + (.18 x 692)**

**Charge = 90 + 124.56**

**Jonathan paid $214.56**

Some businesses have equations to determine how much profit they will make. Belinda owns a hair salon. She has to rent the building, heat it, pay electricity and pay many other expenses. She came up with an equation that shows her how much profit she will make each day. The *n* stands for how many customers she has each day.

**Profit = 18*n* - 72**

Its pretty easy to see that if she has one customer each day she will lose money. I wonder how many customers she needs to break even each day? I'll call her profit 0 and then solve the equation. I call the profit 0 because I am trying to find out how many customers would leave her with no profit and no loss.

**Profit = 18*n* - 72**

**0 = 18*n* - 72**

**72 = 18*n***

**n = 4**

**If Belinda had 4 customers each day, she wouldn't lose money and she wouldn't make any money. She would have zero profit.**

Look at how much money Belinda would make if she had 25 customers in a day.

**Profit = 18n - 72**

**Profit = (18 x 25) - 72**

**Profit = $378**

Sometimes phone companies confuse me with their offers and charges. The Bugyou Phone Company charges $5 per month plus $.07 per minute while the Annoyyou Phone Company charges $25 per month and $.02 per minute. I can't decide what is the better deal.

As you know, it all depends on how many minutes you talk long-distance each month. If you talk a lot, the Annoyyou Company would be the best deal. If you make an expression for the cost charged by each company, watch how easy it is to find out what is the best deal. I am going to call the number of long-distance minutes *m*.

**Bugyou Company---------5 + .07***m*

**Annoyyou company-----25 + .02***m*

Now I am going to find out how many long-distance minutes would make both plans equal. I can do this by making the first expression equal to the second expression.

**Bugyou Company    Annoyyou Company**

$$5 + .07m = 25 + .02m$$

$$.05m = 20$$

$$m = 400 \text{ minutes}$$

So if I talk more than 400 minutes, my choice would be the Annoyyou Company. Algebra sure made that easy!!

Try the following problems:

1) A rental company charges $20 per day for a garden tiller plus an additional $.20 for each minute the tiller is used. What would be the equation for determining the cost of renting the garden tiller? (Let d stand for the number of days and m stand for the number of minutes the tiller is used.)

2) If Ed rented the tiller for 7 days and used it for 13.5 hours, what would the charge be?

3) Bank A charges $5 per month for a checking account plus $.20 for each check written. Bank B charges a $20 monthly fee for a checking account, but has no charge for writing checks. How many checks must you write each month to make Bank B the better choice?

Look at this problem. I could solve it using guess and check, but it would be very time-consuming. Algebra allows me to find the answer very quickly.

Seth has a pile of nickels, dimes and quarters. He has twice as many dimes as nickels and five times as many quarters as nickels. If the pile's value is $16.50, how many nickels does Seth have?

The first thing I want to do is change the problem into the language of algebra. Because I have fewer nickels than dimes or quarters, I will call the number of nickels $n$.

**Number of nickels-------------$n$**

**Number of dimes-------------$2n$**

**Number of quarters----------$5n$**

You've changed the number of coins into the language of algebra. Now I can see that we need to find the value of each kind of coin.

**Value of nickels----------------5 x $n$ ⟶ $5n$**

**Value of dimes-----------------10 x $2n$ ⟶ $20n$**

**Value of quarters------------25 x $5n$ ⟶ $125n$**

*It is easy to find the value of any number of nickels, just multiply by 5. It is also easy to find the value of any number of dimes by multiplying by 10. It is also easy to find the value of any number of quarters by multiplying by 25.*

You can now set up your equation. The value of the coins must add up to $16.50. Because we are talking about cents in our values, we will change the $16.50 to 1650 cents. This is a very important point. When you are dealing with coins, always change the dollar amount to cents.

| nickels | | dimes | | quarters |
| --- | --- | --- | --- | --- |
| 5n | + | 20n | + | 125n = 1650 |

$$150n = 1650$$

$$n = 11$$

**Seth has 11 nickels**

I want to try another problem. This time I'll make a chart so it is less confusing.

Jacob has twice as many nickels as quarters and nine times as many dimes as quarters. If the value of the coins is $11.25, how many dimes does Jacob have?

## *Language of Algebra chart*

| | Number of coins | Value of the coins |
| --- | --- | --- |
| Nickels | 2n | 5 x 2n = 10n |
| Dimes | 9n | 10 x 9n = 90n |
| Quarters | n | 25 x n = 25n |

Equation: **10n + 90n + 25n = 1125**

$$125n = 1125$$

$n = 9$  Jacob has 9 quarters so he must have 81 dimes

There is a kind of problem that is very difficult for me. Could you show me how to do this type of money problem with the language of algebra?

Laurie has a total of 20 coins. If she has only nickels and quarters and the value of the coins is $2.60, how many quarters does she have?

The first thing you need to do is figure out how to write the number of nickels and quarters in the language of algebra. If there are 20 coins, and I call the number of quarters *n*, then the number of nickels must be 20-n.

### Language of Algebra chart

|          | Number of coins | Value of the coins        |
|----------|-----------------|---------------------------|
| Nickels  | 20 − n          | 5 x (20 − n) = 100 − 5n   |
| Quarters | n               | 25n                       |

Equation: $100 - 5n + 25n = 260$

$100 + 20n = 260$

$20n = 160$

$n = 8$  Laurie has 8 quarters

Try the following problems:

1) Juan had dimes and quarters in his pocket. He had three times as many dimes as quarters and the value of the coins was $4.95. How many quarters did Juan have?

2) Diane had nickels, dimes and quarters in her piggy bank. She had 7 times as many nickels as quarters and three times as many dimes as quarters. If the value of the pile is $3.60, how many nickels does Diane have?

3) Pedro found 28 coins that had a value of $1.80. If the coins consisted of only nickels and quarters, how many quarters did Pedro find?

## Algebra and Money                                    Level 1

1) The charge to rent a car is $29.95 per day plus $.08 per mile. Write an expression that shows the cost of renting a car for *d* days and *m* miles.

2) What would be the language of algebra for the value of *n* quarters?

3) A phone company charges $35 per month for a long-distance plan plus a charge of $.03 per minute. Write an expression to show the monthly bill for someone who talks *n* minutes.

4) A bag has only nickels and pennies. If there are a total of 25 coins and you decide to call the number of nickels *n*, what is the language of algebra for the number of pennies?

5) A pile of nickels and dimes is worth $4.25. If there are twice as many dimes as nickels, how many nickels are there?

6) In problem #3, what would be the monthly charge for someone who talked 150 minutes?

7) Jamie had a drawer of money that was worth $375. The money consisted of only $5 and $10 bills. If the number of $10 bills was twice the number of $5 bills, how many $5 bills are there?

8) What is the language of algebra for the value of *n* 5-dollar bills expressed in cents?

9) A child is holding nickels, dimes and quarters in his hand that have a value of $4.95. There are the same number of dimes and quarters, but there are twice as many nickels as dimes. How many nickels are there?

10) Selena's new job pays $15 per day plus $12.50 per hour. Write an expression to show how much money Selena will earn if she works *d* days and *n* hours.

Money earned =

## Algebra and Money                                               Level 2

1) If the number of quarters is **n**, the value of the quarters is **25n**. If the number of quarters is **20 - n**, use the language of algebra to show the value of **20 - n** quarters?

2) Sara is selling soap at a one-day craft show. She has added up all her expenses for the show and the materials to make the soap and determined that her profit equation is as follows:  ***Profit = 1.75n - 162.75 (n = bars sold)*** How many bars of soap must Sara sell to break even at the craft show? (Breaking even means no profit but also not losing money.)

3) In the previous problem, Sara has decided that she will return to next year's craft show if she makes at least a $350 profit at this year's show. How many bars of soap would Sara need to sell to earn enough profit to return next year?

4) Dave had 25 coins that consisted of nickels and quarters. If the value of the coins was $3.45, how many nickels did Dave have?

5) A salesperson sold three times the number of refrigerators as washing machines. The refrigerators sold for $800 each and the washing machines sold for $300 each. If the amount of money collected for these sales was $45,900, how many refrigerators were sold?

6) A hair salon found that it could determine each day's profit by using the following formula:
**Daily Profit = $-.025n^2 + 12n - 140$** (**n** stands for the number of daily customers.)

How much profit or loss would this salon have if they had 10 customers in one day?

7) Jill found a box of pennies, nickels, dimes and quarters that was worth $7.05. The number of nickels was twice the number of pennies while the number of dimes was three times the number of pennies. If the number of quarters was twice the number of nickels, how many quarters are there in the pile of coins?

8) A small post office sold twice as many 20-cent stamps as 34-cent stamps. The number of 5-cent stamps sold was six more than the number of 34-cent stamps. If the value of the stamps sold was $5.83, how many 5-cent stamps were sold?

9) A small rock band made 2000 copies of a CD that contained their most popular songs. If the CDs cost $7500 to make and they sell the CDs for $12 each, what is the equation that shows how much profit or loss they will have if *n* people buy their CD? *Profit =*

10) There is a collection of nickels, dimes and quarters. There are 5 more dimes than nickels and 5 more quarters than dimes. If the value of the collection is $22.60, how many nickels are there?

1) Phone Company A offers long-distance calling for 3 cents per minute but charges an $18 monthly fee in addition to the per minute charge. Phone Company B offers long-distance service for 9 cents per minute with no monthly charge. How many minutes per month must you talk to make Phone Company A the best deal?

2) Connie had six more dimes than quarters. She also had 4 fewer nickels than quarters. If the value of her coins was $3.20, how many nickels does she have?

3) A store had a pile of bills that had a value of $1536. The number of 10-dollar bills was twice the number of 50-dollar bills. The number of 20-dollar bills was the same as the number of 10-dollar bills. There were three times as many 5-dollar bills as 50-dollar bills and the pile contained the same number of 1-dollar bills as 5-dollar bills. How many 50-dollar bills were there in the pile?

4) The Lemon Car Rental Company charges $39.95 per day for its cars with an additional charge of 12 cents per mile. The Kiwi Car Company charges $79.95 per day with no milage fee. How many miles of daily driving would make the Kiwi Car Company a better deal?

5) Pat decided to start his own car repair business. His monthly costs are shown below:

| Rent | $850 | | Water | $35 |
| --- | --- | --- | --- | --- |
| Phone | $60 | | Insurance | $200 |
| Heat | $55 | | Supplies | $300 |
| Electricity | $48 | | Other | $152 |

Pat determined that he makes an average of $45 from each customer that will pay his expenses listed above. If he has enough customers each month, he will make more money than his expenses, which is called his profit. If Pat's shop stays open 20 days per month and he has an average of *n* customers each day, what would the equation be to show Pat's profit each month?

6) Abe had a box that contained 40 coins. The box contained only nickels, dimes and quarters. If the number of dimes was the same as the number of quarters and the value of the coins was $5.00, how many dimes does Abe have?

7) Linus started a lemonade stand because he wanted to make enough profit to buy a new baseball glove. The lemonade costs him 7 cents for each glass and he sells it for 25 cents per glass. He also pays Lucy $2 per day to rent her front yard for the lemonade stand. Write an equation to show the amount of profit Linus makes each day when he has *n* customers.

8) Samatha invested her $10,000 saving at two different banks for one year. She put part of her money in Bank A which paid 8% interest. The rest of the $10,000 was invested at 7% interest at Bank B. At the end of the year she accumulated $735 interest. How much money did she invest at Bank A? Hint: 7% interest on an unknown amount of money is *.07n*.

9) Maria's music group made a CD that has all the songs that they wrote. It cost Maria $2 to buy each empty CD and after she burns the songs onto it, she sells each CD for $15. In addition to the cost of the blank CDs, Maria spent $7514 to rent time in a music studio to record her songs. Write an equation that shows the amount of profit Maria will make if she sells *n* CDs. *Profit =*

10) If Maria sells an average of 4 CDs per day, how many days will it take her to start making a profit?

Last night I saw a streak of light travel across the sky. My friends all started talking about visitors from outer space and UFOs. I just don't know what to think.

There is a rule in science called "Occam's Razor" which suggests that if something strange happens, first try to explain it by using all the simple or down to earth explanations. In this case, I would guess that you saw a meteor or a firecracker.

# Algebra and Physics
## Distance = Rate x Time

The freight train had somehow lost its engineer and was traveling with no one on board. The emergency response team knew that there was very little chance that they could bring the train to a halt, so they decided to concentrate their efforts on making sure that no one would be hurt when and if the train derailed.

With the help of a radar gun, they were able to determine that the train's speed was set at 38 miles per hour. At that speed, the emergency crew knew there was little chance that the train would derail until it reached the town of Demise, 256.5 miles down the track. Unfortunately for the town, the rails had a very sharp curve in them just as they entered the town. When the train reached this curve, it would almost certainly derail and possibly injure scores of people.

The emergency crew had to determine how much time they had to evacuate the town. Several crew members volunteered to use the algebra they knew to come up with the amount of time they had to evacuate the town. With the help of algebra and the formula $D = R \times T$, they were able to quickly establish that the train would be entering the town of Demise in 6 hours and 45 minutes.

With this knowledge, they were able to calmly and efficiently evacuate people from the area around the tracks. Because they knew exactly when the train was going to arrive, they also had time to move several valuable pieces of furniture and paintings from a museum sitting next to the track.

Six and a half hours after the evacuation started, the emergency crew withdrew from the area. 15 minutes later, the train did derail and caused severe damage to the buildings near the curve in the tracks. Even though there was severe damage to several buildings, the town of Demise was very thankful that the proper use of algebra helped save lives and most of their museum pieces.

How were they able to figure out what time the train would pass through the town with the curve?

There is a formula that allows us to use algebra to find distances, amounts of time, and speeds. The formula says that the distance traveled is equal to the amount of time multiplied by the speed. *Distance = Speed x Time* (Rate and speed are almost the same thing so we will use speed instead of rate from now on.)

Watch how I use the formula to figure out how much time they had to evacuate the town. We know the distance to the town was 256.5 miles and the speed of the train was 38 mph. All we need to do is put those numbers into the formula and then solve the equation.

| Step 1: (Formula) | $256.5 = 38 \times \text{Time}$ |
|---|---|
| Step 2: (Equation) | $256.5 = 38n$ |
| Step 3: (Solve) | $\frac{256.5}{38} = \frac{38n}{38}$ |
| Step 4: (Answer) | $n = 6.75$ |
| *The train will arrive in 6 hours 45 minutes* | |

I see how you did that, but what would you do if you had a problem where you knew the distance and the amount of time, but didn't know the speed?

You would solve that problem exactly like the other one except that you would be missing speed. Look at a problem I did where I was trying to find out the speed of my airplane during last summer's vacation.

I left Boston and traveled 6.25 hours on an airplane to San Fransisco. The distance between Boston and San Fransisco is 2985 miles. What was the average speed of the plane?

$D = R \times T$ problems are easy if you just remember that you are doing algebra problems! My parents had the cruise control set for 62 mph for exactly 7 hours. Using the formula, it is easy to see that they traveled 434 miles. I am going to use $D = R \times T$ to solve a lot of fun problems.

| Step 1: | **2985 = Speed x 6.25** |
|---------|------------------------|
| Step 2: | **2985 = 6.25n** |
| Step 3: | $\frac{2985}{6.25} = \frac{6.25n}{6.25}$ |
| Step 4: | **n = 477.6** |

***The average speed of the plane was 477.6 mph***

Try the following **D = R x T** problems. Remember that for this chapter, distances should be in miles and time should always be expressed in hours. If you are given a time such as 12 minutes, you would write it as 12/60 of an hour or 1/5 hour or .2 hours.

1) It took Juanita 30 minutes to ride her bike the 6.25 miles to her school. What was her average speed?

2) It takes light 15 minutes to travel 167,400,000 miles. What is the speed of light?

3) How much time will it take Eric to travel 396.8 miles if he travels at a rate of 64 mph?

4) Sara needs to arrive at work at 8:00. If she travels at a speed of 60 mph and her place of work is 15 miles away, what is the latest time she could leave her home and still arrive at work on time?

5) Jacob pedaled his bike at a speed of 18 mph for 3 hours and 20 minutes. How many miles did he travel?

---

Now I understand how to do
D = R x T problems. I am confused about something though. I know that the time must be written in hours. 15 minutes and 30 minutes are easy to change into hours because they come out even. What *do* I do if I have a time of 17 minutes? How do I change that into hours?

Its easy to change minutes into hours. 17 minutes is $\frac{17}{60}$ of an hour. I always change the fractions to decimals because they are easier to work with. Watch how I do this next problem.

Parker took 16 minutes to ride his bike down a hill that was 8.5 miles long. What was his average speed?

**Distance = Speed x Time**

| |
|---|
| Step 1: **8.5 miles = Speed x $\frac{16}{60}$ hour** |
| Step 2: **8.5 = $n$ x .26666** |
| Step 3: **8.5 = .26666$n$** |
| Step 4: $\frac{8.5}{.26666} = \frac{.26666n}{.26666}$ |
| Step 5: **$n$ = 31.875 mph** |

**Distance = Speed x Time**

| |
|---|
| Step 1: **.25 miles = Speed x $\frac{78}{3600}$ hour** |
| Step 2: **.25 = $n$ x .0216666** |
| Step 3: **.25 = .0216666$n$** |
| Step 4: $\frac{.25}{.0216666} = \frac{.0216666n}{.0216666}$ |
| Step 5: **$n$ = 11.5 mph (Rounded)** |

I ran 1/4 mile in 78 seconds, which set a new record for the slowest time ever at Einstein Elementary School. Watch how I determine my speed. I turned the 78 seconds into $\frac{78}{3600}$ hours because there are 3600 seconds in an hour.

That's right! Because there are 1760 yards in a mile, you ran $\frac{100}{1760}$ of a mile.

If I was trying to find my speed in a 100-yard dash, would I change the 100 yards into $\frac{100}{1760}$ miles?

Try the following problems. Make sure time is always in hours and distance is always in miles.

1) Marissa ran a mile in 8 minutes. What is her speed in miles per hour?

2) Sound can travel a mile in 5 seconds. What is the speed of sound in mph?

3) A frog traveled 440 yards during a 30 minute frog jumping contest. What was its speed in miles per hour?

4) What fraction of an hour is one second?

5) What fraction of a mile is one foot?

I have an interesting piece of knowledge for you that has nothing to do with D = R x T. 99.99% of people think that a kilogram is a measurement of weight just like pounds are a measurement of weight. This is not correct. Kilograms are a measurement of mass, not weight.

If kilograms are a measurement of mass and not weight, then how do I measure my mass using the United States way of measuring things?

You can easily find your mass by dividing your weight by 32. If you weigh 144 pounds, then your mass would be 4.5 slugs. Yes, believe it or not, mass is expressed in something called slugs.

We are finally getting the respect we deserve!!

**Distance = Rate x Time**                                   Level 1

1) If Luke can hike at a speed of 3 mph, how long will it take him to hike 22 miles?

2) A family left on vacation at 9:30 A.M.. They drove until 11:30 P.M. and covered 770 miles. What was the average speed on their trip?

3) A trip from Chicago to Des Moines took $7\frac{3}{4}$ hours. If the average speed was 58 mph, what is the distance between the two cities?

4) Sara took a 12-mile hike in $4\frac{1}{2}$ hours. What was her average speed?

5) Phil drove for 30 minutes on a stretch of highway at a speed of 65 mph. Denzel drove for 30 minutes on this same highway at a speed of 60 mph. How much farther did Phil drive than Denzel?

6) Anna drove west at an average speed of 55 mph. If she started her trip at 8:15 A.M. and ended at 2:45 P.M., how far did she travel?

**Use the following chart to answer questions 7-10**

|  | Boston | Cleveland | Dallas | Detroit | Miami | Washington D.C. |
|---|---|---|---|---|---|---|
| Boston | * | 642 | 1753 | 718 | 1510 | 437 |
| Cleveland | 642 | * | 1180 | 173 | 1251 | 366 |
| Dallas | 1753 | 1180 | * | 1185 | 1305 | 1320 |
| Detroit | 718 | 173 | 1185 | * | 1389 | 525 |
| Miami | 1510 | 1251 | 1305 | 1389 | * | 1074 |
| Washington D.C. | 437 | 366 | 1320 | 525 | 1074 | * |

7) The Kellers were planning a trip from Boston to Cleveland. They usually travel at an average speed of 58 mph. How long will their trip take? (Round to the nearest hour.)

8) Ryan is driving from Detroit to Washington D.C. If he wants to make the trip in 9 hours, what speed must he average?

9) Jose drove round trip between Dallas and Cleveland. On the way to Cleveland, he averaged 60 mph, but on the return trip his car engine was overheating so Jose kept his speed at 40 mph. How long did the entire trip take?

10) Jordon is planning a trip from Cleveland to Washington D.C. and back to Cleveland. If he averages 61 mph, how long will his trip take?

## Distance = Rate x Time          Level 2

1) Two trains leave the station at exactly the same time. One heads north at 60 mph while the other heads south at 45 mph. At 4:30 P.M. the trains are 472.5 miles apart. What time did they leave the station?

2) Apollo 13 traveled 500,000 miles on its perilous voyage to the moon and back. If the entire trip took 5 days and 23 hours, what was the average speed of Apollo 13 on its $\frac{1}{2}$ million mile journey? (Round to the nearest 100 mph.)

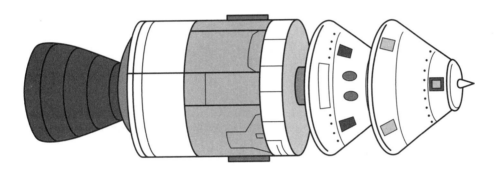

3) Kate is planning a cross country trip of 2970 miles. She is planning to travel from 8:00 A.M. to 4:00 P.M. every day at a speed of 55 mph. If Kate leaves on Monday at 8:00 A.M., on what day and at what time will she arrive at her destination?

4) Stephanie walked through a tunnel at $2\frac{1}{2}$ mph. If the tunnel was 2 miles long, how many minutes did it take her to walk from one end of the tunnel to the other end?

5) A cheetah can run for short distances at a speed of 70 mph. How many miles can a cheetah run in one minute?

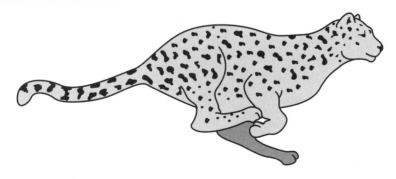

6) Jill departs from the Chicago airport at 8:30 A.M. and travels at a speed of 560 mph. After traveling 2380 miles, she arrives in San Francisco. What is the time in San Francisco when she lands?

7) How long will it take a car traveling at 75 mph to go one mile?

8) Dan needs to ride his bike to soccer practice at a field that is $3\frac{3}{4}$ miles from his home. If Dan pedals his bike at a constant 15 mph, what time should he leave his house if he must arrive at practice at 5:00?

9) At what speed must you travel to cover 325 miles in 12 minutes?

10) Mr. Rodent can canoe at 2 mph in still water. If he travels for 3 hours down a river with a 1 mph current and then turns around and returns to his starting point, how long will his canoe trip last?

Distance = Rate x Time                    Einstein Level

1) Running a mile in 4 minutes is a remarkable feat. What is the average speed in mph when a mile is run in 4 minutes?

2) A peregrine falcon can reach speeds of 200 mph while it is diving. If a peregrine falcon that is circling a rabbit at an altitude of 660 feet turns and dives at an average speed of 200 mph, how many seconds will it take to reach the rabbit?

3) The world record in the 100-yard dash is under 10 seconds. When the 100-yard dash is run in a time of exactly 10 seconds, what is the speed of the runner in miles per hour?

4) How quickly could a rat finish a 100-yard dash? (Assume it averages 12 mph over the 100 yards, and round to the nearest second.)

5) Civil War soldiers were standing on a riverbank across from a cannon. When they saw the flash of the cannon, it took 2 seconds before the cannon ball hit their side of the river. If the cannon was $\frac{1}{4}$ mile away, at what speed did the cannonball travel?

6) If sound travels 1100 feet per second, what is its speed in miles per hour?

7) Warren and Kevin entered a 6.3 mile race. If Warren ran at 7 mph and Kevin ran at 9 mph, how far was Warren from the finish line when Kevin won the race?

8) A greyhound dog can race at a speed of 40 mph. How many seconds does it take a greyhound to finish a $\frac{1}{4}$ mile race?

9) Fritz was wondering what it would have been like if cheetahs chased dinosaurs, so he made the following problem: A cheetah traveling at 70 mph is chasing a dinosaur that is traveling at 55 mph. If the cheetah starts out $\frac{1}{2}$ mile behind the dinosaur, how close is it after chasing the dinosaur for one minute?
(I don't think we want to know what would happen to the cheetah if it ever caught the dinosaur.)

10) Laura did not have a speedometer for her bike so she decided to go to the high school track and time how long it took her to bike the $\frac{1}{4}$ mile oval. If it took her 24 seconds, what was her speed in miles per hour?

# A Different Kind of Average Speed

## What Amoeba Wants to Win a Million Dollars?

| |
|---|
| **$1,000,000** |
| $500,000 |
| $250,000 |
| $125,000 |
| $64,000 |
| $32,000 |
| $16,000 |
| $8,000 |
| $4,000 |
| $2,000 |
| $1,000 |
| $500 |
| $300 |
| $200 |
| $100 |

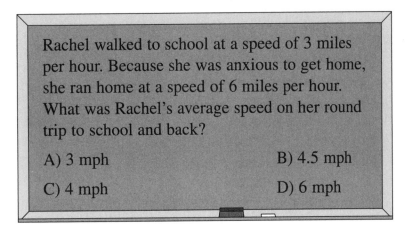

Rachel walked to school at a speed of 3 miles per hour. Because she was anxious to get home, she ran home at a speed of 6 miles per hour. What was Rachel's average speed on her round trip to school and back?

A) 3 mph          B) 4.5 mph

C) 4 mph          D) 6 mph

The announcer asked for the answer to the million dollar question. Amy the Amoeba was pretty sure she knew the right answer, but something was bothering her. This was the million dollar question, but it appeared that it was a simple average question. The average of 3 mph and 6 mph was 4.5 mph. She was about to pick the letter B when she remembered she was allowed to make a phone call to a friend. Fortunately for Amy, Algebra Woman was on her list of friends to call.

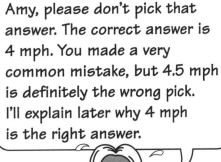

Hi Algebra Woman. I am about to win a million dollars if I get this question right. I think I know the answer, but I thought I would call you just to check. If someone went to school at 3 mph and then returned home at 6 mph, her average speed would be 4.5 mph. Right?

Amy, please don't pick that answer. The correct answer is 4 mph. You made a very common mistake, but 4.5 mph is definitely the wrong pick. I'll explain later why 4 mph is the right answer.

It seems like you would just add 3 and 6 and then divide by two. As you know I did pick your answer and won the million dollars, but why is my thinking wrong?

When you are figuring speed averages, you must think differently than you normally do. You must think in blocks of time. Because 3 mph is two times slower than 6 mph, the time the girl spent walking to school was two times longer than the time she spent going home from school. Because of this, you must count the 3 mph twice when you are finding averages. An easy way to do this is to give the 3 mph two blocks of time.

**Walking**    **3**  **3**

**Running**    **6**

To find the average speed, you simply add up the numbers inside the blocks and then divide by three. (The number of blocks of time)   Her average speed was *12 ÷ 3 = 4 mph*.

Look at the next example:

If Kristin walked halfway to school at 10 mph and then ran the rest of the way at 20 mph, what was her average speed?

Because Kristin spent twice as much time walking, make sure walking gets two blocks of time.

**Walking** $\boxed{10}$ $\boxed{10}$

**Running** $\boxed{20}$

**Adding** $10 + 10 + 20 = 40$

$40 \div 3 = 13\frac{1}{3}$ mph

Let's try a slightly harder problem:

> A student was driving to school at 40 mph.
> A third of the way there he ran out of gas.
> If he ran the rest of the way at 10 mph,
> what was his average speed?

Draw a picture to represent his trip:

| 40 | 10 | 10 |
|----|----|----|

As you can see, the student spent much more time going 10 mph, and very little time going 40 mph. When you look at the picture it is very clear that each section of 10 mph should have 4 blocks of time.

$\boxed{40}$    $\boxed{10}\boxed{10}\boxed{10}\boxed{10}$    $\boxed{10}\boxed{10}\boxed{10}\boxed{10}$

Why does each 10 mph section have 4 blocks of time?

Remember, when he travels a section at 10 mph, he spends four times as much time as when he does that same section at 40 mph.

Adding all the blocks:    $120 \div 9 = 13\frac{1}{3}$ mph

What happens if I have speeds like 5 mph and 7.5 mph. How can I use blocks of time with weird combinations like these?

Sometimes you have to use a new number for the block of time. I'll turn your example into a word problem and solve it by picking another number for the block of time.

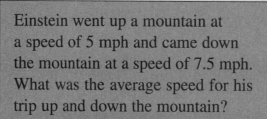

Einstein went up a mountain at a speed of 5 mph and came down the mountain at a speed of 7.5 mph. What was the average speed for his trip up and down the mountain?

Our block of time in this case will be 15 because both numbers fit evenly into it. You probably noticed that 15 is the least common multiple of 5 and 7.5.

**15**

**5** **5** **5** **7.5** **7.5**

**5 + 5 + 5 + 7.5 + 7.5 = 30**

**30 ÷ 5 blocks = 6**

**Einstein's average speed is 6 mph**

I'll always remember to use blocks of time when I am doing average speeds. I'll also always remember how close I was to losing the million dollars. Thank you for your help!

*Remember that when you find the average speed, you must take into account the amount of time spent traveling at each speed. If you walked two minutes at 3 mph to an airplane and then traveled 6 hours at 597 mph, you certainly wouldn't think your average speed would be 300 mph. Your average speed would be very close to 597 mph because you spent most of the time traveling at that speed.*

## A Different Kind of Average Speed                                    Level 1

1) Buffy climbed Mt. Washington at an average speed of 1 mph. On her way down she averaged 5 mph. What was her average speed for the entire trip?

2) Mike is kicking a soccer ball with his dad.  Mike kicks the ball at 12 mph while his dad kicks the ball at 60 mph. What is the average speed of the ball as it goes from Mike to his dad and then back to Mike?

3) Larry rode his bike to school at 6 mph. When he was halfway there his chain broke and he rode in his dad's car the rest of the way at 48 mph. What was his average speed on his trip to school?

4) Fritz rode his bike at 15 mph on his way to soccer practice. Because he was tired from playing soccer, he could only pedal his bike at 10 mph on his way home. What was his average speed for the round trip?

5) Anty was riding his bike to school at a speed of 12 mph. When he was $\frac{2}{3}$ of the way there, he got a flat tire.  His mother drove him the rest of the way at a speed of 48 mph. What was his average speed?

## A Different Kind of Average Speed                                  Level 2

1) Juan decided to drive up the Pikes Peak Road. If he went up at 40 mph and down the mountain at 60 mph, what was his average speed for the entire trip?

2) Kyle can climb up a 30-foot rope in his physical education class at a speed of 1 mph. When Kyle goes down the rope, he travels at 3.5 mph. What is Kyle's average speed for his trip up and down the rope?

3) Luke can canoe at a speed of 3 mph on a still lake. Luke took a canoe trip down a river with a current that flowed at 2 mph. He then returned by paddling upstream to his starting point. What was his average speed for the trip?

4) Sara walked halfway to school at 5 mph. She then ran the rest of the way at 8 mph. If she rode home with her dad at a speed of 40 mph, what was the average speed for Sara's trip to and from school?

5) Richard entered a marathon in which he ran the first half at an average speed of 7 mph. He then walked the rest at an average speed of 1.75 mph. What was his average speed for the entire marathon?

## A Different Kind of Average Speed                    Einstein Level

1) A student decided that she wanted to travel to school on her birthday in four different ways: Walking, running, skateboarding, and by car. She walked the first quarter of the way at a speed of 3 mph and then ran the next quarter at 6 mph. She rode her skateboard at a speed of 16 mph for the next section and then drove the last quarter at 48 mph. What was her average speed on her trip to school? (Round to the nearest whole number.)

2) Kate had a noon doctor's appointment 64 miles from her home. Kate left her home at 11:00 and traveled 1/4 of the way to the appointment at a speed of 40 mph. At what speed does Kate need to travel for the rest of the trip to arrive at exactly 12:00?

3) Nancy drove at a speed of 60 mph for a distance of 100 miles so she could catch a plane at her favorite airport. If the plane traveled 360 mph for 400 miles, what was Nancy's average speed for her car and plane trip?

4) Erin took an 1800 mile trip. She averaged 55 mph for the first 16 hours of the trip and then because of poor roads, averaged 46 mph over the rest of the trip. What was her average speed for the entire trip?

5) Marissa and Nathan joined a relay race with their pet rats. Marissa's rat ran the first half of the race at a speed of 2 mph. Unfortunately, Nathan's rat ran his half of the race at a speed of 1.5 mph. The winning team's average speed was 1.75 mph. What was the average speed of Marissa and Nathan's team?

# Distance = Rate x Time

The sailboat was being pounded by 30 foot waves as it raced toward the safety of shore. Suddenly a wave of monstrous size crashed over the struggling boat. The situation had suddenly turned desperate as the boat slammed sideways into the water. When it righted itself, the mast was gone and water poured through the formerly airtight cabin. It became very clear that the boat would never make it to shore without help.

The Coast Guard in Boston picked up a desperate plea for help. "We are 56 miles from shore, traveling at 18 mph, but we are taking on water and will last only an hour more."

As the Coast Guard captain headed out into the storm, he knew the situation was desperate. The top speed that he could travel through the frightening waves was 46 mph. If the sailboat traveled toward him at 18 mph, could he reach it in time?

He thought to himself that it was lucky that he knew the math "language of algebra." He wrote down all the information that he knew and then translated it into an algebra problem. He then radioed the captain of the sinking sailboat. "Try to hold on, I'll arrive in $52\frac{1}{2}$ minutes."

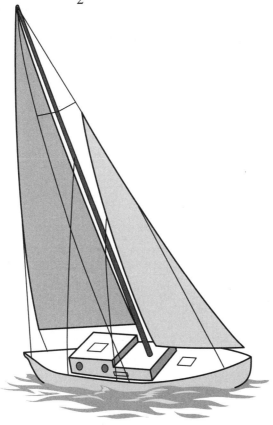

Distance, speed and time problems have always given me a lot of trouble. Is there any way to make them easier?

When you are solving complicated problems that have to do with speed, distance, and time, it is much easier to find the correct equation if you make a chart. Look at the problem below.

Rachel starts from Boston and drives her car west at 45 mph. Her dad starts 2 hours later from the same place and drives west at 60 mph. How long until Rachel's dad catches up to her?

Watch how I use a chart to solve the problem. I don't think my brain could handle this problem without a chart.

I think I see how you are using the chart. You put in all the information you know. You put in speed and time. That was very clever putting in $n+2$ for Rachel's time. Her dad's time is n and because Rachel got a 2-hour head start, her time is $n+2$.

|        | **Rate** (mph) | **Time** (in hours) | **Distance** (in miles) |
|--------|----------------|---------------------|-------------------------|
| Rachel | 45 mph         | $n + 2$             |                         |
| Dad    | 60 mph         | $n$                 |                         |

Now the chart is starting to make the problem clear. When we find what we need to fill in the distance box, we will be ready to solve the problem. Because *distance = rate x time*, all we need to do is multiply to find the distance. Rachel's distance will be 45(*n*+2) and her dad's distance will be 60*n*.

I think I know how to write the equation. When her dad catches up to her, they will have gone the same distance. Our equation will be Rachel's distance equals her dad's distance.

|  | **Rate** (mph) | **Time** (in hours) | **Distance** (in miles) |
|---|---|---|---|
| Rachel | 45 mph | $n + 2$ | $45\,(n + 2)$ |
| Dad | 60 mph | $n$ | $60n$ |

$$45(n+2) \quad = \quad 60n$$
Rachel's distance        Dad's distance

$$45n + 90 = 60n$$

$$90 = 15n$$

$$n = 6 \quad \text{Rachel's dad will catch her in 6 hours}$$

Let's look at another problem where we can use a chart:

A train leaves Boston at 3:00 P.M. and heads for New York at 35 mph. At the exact same time, another train leaves New York and heads for Boston at a speed of 45 mph. If the distance between New York and Boston is 240 miles, how long will it be before the trains meet?

The first thing we need to do is make our chart. The speeds are easy and since the amount of time traveled will be the same for both trains, we can call the times $n$.

Because *distance* is equal to *speed x time*, we can easily find our distance.

|  | **Rate** | **Time** | **Distance** |
|---------|------|------|----------|
| Train A | 35 | $n$ | $35n$ |
| Train B | 45 | $n$ | $45n$ |

If we draw a picture, it will become very clear what our equation needs to be.

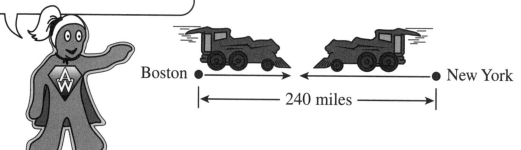

Boston ●→ ←● New York

240 miles

The distance traveled by Train A plus the distance traveled by Train B equals 240 miles.

$35n + 45n = 240$

$80n = 240$

$n = 3$    The trains will meet in 3 hours

Let's look at a very confusing problem that can be solved by making a D = R x T chart.

Ryan made a trip to the mall that took 2 hours. Ryan spent an hour at the mall and then because of road construction, returned home at a speed 20 mph less than the speed he traveled to the mall. If the entire time Ryan was gone was 6 hours, what was his speed on his trip to the mall?

Speeds are easy. We'll call his trip to the mall $n$ and his return trip $n-20$ because he went 20 mph slower on his return trip from the mall.

The times are also easy. The problem said it took 2 hours to get to the mall. Since he spent an hour at the mall and the total trip was 6 hours, then his return trip must have taken 3 hours.

|         | Rate    | Time | Distance    |
|---------|---------|------|-------------|
| To Mall | $n$     | 2    | $2n$        |
| Return  | $n - 20$ | 3    | $3(n - 20)$ |

Because the distance to the mall is identical to the distance back, we can set up an equation with the distances equal to each other.

$2n = 3(n - 20)$

$2n = 3n - 60$

$n = 60$    Ryan's speed going to the mall was 60 mph.

*Remember to use the equation **D = R x T** when you have problems that have to do with time, distance or speed. Some students get confused by the **R** in the equation. Remember that when we use rate in this formula, we are talking about speed.*

**D = R x T**                                                    Level 1

1) Ryan was bragging to his brother about how fast he could ride his bike. If Ryan travels at 12 mph while his brother travels at 8 mph, how long will it take Ryan to catch his brother if he gives him a 3 hour head start?

2) Stephanie leaves school at 3:00 on her bike and travels at a speed of 10 mph. If her mom leaves home at the same time and drives toward school at 40 mph, what time will they meet if the distance between home and school is 10 miles?

3) Kate is running a race at a speed of 13 mph while Erin runs the race at 5 mph. If Erin is given a 2 hour head start, how long will it take Kate to catch her?

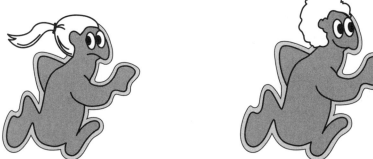

4) Joey and Josh are 600 miles apart. If Joey travels towards Josh at 22 mph and Josh travels toward Joey at 26 mph, how long until they meet?

5) Dan and Luke are running in a 20 mile charity benefit race. If Dan runs at 3 mph and Luke runs at 4 mph, how long until their total mileage equals 20 miles?

**D = R x T**                                                          Level 2

1) Steve and Jordan are riding bikes. Jordan is riding at 7 mph and Steve is riding at 6 mph. If Jordan is 5 miles behind Steve, how long will it take for Jordan to catch up to Steve?

2) A sailboat is taking on water during a storm and is in danger of sinking. After calling the Coast Guard, the sailboat turns towards shore and travels at 17 mph towards Boston which is 123.9 miles away. At the same time, a Coast Guard cutter leaves Boston and heads towards the floundering sailboat at a speed of 42 mph. How long until the Coast Guard reaches the sailboat?

3) Megan and Kate decided to race their bikes. If Megan can ride at 12 mph and Kate can ride at 16 mph, how long until they are $1\frac{1}{2}$ miles apart?

4) A member of the highway patrol clocked a speeding motorist at 80 mph. By the time the patrolman began his chase, he was 2 miles behind the speeding vehicle. If the patrolman traveled at 100 mph, how long until he catches the speeding motorist?

5) Josh told his sister that he could beat her in a 10 mile race where she rides her bike and he runs. The only advantage that he wanted was a half hour head start. If Josh runs at 8 mph and his sister rides at 15 mph, who will win the race and by how many minutes?

**D = R x T**             **Einstein Level**

1) It took Steve 2 hours to ride his bike to school. Because he was tired, Steve took 3 hours to pedal home. If Steve rode his bike 5 mph slower on the way home, what speed did he travel on his way to school?

2) A horse and a chicken are standing at a point on a 1/4 mile track. The horse heads in one direction at 26 mph while the chicken heads in the opposite direction at 4 mph. How many seconds will pass before they meet again?

3) A turtle and a rabbit are standing at a point on a 1/4 mile track. The rabbit heads in one direction at 8 mph and the turtle heads in the other direction at 2 mph. How many minutes will pass before they meet *twice*?

4) Two planes leave from Chicago at noon. One heads directly east at 420 mph while the other heads west at $413\frac{1}{3}$ mph. At what time will they be 2000 miles apart?

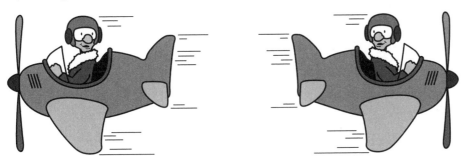

5) Dan and Luke decided to take part in a twenty mile race. Luke runs at 5 mph while Dan runs at 4 mph. When Luke crosses the finish line, how far will Dan be from finishing?

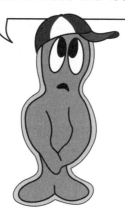

When I cook food in a microwave, the inside of the microwave oven doesn't get hot. How in the world does the food cook?

If you rub your hands back and forth, heat is generated. Microwave ovens force the molecules in the food to move back and forth. The heat that is generated by this movement cooks the food.

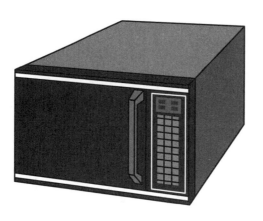

# Algebra and Work
## Work = Rate x Time

I remember a contest at a State Fair when I first saw how powerful algebra was for making predictions. A large tub was to be filled by a large hose and a small hose. There was a note by the small hose that said it was able to fill the tub last week in four hours. The large hose had a note next to it that said it took only two hours to fill the tub. Everyone at the fair was allowed to make one guess as to how long it would take the tub to fill if both hoses were running at the same time. My first thought was that it would take three hours if both hoses were used, but then I realized that the large hose could fill the tank in two hours, so the time for both hoses must be shorter than two hours.

My mind was starting to spin when my grandmother came over and mentioned that algebra could help me. She reminded me of the many formulas for figuring out things in algebra such as **D = R x T**. She then shared with me one of her favorite formulas: **Work = Rate x Time.**

It was hard at first to see what work was being done, but it soon became clear that the hoses were doing a kind of work as they filled the tank. I also remembered that **Rate** is like speed so I wrote down the rates of each hose. Just like in the formula **D = R x T**, I made my rates in tanks per hour. Because it takes the large hose two hours to fill the tank, it fills 1/2 tank in one hour, so its rate is 1/2 tank per hour. Because it takes the smaller hose four hours to fill the tank, it fills 1/4 tank in one hour, so its rate is 1/4 tank per hour. Because time was what I was looking for, I called time $t$.

Large hose rate: 1/2 tank per hour
Small hose rate:  1/4 tank per hour
Time: $t$

Because **Work = Rate x Time**, I knew that the amount of work done by the large hose was $\frac{1}{2}t$ and the amount of work done by the small hose was $\frac{1}{4}t$. Now things were starting to become clear. The amount of work that needed to be done was one tank, so the equation was easy to write.

Equation: 1 tank $= \frac{1}{2}t + \frac{1}{4}t$  or  $1 = \frac{3}{4}t$
Solving: $t = 1\frac{1}{3}$ hours.    The tank would be filled in 1 hour and 20 minutes.

That was amazing! I don't think I could ever figure something like that out without algebra.

Could you show me how to answer this problem that I once had on a math contest. It seems like using the formula *Work = Rate x Time* would help.

I did win the contest with my answer. There was something very odd about the guesses people made. Most guesses were three hours, so it was pretty clear that people were not making sure their answers made sense.

Ali can paint a fence in 3 hours while his sister takes only 2 hours. If they work together, how long will it take them to paint the fence?

Ali's rate: 1/3 fence per hour
Sister's rate: 1/2 fence per hour
Time: $t$

Equation: 1 fence = $\frac{1}{2}t + \frac{1}{3}t$
Solve: 1 = $\frac{5}{6}t$
   $t = \frac{6}{5}$
   $t = 1.2$ hours  or 1 hour 12 minutes

Watch how I find each person's rate and then make an equation. Remember that you can change fractions of an hour into minutes by multiplying by 60.

Now that I know how to do that kind of problem, could you show me how to do a very confusing type of problem? What do I do with this problem when work is being done and at the same time work is being undone?

A pump can empty water in a basement that is 6 inches deep in 4 hours. The water leaking into the basement takes 6 hours to reach the 6 inch level. With the pump running and water continuing to leak into the basement, how long will it take before the pump takes away the 6 inches of water from the basement?

This type of problem is also easy to do when you use the formula W = R x T. Watch how I write down the rate for the pump and the rate for the leak. Of course the rate for the leak will be a negative number because work is being undone.

Pump's rate: 1/4 job per hour
Leak's rate: −1/6 job per hour
Time: $t$

Because **W = R x T** , we can write the amount of work as shown below:

Pump's work: $\frac{1}{4}t$

Leak's Work: $-\frac{1}{6}t$

Equation: $1 \text{ job} = \frac{1}{4}t - \frac{1}{6}t$

Solve: $1 = \frac{1}{12}t$        $t = 12$ hours

## Work = Rate x Time                                    Level 1

1) Armando can paint a fence in 4 hours while his sister can paint the same fence in only 2 hours. If they work together, how long will it take them to paint the fence?

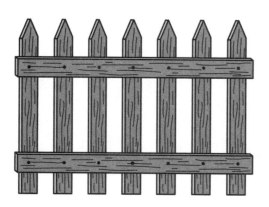 

2) A swimming pool's large drain will empty the pool in 3 hours while its smaller drain takes 6 hours. If both drains are opened, how long will it take to empty the pool?

3) Three highway maintenance workers must pick up trash on a 2 mile stretch of highway. The first worker takes 2 hours to complete the job while the second worker takes 3 hours. The third worker is new at the job and takes 6 hours. The day before a holiday, their boss decided to let them work together so they could finish earlier. How long does it take them to pick up trash on this 2 mile stretch of highway if they all work together?

4) A pond is being filled by two water lines. The first water line can fill the pond in 2 hours. If the second water line is used, it takes 6 hours to fill the pond. How long would it take to fill the pond if both water lines are used?

5) A backyard swimming pool takes three hours to fill with a garden hose. When the drain is opened, it takes 4 hours for the pool to empty. One year Larry started filling the pool, but forgot to close the drain. He noticed that it took a long time for the pool to fill. How long did it take?

**Work = Rate x Time**       **Level 2**

1) Jamal owns a construction company and is trying to figure out how long it will take for his 2 bulldozers to flatten a 1/4 mile stretch of land. He knows that his large bulldozer does the job in 3 hours while the smaller bulldozer can do the job in 5 hours. How long will it take the two machines to flatten the 1/4 mile stretch of land if they work together?

2) It takes Lamar 50 hours to paint a house while Claudia can paint the house in 30 hours. How long would it take them to paint the house if they worked together?

3) It takes Gregg only 2 hours to sew labels on a pile of 100 shirts. His co-worker takes 8 hours to do the same job. How long will it take to sew labels on 100 shirts if Gregg and his co-worker do the job together?

4) The Sine Tunnel Building Company can build a 1/4 mile tunnel through a hill in 50 days while the Tangent Tunnel Building Company takes 200 days to build the 1/4 mile tunnel. If both companies work together from opposite ends of the hill, how long will it take before they meet?

5) Roberto has four car painters who work for him. The chart below shows how fast each worker can paint a car.

Worker 1: 2 hours
Worker 2: 4 hours
Worker 3: 8 hours
Worker 4: 8 hours     Roberto's four painters need to paint a total of three cars. How long will take them if they work together?

1) Lennox and his dad are bricklayers. It takes them 2 hours and 24 minutes to build a 10 foot by 4 foot wall when they work together. If it takes Lennox 6 hours to build this wall by himself, how long would it take for his dad to build the wall alone?

2) Alomar unloads a truck of lumber in 7 hours. When Jon helps him, they can unload the truck in 2 hours and 6 minutes. How long would it take Jon to unload the truck alone?

3) A large city swimming pool had a leak that caused the pool to lose all its water in 20 hours. The city decided to fill the pool without fixing the leak by turning on two hoses. Hose A normally takes 4 hours to fill the pool when there is no leak. Hose B normally takes 5 hours to fill the pool when there is no leak. With both hoses turned on and the leak unrepaired, how long will it take to fill the pool?

4) 2-person teams were entered in a pancake eating contest that required each team to eat 25 pancakes. Derek can eat 25 pancakes in 2 hours while his teammate takes $3\frac{1}{2}$ hours. If they work together, how long will it take them to eat the 25 pancakes? (Round to the nearest minute.)

5) Lenny can mop the gymnasium floor at Einstein Elementary School in 30 minutes while it takes Abe 60 minutes. If Melody can mop the floor in 20 minutes, how long will it take to mop the gymnasium floor if they all work together?

# Simultaneous Equations

Kate was excited when she found the wooden box sitting on her porch. Her grandfather always gave her something exciting for her birthday and it looked like this year would again be special. The lid had a large question mark on the top with a carving underneath that said X or Y.

When Kate opened the box, she saw a short poem attached to the inside that read:

> X or Y
> One letter you must chose
> But be very careful
> Because money you can lose
>
> To help with your selection
> I have given two clues
> If you study your algebra
> You won't get the blues

It appeared that Kate's grandfather was giving her some money for her birthday and to determine how much money she was going to get depended on whether she picked *x* or *y*. Kate hoped that the two clues would help her decide which letter had the higher amount of money. When Kate took the poem out of the box, she saw two equations carved into the bottom of the box. Kate knew instantly that these equations were her clues.

$$3x + 4y = \$2950$$
$$3y + 4x = \$3525$$

Kate knew exactly what she had to do because she had been studying a part of algebra called "Solving Simultaneous Equations." Kate did some calculations and then wrote down: x = $750 and y = $175. She then ran to the phone and called her grandfather. "Grandpa, I would like to have *x* for my birthday."

How did Kate find out what the value of x and y was? It seems like she did something that is impossible.

Up to now we have been working with problems with only one unknown. In this chapter you will learn how to solve problems just like Kate did. You will learn how to solve problems with two variables.

*We have been using the letter **n** to take the place of our unknown. In this chapter we will use **x** and **y** for our two unknowns. Mathematicians call these letters variables.*

Look at the equations shown below. What values of $x$ and $y$ will make both equations true?

$$x + y = 15 \qquad x - y = 5$$

The first equation has a lot of possible answers. In fact, I think there are an infinite number of possible answers that make equation one true. I've listed some possible numbers for x and y that make x + y = 15. I can see now that my list could go on forever.

| | |
|---|---|
| x = 1 | y = 14 |
| x = 2 | y = 13 |
| x = 3 | y = 12 |
| x = 4 | y = 11 |
| x = 5 | y = 10 |
| x = 6 | y = 9 |
| x = -5 | y = 20 |

The second equation also has an infinite number of possible answers. I've listed some values for x and y that make the equation x - y= 5 true.

| | |
|---|---|
| x = 20 | y = 15 |
| x = 15 | y = 10 |
| x = 10 | y = 5 |
| x = 8 | y = 3 |

*There are an infinite number of solutions for x + y = 15 and there are also an infinite number of solutions for x - y = 5. What is important though is that there is only one solution that will make both equations true. We do not want to use guess and check to find that one solution because it could take a very long time, so we use a special method called "getting rid of one of the variables."*

Einstein calls this method the "getting rid of one of the variables" method. If you want to impress your friends, you can call it the elimination method.

One very important rule of algebra that we learned is that you can add or subtract the same thing from each side of an equation. Because x - y and 5 are equal to each other, we can add the two equations. Notice that something very interesting happens.

$$x + y = 15$$
$$+ \quad \underline{x - y = 5}$$
$$2x + 0 = 20$$

That was incredible!! The y's just disappeared. Now it is easy to find the value of x.   x must equal 10.

When you are working with two equations and two variables, you try to get rid of one of the variables. This is called the elimination method of solving equations. Look at this next problem. There is something a little tricky about it.

$$4x + y = 30$$
$$2x + y = 16$$

If we add these equations, we end up with 6x + 2y = 46. That doesn't help us at all.

You've noticed that adding doesn't help. We have to be a little clever here. According to the rules of algebra, we can add or subtract the same thing from each side of the equation. Look what happens when we subtract the equations.

$$4x + y = 30$$
$$-\ (2x + y = 16)$$
$$\overline{\quad 2x + 0 = 14}$$

$$x = 7$$

It worked!! Now we have two different ways to make variables disappear. We can add equations or subtract equations.

Because you know that x = 7, you can find the value of y by using 7 for x in either one of the equations.

$$4x + y = 30$$

$$(4 \times 7) + y = 30$$

$$28 + y = 30$$

$$y = 2$$

Use the elimination method to make one variable disappear. Then find the value of **x** and **y**.

1)    $4x + y = 44$
      $x + y = 20$

2)    $3x + 2y = 61$
      $9x - 2y = 23$

3)    $x + y = 27$
      $x - y = 1$

4)    $\frac{1}{2}x + 3y = 76$
      $1\frac{1}{2}x + 3y = 126$

5)    $x + 2y = 18$
      $x + y = 9$

6) A store had a sale on pencils and pens. Look at the sale sign and then determine the price of one pencil and one pen.

> 2 pencils + pen = $1.63
> 10 pencils - pen = $.41

7)  A coat and a pair of mountain boots together cost $112. Collin bought a coat and returned a pair of mountain boots he received for a Christmas present. Because he returned the boots, the store only charged him $66 for the coat. (Coat - Boots = $66) Collin's friend liked his coat so much that he went to the store to buy the same coat. How much did he pay?

8) Stephanie bought a mouse and a porcupine for $12.50. Kate went to the same store and bought 2 mice and a porcupine for $20. What is the cost of one mouse?

9) Erin told her friends that she had two favorite numbers. She decided to give 2 clues so her friends could try and guess the numbers. What are Erin's favorite numbers?
Clue 1:  Twice the first number minus the second is equal to 21.
Clue 2:  Twice the first number plus the second is equal to 23.

10) Ryan's age plus three times Steve's age is equal to 34. Seven times Steve's age minus Ryan's age is equal to 36. What is Ryan's age?

Sometimes the equations we are working with are complicated and we have to do a little extra work. Look at the two equations below:

$$4x + y = 21$$
$$2x + 3y = 33$$

If we add the equations, no variable will disappear. Subtracting doesn't help either. What can we do to solve the equations?

Let's try multiplying each side of the top equation by 3. That way we will get a 3y in the top equation. Of course we are allowed to do this because of the fairness rule of algebra.

$$3(4x + y) = 3(21)$$

$$12x + 3y = 63$$
$$2x + 3y = 33$$

That was brilliant!! Now we can subtract and make the y's disappear.

$$12x + 3y = 63$$
$$-\ (2x + 3y = 33)$$
$$\overline{10x + 0 = 30}$$

$$x = 3$$

*Sometimes you must change one of the equations to make variables disappear. You may even have to change both equations occasionally.*

Look at these equations:

$$5x + y = 37$$
$$x + 2y = 11$$

It is clear that adding or subtracting will not help. If I can turn the y in the top equation into 2y, then I can get rid of the y's.

Just like in the last example, we can multiply the top equation by 2. This isn't so hard is it?

$$2(5x + y) = 2(37)$$

$$10x + 2y = 74$$
$$-\ (x + 2y = 11)$$
$$\overline{9x + 0 = 63}$$

$$x = 7$$

Einstein said that both equations need to be changed sometimes. Look at the following equations:

$$3x + 2y = 43$$
$$2x - 3y = 7$$

I can see the problem here. I will need to change both equations to get rid of the x's or the y's. I can easily do that by multiplying the top equation by 3 and the bottom equation by 2. When I do that I end up with 6y on the top and on the bottom.

$$3(3x + 2y) = 3(43)$$
$$2(2x - 3y) = 2(7)$$

$$9x + 6y = 129$$
$$+\ 4x - 6y = 14$$
$$\overline{13x + 0 = 143}$$

$$x = 11$$

Change one or both equations to make one of the variables disappear. Find the value of $x$ and $y$.

1) x + y = 79
   3x + 4y = 284

2) 4x + 3y = 14
   3x + 4y = 17.5

3) x + y = 3.75
   14x - 2y = 4.5

4) 2x - y = 0
   4x + 3y = 60

5) 2x + 3y = 40.5
   3x + 2y = 39.5

6) Four cats and three dogs cost $135. At the same store three cats and four dogs cost $145. What is the cost of one cat? (At this store all cats sell for the same price and all dogs sell for the same price.)

7) Stacy and Linsey gave clues to Dan about their ages. Using the clues, determine both their ages.
   Clue 1: When you add twice Stacey's age to Linsey's age, you get 54.
   Clue 2: When you add Stacey's age to twice Linsey's age, you get 45.

8) Scott bought two tape dispensers and two pencils for $13.08. The next day he bought 3 tape dispensers and 4 pencils for $19.81. What is the cost of one tape dispenser?

  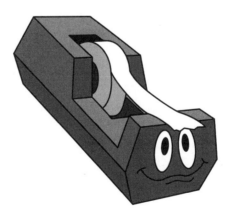

9) Find two numbers such that three times the first plus two times the second equals 37 and also two times the first plus three times the second equals 38.

10) Jacob bought 6 angelfish and two goldfish for $9.52. Steve bought 6 goldfish and two angelfish for $7.92. What was the price of one angelfish?

## Simultaneous Equations                                    Level 1

1) A pair of shoes and a pair of socks together cost $39.75. This same pair of shoes minus a pair of socks cost $31.25. What is the price of the shoes?

2) A math book plus two science books cost $80.50. Five math books minus the price of two science books is $60.50. What is the price of one science book?

3) Half of Ed's weight plus Luke's weight equals 250 pounds. Half of Luke's weight plus Ed's weight equals 282.5 pounds. How much does Luke weigh?

4) Donna and Jay were saving for a $54 bike. When they combined their money, they had exactly the right amount of money. They also knew that they could buy a $137 racing bike if Donna doubled her money and Jay tripled his. How much money does Jay have?

5) Anna and Claire found out that they were not only the same height, but they weighed the same too. They decided to see if their algebra class could guess their height and weight with two clues. Use the clues and determine Anna and Claire's height and weight.

Clue 1: When one of our weights is added to one of our heights (in inches) the number you would get is 144.
Clue 2: If you triple Anna's weight and then subtract her height (in inches), you would get 184.

6) Ben's allowance plus his friend's allowance equals $11.25. If Ben's allowance is tripled, their allowances would total $27.25. How much is Ben's allowance?

7)  Maria's height in inches plus her weight is equal to 155. Maria's weight minus her height is equal to 31. How tall is Maria?

8) Rosa gave two clues to her friends so they could guess her age and her mother's age. Use the two clues to find Rosa's age and her mother's age.
Clue 1:  My age plus my mother's is equal to 57.
Clue 2: If you subtract my age from my mother's, the answer is 39.

9) The perimeter of an Isosceles triangle is 34 inches.  When you add the base of the triangle to one of the equal sides the sum is 18. What is the length of the base of the triangle?

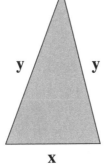

10) The perimeter of a rectangle is 92 inches. When you subtract the width from the length the difference is 24 inches. What is the width of the rectangle?

## Simultaneous Equations                                    Level 2

1)  3 dogs plus 5 cats cost $365
    5 dogs plus 3 cats cost $491        What is the cost of one cat?

2) Dan bought a computer game and returned a coffee mug that he didn't need.  Dan wrote a check for $75. Scott bought the same computer and also bought a coffee mug. He wrote a check for $90. How much did the computer game cost?

3)      $2x + 18 = y$
        $x + 7 = -y$        Find the value of x

4)      $3\frac{1}{2}x + 2y = 43$
        $2x + 3\frac{1}{2}y = 25\frac{3}{4}$    Find the value of x

5) When you add the digits of a two-digit number, the sum is 12. When you subtract the second digit from twice the first, the answer is 15. What is the number?

6) Tickets for a school musical were $4 for adults and $3 for children. The school took in $2778 in ticket sales. If the total number of people attending the play was 722, how many children attended?

7) Amadeus bought a certain number of 5-cent stamps we'll call *x*. He also bought a certain number of 3-cent stamps we'll call *y*. Altogether he paid $1.26. Jay bought *x* 3-cent stamps and *y* 5-cent stamps and paid $1.14. How many 3-cent stamps did Amadeus buy? (Hint: When you buy *x* 5-cent stamps, the cost of that purchase is *5x*.)

8) Three years ago Luan and Jordan had saved a total of $2850. Luan decided to invest his money in the stock market and doubled his money. Jordan, who decided to invest his money in a chicken farm, ended up tripling his money. When they put their money together now, they have $7340. How much money did Jordan start with?

9) A bag of nickels and dimes contained 83 coins. If the value of the coins was $7.30, how many nickels are there? (Hint: If you call the number of nickels *x*, then the value of the nickels is *5x*. If you call the number of dimes *y*, then the value of the dimes is *10y*.)

10) Cheryl has a horse and cow ranch that contains 100 animals. The value of each horse is $500 and the value of each cow is $200. If the total value of the 100 animals is $31,100, how many horses does Cheryl have on her ranch? (Hint: Call the number of horses *x* and the number of cows *y*.)

**Simultaneous Equations**                                    Einstein Level

1) A barn was the home for ducks and cows. If there were 97 animals in the barn and there were 354 legs in the barn, how many cows are in the barn?

2) A horse and a saddle together normally cost $960. During a sale where horses are 30% off and saddles are 25% off, the total cost was $672.50. What is the regular price of a saddle? (Hint: When an item is discounted 30%, the new price is 70% of the regular price or .7*n*.)

3) Mike and Juanita worked the same number of hours during a week of road construction. Mike made $6 per hour and Juanita made $10 per hour. Their boss was so pleased with their work that she gave them each a bonus in addition to their hourly wage. (Their bonuses were the same.) If Mike made a total of $333 that week and Juanita made $481, how many hours did they each work? (Hint: Call the bonus *y*.)

4) Erin bought a bike and hiking boots in a state with a sales tax of 5%. The total cost of the items, including tax, was $116.13. Steve bought 2 bikes and hiking boots and paid $180.60 ***without*** tax. What was the price of the bike without tax?

5) Larry had the same number of nickels and
dimes in his left pocket. In his right pocket, he
had an equal number of quarters and half-dollars.
When Larry counted all the nickels and half-dollars,
it totaled $16.35. When he counted the dimes and
quarters, it totaled $10.20. How many quarters
does Larry have?

6) Brianna and her sister each have a savings account and they each owe
money to a credit card company. Brianna owes $1660 while her sister owes
$2136. "If you  give me just 15% of your savings, I can combine it with my
savings and pay off my debt," Brianna said.  Her sister replied, "If you give
me just 10% of your saving, I can combine it with my savings and pay off my
debt." How much money is in Brianna's savings account?

7) Cliff had a total of $100,000 to invest. He put some of the money in Bank
A that paid 4% interest and the rest in Bank B which paid 5% interest. After a
year, the amount of interest he earned was $4850. How much money did
Clifford invest in Bank A?

8) Latisha bought a bike and a helmet for $105 without sales tax. Amanda
went to the same store the following day and found that bikes were 25% off
and helmets were selling for 40% off. Amanda bought a bike and a helmet
and paid $75 without sales tax. What did Latisha pay for her bike?

9) Find the angle measurements in the two triangles shown below.

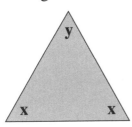
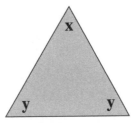

10) The perimeter of the first rectangle is equal to 50 inches. The perimeter of
the second rectangle is 74 inches. What are the dimensions of the first rectangle?

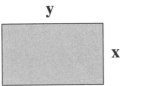
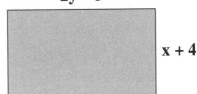

My parents sometimes suggest that I dig a hole in our backyard and see if I can make it go all the way to China. After a few feet, I usually give up. If I kept digging, would I eventually reach China?

If you dig a hole straight through the Earth from anywhere in the United States, (Except for two exceptions where you would end up on a couple small islands) you will end up in the ocean. I'm curious, what were you doing when your parents suggested that you try to dig a hole all the way to China? You weren't annoying them were you?

# Fun With Variables

A person who is eccentric is someone who does things differently than most people. The local fruit stand is owned by an eccentric mathematician who does not list prices for the fruit he sells. Instead of prices, he has a list of three equations that gives the value of the fruit. Using the equations, see if you can find how many pears are equal to a cantaloupe?

*cantaloupe - 2 apples = pear*

*2 bananas + pear = apple*

*2 pears = apple*

This problem looks confusing, but is actually quite easy. The first equation has cantaloupe, pears, and apples in it. You need to get rid of the apples. Because you know that 2 pears equal one apple, you can replace the 2 apples in the equation with 4 pears. All I do now is get rid of the pears on the left side.

*cantaloupe – 2 apples = pear*

*cantaloupe – 4 pears = pear*
         *+ 4 pears    + 4 pears*

*cantaloupe = 5 pears*

Some problems with many variables can be difficult. See if you can see how I solved this problem. You have to be a little clever sometimes to find out the right way to get rid of some of the variables, but if you use what you learned in the chapter on simultaneous equations, you should be able to figure them out.

*4 snakes + dog = rat*
*3 cats = rat*
*dog + snake = cat*

**How many dogs equal a rat?**

| | |
|---|---|
| | *4 snakes + dog = rat* |
| | *dog + snake = cat* |
| Step 1: Getting rid of snakes | *4 snakes + dog = rat* |
| | *4(dog + snake = cat)* |
| Step 2:  Subtract equations | *4 snakes + dog = rat* |
| | *4 dogs + 4 snakes = 4 cats* |
| (Snakes are gone) | *– 3 dogs = rat – 4 cats* |
| Step 3:  Get rid of cats | *3(–3 dogs = rat – 4 cats)* |
| | *4(rat = 3 cats)* |
| | *–9 dogs = 3 rats – 12 cats* |
| | *4 rats = 12 cats* |
| Step 4:  Add equations (Cats are gone) | *4 rats – 9 dogs = 3 rats* |
| | *rat = 9 dogs* |

*Remember to use the rules you learned in simultaneous equations to get rid of the variables you don't want. Eventually you will be left with only the variables that you need to answer the question.*

**Fun With Variables**                                              **Level 1**

1)  2 Apples + Cherry = Pear
    3 Cherries - 2 Apples = Pear

    How many cherries equal a pear?

2)  Banana + Pear = Apple
    3 Bananas = Apple

    How many pears would it take to make 2 apples?

3)  If three snails weigh as much as a snake and 18 ants
    weigh as much as a snake, how many ants equal a snail?

4)  Two tomatoes weigh the same as a grape and a peach. The peach weighs
    the same as nine grapes. How many grapes weigh as much as one tomato?

5)  A dog and a cat sell for the same price as 12 hamsters. Five cats sell for the
    price of one dog. How many hamsters would it take to equal the price of
    one dog?

## Fun With Variables                                    Level 2

1) 2y + 4z = 2x
   3x - 2y = 10z                    How many z's equal an x?

2) 4 dogs + parrot = cat
   cat - 3 parrots = 3 dogs
   dog + 7 parrots = cat           How many parrots equal a cat?

3) 3 camels - 2 deer = turtle
   2 deer + camel = turtle         How many deer are equal to a camel?

4)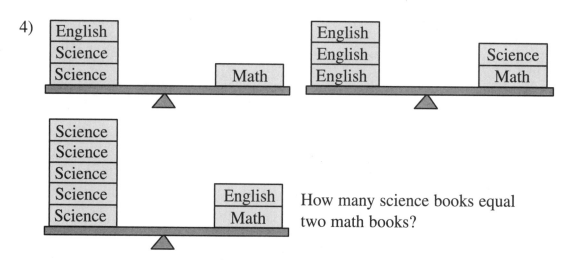

How many science books equal two math books?

5) Jody and Amber were trading baseball cards. Jody traded six of her Garcias for four of Amber's Robinsons. She also traded 2 of her Robinsons for one of Amber's Mays. How many Garcias would be equal to one Mays?

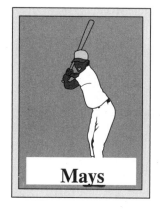

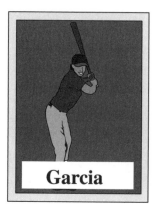

**Fun With Variables**                                    **Einstein Level**

1) 2 squares + triangle = rectangle
   2 circles - triangle = square
   3 circles + 2 triangles = rectangle

   How many triangles
   equal a rectangle?

2) 3 worms + salamander = lizard
   snake + salamander = worm
   lizard - 5 snakes = salamander

   How many salamanders
   equal 2 worms?

3) 2x + 2y = z
   y - 3r = x
   2x + 10r = z

   How many x's equal z?

4) 2 termites - ant = beetle
   2 beetles - termite = 2 ants

   How many termites
   equal 4 ants?

5) A camp made its own coins to use for buying food from the camp store.
The coins were called bats, bees and mosquitoes.  How many bees would a
camper get for 6 bats?

I've heard that a small part of a neutron star would be very, very heavy. Could I lift a piece the size of a marble?

A neutron star is so dense and heavy that it is very hard to believe how much a small piece weighs. To give you an idea of how dense a piece of neutron star is, if the small ball at the end of your pen was made of matter from a neutron star, that small piece would weigh 100,000 tons.

That's amazing! A piece of neutron star the size of a marble would probably weigh over 10,000,000 tons!

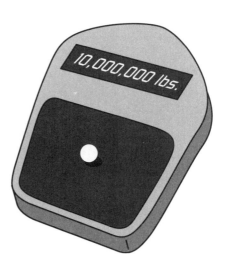

10,000,000 lbs.

# Order of Operations

When you do math problems, you find out very quickly that your answer to a problem changes if you do addition before multiplication or subtraction before division. It didn't take mathematicians long to realize that they needed rules to make sure everyone did math problems the same way. That is why we have "order of operations rules."

A long time ago my grandmother told me a story to help me remember the math rules for order of operations. The story seems awfully silly now, but it was a big help when I tried to remember the correct order of operations. Here is my grandmother's story.

A long, long time ago, when people were deciding what operations would go first, there were arguments every night as to what operation was most important and why. Parentheses Man said that his operation was the most important because he could include all the other operations inside him. Exponent Woman argued furiously that her operation was the most important because she could multiply numbers by themselves.

I am the most important because I can put all of you inside parentheses.
$(5^2 + 6 \times 9 \div 6 - 3)$

I am the most important because I can multiply numbers by themselves.
$6^2 = 36 \qquad 6^3 = 216$

As you might expect, the Multiplication and Division Twins thought they were most important because multiplication could make numbers get very large and division could split things into pieces. The one thing that they wanted everyone to know was that they thought multiplication and division were of equal importance.

The other set of twins, the Addition and Subtraction twins, knew that they weren't nearly as powerful as everyone else so they remained very quiet. They were very impressed with the Multiplication and Division Twin's statement of equality so they decided that even though they weren't powerful, they were equal to each other in importance.

The arguments went on for a long time, so it was decided that there would be a race to determine the order of operations. As expected, Parentheses Man came in first and Exponent Woman came in second. The Multiplication and Division Twins crossed the finish line at the same time so it was decided that as a math problem is worked on, parentheses would be done first, exponents second, and then multiplication and division would be done in the order they appear in the problem. If multiplication is before division in the problem, it would be done first. If division is before multiplication, it would be done first. The Addition and Subtraction Twins came in last, so of course they would be the last operations to be done. They also crossed the finish line together so it was decided that whichever one was first in the problem would be done first.

**Order of Operations**

(1) Parentheses

(2) Exponents

(3) Division and Multiplication

(4) Addition and Subtraction

When I solve problems using the order of operation's rules, I circle the part I am working on so I don't make so many careless mistakes. Watch how I do these two problems.

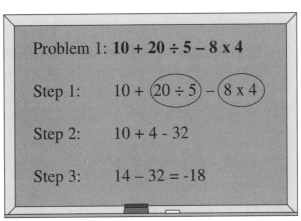

Problem 1: **10 + 20 ÷ 5 − 8 x 4**

Step 1:      10 + (20 ÷ 5) − (8 x 4)

Step 2:      10 + 4 - 32

Step 3:      14 − 32 = -18

Problem 2: **(9 + 5) ÷ 7 + 6 x 3**

Step 1:      (9 + 5) ÷ 7 + (6 x 3)

Step 2:      (14 ÷ 7) + 18

Step 3:      2 + 18 = 20

## Order of Operations                                              Level 1

1) $60 + 15 \div 3 - 6 =$

2) $8 \times 4 - 10 \times 2 =$

3) $35 - 35 \times 2 =$

4) $6 + 6 \div 6 \times 6 - 6$

5) $10 + 10 \div 10 - 11$

6) $4 \times 5 + 3 - 2 \div 2 =$

7) $6 \div 3 \times 7 \div 7 =$

8) $20 - 18 \div 9 - 18$

9) $10 \div 5 + 5 \times 5$

10) $5 + 5 - 5 - 5 \div 2$

## Order of Operations                                              Level 2

1) If you can insert one pair of parentheses, what is the largest number you can make out of the following:    *8 – 4 x 5 + 10*

2) Insert parentheses to make the following statement true:  *5 x 7 + 3 = 50*

3)  Insert parentheses to make the following statement true: *6 x 5 + 5 ÷ 1 = 60*

4) If *n* is equal to 7, what is the value of the following:      *2n² + 6(5 -n)*

5) If you can insert one pair of parentheses, what is the largest number you can make out of the following:   *6 x 5 + 12 – 3*

6) If *n* is equal to 5, what is the value of   *2(n²)²?*

7) $5 + 5 \div \dfrac{1}{5} \times 5$

8) $3 + 3 - 3 - 3 \div \dfrac{1}{10}$

9) $1 + 1 \times 1 \div 1 - 1$

10) $\dfrac{1}{8} \div 8 + \dfrac{63}{64}$

## Order of Operations                    Einstein Level

1) $5n = 6 \times 9 \div 9$

2) $(-4)^2 \div 2 + 8 \times 4$

3) Add one pair of parentheses to make the expression as large as possible. What is the value?

$$5 \times 2 + 1000 \times 4$$

4) $-5^2$

5) $6 - 9^2$

6) Add one pair of parentheses to make the expression as small as possible. What is the value?

$$100 \div \frac{1}{4} \div 2 - 9$$

7) Add one pair of parentheses to make the expression as large as possible. What is the value?

$$100 \div \frac{1}{4} \div 2 - 9$$

8) $\left[\left(\frac{1}{4}\right)^2 + \frac{15}{16}\right] \div 1 \times \frac{1}{4} + \frac{3}{4}$

9) $9 \div 3 \times 3 + 9 \div 3 \times 3 \div 9$

10) $3(5-9)^2 \times 2 + 4$

Why were all the great thinkers and philosophers of ancient Greece also mathematicians?

There were so many things that people of that time didn't understand. Philosophers and thinkers of the time loved mathematics because it showed them the truth about many things. For example, people thought that the moon and the sun were very close to the earth until mathematics showed them that both were quite far away.

# Fun With Formulas

The children of Einstein Middle School were all gathered around a large tire that was in their playground. The tire towered over the school and seemed to be as tall as some nearby trees. The tire was part of the field day contest that the entire school was engaged in. The task for each class was to try and determine how many inches around the tire was.

Most of the students thought that making an educated guess was about all that they could do. Brianna's class was sitting in a group discussing various ways of determining the circumference of the tire when suddenly one of the children jumped to her feet.

The problem is difficult because we need to go through two steps. We can use shadows and ratios and proportions to find the height of the tire. Then because the height of the tire is the same as the diameter of the tire, we can use the formula for finding the circumference of a circle.

$$C = \pi D$$

I am five feet tall and have a shadow of four feet. Because the tire has a shadow of 40 feet, it must be 50 feet tall. Then I use the formula $C = \pi D$. The circumference of the tire must be 157 feet. Formulas sure made it easy to find the circumference of the tire!!

There are many formulas that we use to find out important information. For example, we can get a very close estimate to what the temperature is in Celsius by using this formula that has to do with how many times a cricket chirps. Look at how easy it is to figure the temperature if a cricket chirps 33 times in a minute.

**Formula**

$$\text{Temperature in Celsius} = \frac{\text{Chirps per minute} + 30}{7}$$

$$\text{Temperature in Celsius} = \frac{33 + 30}{7}$$

$$\text{Temperature in Celsius} = \frac{63}{7} = 9°C$$

I am used to temperatures in the Fahrenheit scale. I can even use a formula to change that temperature from Celsius to Fahrenheit.

**Formula**

**Fahrenheit = 1.8 x Celsius + 32**

**Fahrenheit = 1.8(9) + 32**

**Fahrenheit = 16.2 + 32**

**Temperature = 48.2˚F**

We talked earlier in the book about how to use our weight to determine what our mass is. It's fun to tell people that my mass is 4.5 slugs. Watch how I use the weight to mass formula to find out how many slugs 144 pounds is equal to.

**Formula**

$$\text{Mass} = \frac{\text{weight}}{32}$$

$$\text{mass} = \frac{144}{32}$$

**My mass is 4.5 slugs**

Why does everyone laugh at the fact that the label for mass is the slug. I see nothing at all humorous about it.

People are always converting my weight of 88 pounds into 40 kilograms. This bothers me because kilograms are a unit of mass and not weight. The metric system uses the *newton* as a unit of weight. I can use the following formula to change kilograms into newtons: *Kilograms x 9.8 = Newtons*

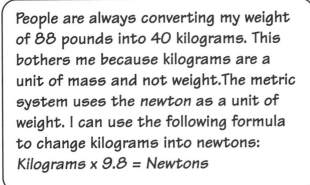

**Formula**

**Kilograms x 9.8 = Newtons**

**40 x 9.8 = 392 newtons**

**I weigh 392 newtons**

When I climb an observation tower, it seems like I can see forever. I know I can't because the earth is round, but I can see much farther than when I am on the ground. Is there a way to tell how far I can see when I am up on a tower or even at the top of a mountain?

Yes, there is even a formula to help you determine how far you can see when you are in a tall building or at the top of a mountain. The formula is a little confusing, so I'll show you how to solve a couple problems.

A girl was standing at the top of an observation tower that was 25 meters tall. How far can she see on a clear day?

### Formula

Distance you can see in kilometers = $3.5 \sqrt{\text{height in meters}}$

Distance = $3.5 \sqrt{25}$

Distance = 3.5 x 5

**The girl can see 17.5 kilometers**

Luke climbed Mt. Washington, which is about 2000 meters high. When he reached the top, about how many kilometers could Luke see in the distance?

Distance you can see in kilometers = $3.5 \sqrt{\text{height in meters}}$

Distance = $3.5 \sqrt{2000}$

Distance = 3.5 x 44.7

**Luke can see 156.45 kilometers**

**Fun with Formulas**                                                Level 1

Distance in kilometers = $3.5 \sqrt{height\ in\ meters}$

Temperature in Celsius = $\dfrac{Chirps\ per\ minute + 30}{7}$

Fahrenheit = 1.8C + 32

Mass = $\dfrac{Weight}{32}$

Newtons = 9.8 x Kilograms

1) On a clear day how far can you see from a building that is 225 meters high?

2) If a cricket chirps 110 times in a minute, what is the approximate temperature expressed in Celsius?

3) A football player weighs 336 pounds. What is the mass of the player expressed in slugs?

4) A baby who was not feeling well had a temperature of 37° C. Is this temperature cause for concern?

5) A student who liked science was very annoyed when his doctor wrote his weight as 86 kilograms. This student knew that kilograms was a measurement of mass and not weight so he asked the doctor to write his weight using newtons. What is this student's weight expressed in newtons?

**Fun with Formulas**    Level 2

$$\text{Distance in kilometers} = 3.5 \sqrt{\text{height in meters}}$$

$$\text{Temperature in Celsius} = \frac{\text{Chirps per minute} + 30}{7}$$

$$\text{Fahrenheit} = 1.8C + 32$$

$$\text{Mass} = \frac{\text{Weight}}{32}$$

$$\text{Newtons} = 9.8 \times \text{Kilograms}$$

1) The boiling point of water on top of Mount Everest is 159.8° F. What is this temperature expressed in Celsius?

2) If you can see 35 kilometers from the top of a building, how tall is the building?

3) If the temperature is 18°C, how many cricket chirps would you expect each minute?

4) If a student weighed 490 newtons, what is his mass?

5) If a book had a mass of .03125 slugs, what is its weight in pounds?

**Fun with Formulas**　　　　　　　　　　　　　**Einstein Level**

Distance in kilometers = 3.5 $\sqrt{\textit{height in meters}}$

Temperature in Celsius = $\dfrac{\textit{Chirps per minute} + 30}{7}$

Fahrenheit = 1.8C + 32

Mass = $\dfrac{\textit{Weight}}{32}$

Newtons = 9.8 x Kilograms

1) If you are in an airplane and can see 126 kilometers, how high is the plane? (Express your answer in kilometers.)

2) Serena has a mass of 52 kilograms. What is Serena's mass expressed in slugs? (Each kilogram is 2.2 pounds.)

3) How many newtons would a 200-pound man weigh?

4) There is one temperature that is the same in both the Fahrenheit and Celsius scales. What is that temperature?

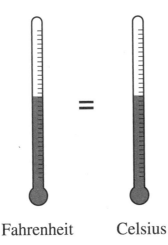

Fahrenheit　　　Celsius

5) Determine the formula for finding the temperature based on the chirping of a cricket in Fahrenheit. Hint: C= $\frac{F-32}{1.8}$ (Plug this in for C in the cricket formula.)

When a lion tamer snaps his whip, there is a loud noise that sounds almost like the loud crack of thunder during a storm. The whip doesn't hit anything so how does the lion tamer make such a loud noise?

The sound that you hear is actually a small sonic boom. Believe it or not, the tip of the whip is traveling faster than the speed of sound when it makes the loud crack.

# Function Machines

I remember very clearly the first time I heard of function machines. One of my math teachers would put an extra credit problem on the board when there were only five minutes left of math class. The problem wasn't hard if you had three or four hours to solve it, so it was very frustrating to never be able to have the time to find the answer and get the extra credit.

> It is very easy to find the 6th number in the following sequence. I want you to find the 5000th number.
>
> 7,    11,    15,   19,   23.................
> 1st   2nd   3rd   4th   5th

After I told my grandmother about the type of problem the teacher was expecting us to solve in five minutes, she took me up into her attic where she kept hundreds of function machines. I can still remember what she said as I looked at the mysterious machines lined up against the wall. "These machines will not only give you the speed to answer those kinds of questions in less than a minute, but they will help you understand the advanced math that you will be taking when you are a little older."

Each machine had an opening into which a number was placed. After a few seconds of rumbling and whirling, a number came out an exit pipe. The machine did something to the number you put into it as it changed it into a new number. All the function machines in grandmother's attic did something different. Some were complicated like the function machine that squared the number, multiplied the answer by five and then subtracted seven. Others were simple like the function machine that just multiplied by two.

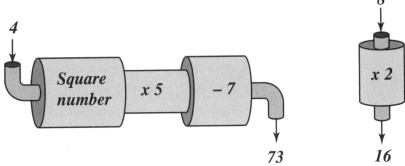

The fun part of playing with the function machines was putting numbers into it, seeing what came out and then trying to guess what the function machine did to the number. The way I tried to figure out what each machine did was to make a chart. I would send a few numbers through the machine and write down what came out. After I made my guess, grandmother would open the function machine with a key so I could see inside of it and check whether I was right or not.

| In | Out |
|----|-----|
| 1 | 6 |
| 2 | 12 |
| 3 | 18 |
| 4 | 24 |

My guess is that this function machine multiplies by six.

Because there is a difference of five between each output number, I know that there is a x 5 in the function machine. If I put a 1 in the machine, 1 x 5 = 5 but the output is a 4 so all I need to do is put a *subtract one* in the function machine. Now I'll check my other numbers. 2 x 5 -1 = 9
3 x 5 - 1 = 14   It works!!!!

| In | Out |
|----|-----|
| 1 | 4 |
| 2 | 9 |
| 3 | 14 |
| 4 | 19 |

| In | Out |
|----|-----|
| 1 | 1 |
| 2 | 4 |
| 3 | 9 |
| 4 | 16 |

This function machine gave me a lot of trouble because after I put the 1 in, it looked like the machine didn't do anything because a 1 came out. Then I noticed that there was something special about all the output numbers. They were all perfect squares. I was pretty sure then that the function machine was squaring the numbers.

After I practiced a little on the function machines, my grandmother said that I was ready to solve the extra credit problem from school. She told me that I could draw a function machine and it would work just as well as her machines. I made up a chart for the extra credit problem and it wasn't long before I could see what I needed to do.

It is very easy to find the 6th number in the following sequence. I want you to find the 5000th number.

7,   11,   15,   19,   23.................
1st 2nd 3rd 4th 5th

| In | Out |
|----|-----|
| 1 | 7 |
| 2 | 11 |
| 3 | 15 |
| 4 | 19 |
| 5 | 23 |

Because there was a difference of four between each output number, I knew there was a x 4 in the function machine. 1 x 4 = 4 but the output was 7 so all I had to do was add + 3 to the function machine.

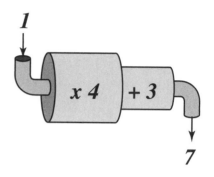

When I checked all the other numbers, the function machine worked perfectly. Now I knew exactly what to do. I needed to send the number 5000 through the function machine because the problem asked for the 5000th number.

2 x 4 + 3 = 11
3 x 4 + 3 = 15
4 x 4 + 3 = 19
5 x 4 + 3 = 23

**5000**

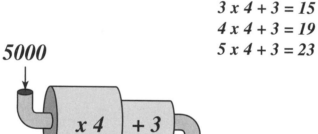

**20003**

That was incredible!! Function machines can quickly find answers to problems that would take hours.

Draw your own function machines as you solve the following problems. When the problem asks for the 100th term , it is asking for the 100th number in the sequence.

1) Find the 100th term in the following sequence:  2, 5, 8, 11................

2) Find the 1000th term in the following sequence: 0, 12, 24, 36.........

3) Find the 500th term in the following sequence: 6, 12, 18, 24.............

4) Find the 25th term in the following sequence: 1, 4, 9, 16, 25..............

5) In the sequence 3, 9, 15, 21........ you will eventually reach the number 1047. What term of the sequence is the number 1047?

I was doing great until problem number 5. It was easy to make the function machine, but in this problem you are given the output and you need to find the input. How in the world do you do that?

If you ever have to go backwards through a function machine, all you do is use the opposite operation. Watch what I do when I go in the reverse direction through this function machine. 1047 is the 175th term of the sequence.

*Do the opposite operation*

Try the following function machine problems where you need to send numbers through the function machine in the opposite direction. Remember that when you go in a reverse direction, you need to do the opposite operation. Addition turns into subtraction and multiplication turns into division.

1) In the sequence 1, 4, 9, 16....... What term is the number 2304?

2) In the sequence 9, 15, 21, 27.......What term is the number 4863?

3) In the sequence 5, 10, 15, 20.........What term is the number 23,945?

4) In the sequence -4, 6, 16, 26.........What term is the number 9986?

5) In the sequence 8, 4, 2, 1............What term is the fraction $\frac{1}{32}$? (There are some problems where function machines don't help you.)

There was one function machine at grandmother's house that I could not figure out. I sent numbers through the machine and made the chart that I'm showing you, but I just couldn't figure out what the machine was doing to the numbers.

| In | Out |
|----|-----|
| 1  | 11  |
| 2  | 16  |
| 3  | 23  |
| 4  | 32  |

I got so frustrated at not being able to find out what the machine was doing to the numbers I put through it that I drew the letter $x$ and sent it through the machine. When I saw the output, I suddenly realized what the function machine was doing to the numbers. I also realized that I didn't have to make a chart anymore to find out what any function machine did to numbers. All I had to do was send a letter through. See if you can guess what the function machine is doing to the numbers that are sent through it.

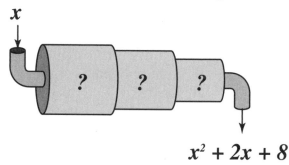

$x^2 + 2x + 8$

## Function Machines       Level 1

1) Find the 1000th term in the sequence 4, 7, 10, 13..................................

2) What is the next number in the following sequence? 1, 4, 9, 16,___

3) The number 2002 is what term in the following sequence?

| 6 | 10 | 14 | 18 | | 2002 |
|------|------|------|------|---|------|
| 1st | 2nd | 3rd | 4th | | nth |

4) Find the millionth term in the sequence 5, 10, 15, 20.............

5) What is the next number in the following sequence? 5, 25, 125, 625.......

6) What is the next term in the following sequence? 6.1, 6.4, 6.8, 7.3..........

7) How many squares of any size are in the figure shown?

8) What is the 100th term in the following sequence? 0, 7, 14, 21,............

9) There were three mosquitoes on June 1st, six on June 2nd and nine on June 3rd. If this pattern continues, how many mosquitoes will there be on June 30th?

10) What is the 10th term of the following sequence?

23, 17, 11, 5,.............

## Function Machines                                              Level 2

1) What is the next number in the following sequence? 1,8,27,64..........

2) What is the 100th term in the sequence? 2,5,10,17..........

3) Find the 1000th term in the following sequence: 0,3,8,15...............

4) How many squares of any size are in the following figure?

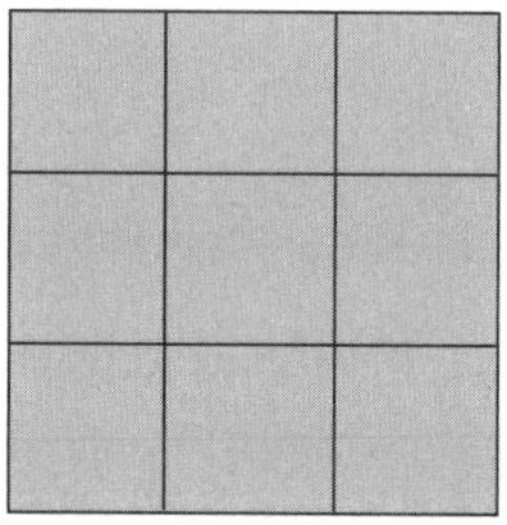

5) Which term of the following sequence is 424? 4, 9, 14, 19, .....................424

6) An amoeba population triples every 10 minutes. If a petri dish is completely filled after 7 hours, how long did it take for the petri dish to be a third filled?

7) What is the next term in the sequence? 4, 16, 64, 256,.............

8) If the radius of a circle is doubled, the area is four times as large. If the radius of a circle is tripled, the area of the circle is nine times as large. What happens to the area of a circle when the radius is quadrupled?

9) What is the 500th term of the following sequence? -7,-4,-1, 2, 5, 8............

10) What term in the sequence shown below is the number 498?

-6, 0, 6, 12, 18, 24...............................498

Function Machines                                    Einstein Level

1) Find the 100th term in the following sequence:  2,6,12,20............

2) You are given a penny on May 1st, two pennies on May 2nd, four pennies on May 3rd, eight pennies on May 4th and so on. How much money would you be given on May 31st?

3) How many squares of any size are in this figure?

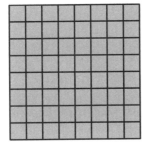

4)  A bookworm read books in the given pattern. If she continues to read in the same pattern, what year of her life would she read 6561 books?

1st year of her life......1 book
2nd year of her life.....4 books
3rd year of her life......9 books
4th year of her life......16 books

5) Scientists are worried about the hot gases in a rocket burning through the rubber gasket that is supposed to seal them inside the rocket. They noticed that the colder the temperature during the launch, the more burn-through there is of the rubber gasket. The scientists are very concerned because if the rubber gasket burns through completely, the rocket could explode. Using the following data they collected, predict the temperature at which the rubber gasket will burn completely through.

60°------------8% burn-through
55°------------11.5% burn-through
50°-----------18.5% burn-through
45°-----------32.5% burn-through
40°-----------60.5% burn-through

6) What is the 500th term of the following sequence? $3, 3\frac{1}{2}, 4, 4\frac{1}{2}, 5, \ldots\ldots$

7) What is the 1000th term of the sequence? $8, 11, 16, 23\ldots\ldots\ldots$

8) A triangle has interior angles that add up to 180°. A quadrilateral has interior angles that add up to 360°. A pentagon has interior angles that add up to 540° while a hexagon has interior angles that add up to 720°. What is the total number of degrees of the interior angles in a polygon with one hundred sides?

3-sided-------180°
4-sided-------360°
5-sided-------540°
6-sided-------720°

9) Find the 500th term in the following sequence? $15, 10, 5, 0, -5, -10\ldots\ldots\ldots$

10) A mouse population grew from one mouse to two mice in a week. The mouse population then grew to four mice in another week. How many total weeks would it take for the mouse population to grow from one mouse to a million mice if it continues to double every week?

# Math Contest 1

1) A very wealthy individual donated 100 million dollars to the United Nations for hunger relief. Because this individual is worth 50 billion dollars, the donation caused him very little hardship. A student who owned $100 wanted to donate to charity the same proportional amount of money as the wealthy person. How much should her donation be?

2) Einstein Elementary School is in such poor condition that it must be replaced. The only way that it can be replaced is if voters in the community pass

a bond issue to raise the 8 million that is needed for a new school. In order for the bond issue to pass, over 60% of the voters must vote yes. If 5613 votes are cast, how many must be yes votes for the children of Einstein Elementary School to get their new school?

3) Renee drove the 673.75 miles to her mother's house at an average speed of 55 mph. If she arrived at 11:00 P.M., what time did she start her trip?

4) Bonnie is planning to put an outdoor carpet on her deck. The deck is in the shape of a trapezoid as shown below. She needs to find the size of the two unknown angles so she can accurately cut the carpet. Angle a is 10° larger than angle b. What is the measurement of each angle?

5) A pile of coins contained nickels, dimes and quarters. There were 4 times as many dimes as nickels and twice as many quarters as dimes. If the value of the pile is $4.90, how many quarters are in the pile?

# Math Contest 2

1) Three sisters decided to jointly buy a car. Karen earns three times as much per hour as Sara. And Claudia earns twice as much per hour as Sara. When they had each worked 500 hours, they had enough money to buy an $18,000 car. What is Sara paid per hour?

2) The election for a tax increase to pay for a new Einstein Elementary School is about to take place. The supporters of the tax have lined up 568 voters who they are sure will vote to support the school. The group of people who are hoping that the new school will not be built are trying to figure out how many no votes it will take before the election is lost. How many no voters must they line up in order to defeat the tax increase if the supporters of the school line up 568 yes votes? Remember that in order for the tax increase to pass, the yes votes must be 60% of the total votes.

3) Jesse needed to find out how many times his heart beat per minute. He didn't want to count his heartbeats for a full 60 seconds, so he decided to count them for a short period of time and then use math to find out how many beats there would be in a full minute. Jesse counted 21 beats in 17 seconds. How many times would Jesse's heart beat in a minute?

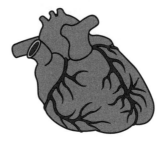

4) Isaac bought four pencils and one pen and paid $1.65. Travis bought one pencil and four pens and paid $3.75. What is the cost of one pen?

5) Stacy hiked up Pikes Peak at a speed of 3 mph. She then rode a trail bike down at a speed of 9 mph. What was her average speed for the round trip?

# Math Contest 3

1) A fruit stand owner ordered 20,000 apples for her roadside store at a cost of 12.4 cents per apple. She was given a bill for $2480. When the apples arrived and were unloaded from the truck, the fruit stand owner found that there were 15 bad apples for every 90 that were unloaded. She is demanding an adjustment in the $2480 bill because it is clear that 15 out of every 90 apples are so damaged that they can not be sold. What should the new bill be?

2) The total cost of a book, including an 8% sales tax, was $26.19. What is the cost of the book without tax?

3) Four consecutive numbers add up to 450. What is the smallest number?

4) The smallest side of a trapezoid is 8 inches smaller than the largest side. The second to the largest side is 3 inches smaller than the largest side while the remaining side is 2 inches larger than the smallest side. If the perimeter of the trapezoid is 59 inches, what is the length of the largest side?

5) Alen Webb, a talented high school track star, ran a mile in 3 minutes 53.43 seconds. Express this speed in miles per hour. (Round to the nearest tenth.)

# Math Contest 4

1) A 75 pound child and a 60 pound child are playing on a 16 foot see-saw. If the 60 pound child sits on one end of the board, how far from the fulcrum must the 75 pound child sit for the see-saw to balance?

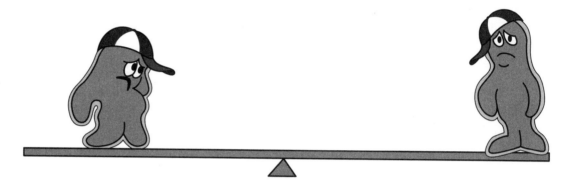

2) If a television that normally sells for $180 is on sale for 15% off, what is the total price for the television including tax? The sales tax rate is 8%.

3) If a glove and a ball together cost $50 and the glove cost $45 more than the ball, what is the price of the ball?

4) Solve:  20 + 5 ÷ 5 x 81 =

5) The distance between Westown and Northboro is 91 miles and the distance between Northboro and Eastown is 35 miles. How many miles shorter is it to take Route 3 directly from Westown to Northboro instead of first traveling to Eastown and then going to Northboro?

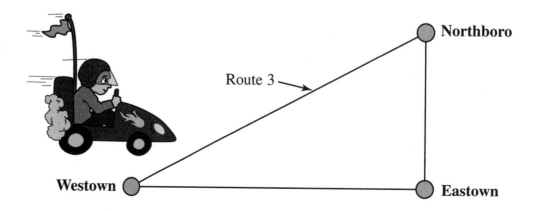

# Math Contest 5

1) A 92 mile trip used 6 gallons of gas. If gas was consumed at the same rate, how many gallons of gas would be used on a 158 mile trip?

2) Two cyclists are starting on a trip at the same time. If one travels at 24 mph and the other at 20 mph, how long until they are 5 miles apart?

3) Dan types 50 words a minute. He found out that there are an average of 300 words on each page that he types. How many hours would it take Dan to type *n* pages? Hint: How many hours does it take Dan to type one page? 10 pages? *n* pages?

4) Is the following triangle a right triangle?

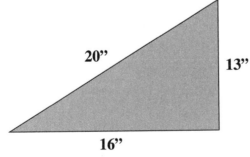

5) When 5 squares of equal size are placed next to each other in a row, the perimeter of the rectangle is 84 inches. What is the measurement of one side of one of the squares?

# Math Contest 6

**Distance in kilometers = 3.5 $\sqrt{h}$**  (*h* is your height in meters above the ground.)

**Temperature in Celsius =** $\dfrac{\text{Chirps per minute} + 30}{7}$

**Rate x Time = Work**

1) Steve paints a car in 2 hours while Jill paints the same car in 4 hours. If they work together, how long will it take them to paint the car?

2) Lyn is at the top of a 64 meter tower. Assuming the air is clear, how many kilometers away can she see?

3) If you are in an airplane 10,000 meters above the ground, how far can you see?

4) If a cricket chirps 180 times per minute, what is the approximate air temperature in Celsius?

5) If the air temperature is 100° C, how many chirps per minute would you expect?

# Math Contest 7

1) The part of an iceberg that is below water has been estimated to be seven times the amount that shows above the water. What percent of the iceberg is below the water?

2) Debra can paint a 25' x 80' wall in 6 days. What fraction of the wall can she paint in 1 day? How much of the wall can she paint in *n* days?

3) The angles in a triangle are in a ratio of 2:5:17. What is the measurement of the largest angle?

4) Janelle can pick 17 bushels of apples in an hour. Her hourly wage is $8.75. Sam can pick only 11.5 bushels of apples per hour. To be paid fairly (based on the amount of apples picked) what should Sam be paid per hour?

5) Ten apples plus twenty oranges cost $12.70. Ten oranges plus twenty apples cost $13.70. What is the cost of one apple?

# Math Contest 8

1) Brianna is trying to find out how tall a tree is near her house so she can determine if it will hit the house if she cuts it down. The tree has a shadow of 62 feet and at the same time a yard stick is casting a shadow of 23 inches. If the tree is 95 feet from her house, is it safe to cut it down? Why?

2) A car rental company charges $20 per day plus 8 cents per mile. Another company charges $48 per day but doesn't charge for the miles driven. How many miles would a customer have to drive to make the charge from each company exactly the same?

3)  8 + 4 x 8 - 7 ÷ 7 = n   What is the value of n?

4) Tom weighs 15 pounds more than Steve who weighs 20 pounds more than John. If their combined weight is 490 pounds, how much does Steve weigh?

5) Tonya and Donna are sitting on opposite ends of a 14 foot see-saw. If Tonya weighs 60 pounds and Donna weighs 80 pounds, how far should the fulcrum be placed from where Donna is sitting?

# Math Contest 9

1) Sara was shopping at a bookstore when she saw a shelf of books with a sign that said 75% off all books on this shelf. As she looked through the books, she spotted a book she always wanted but didn't want to spend the $50 that it normally cost. When Sara picked the book up, she saw a note on the book that said "Take an additional 20% off today." Sara quickly took the book to the cashier expecting to have the book discounted 95% to a price of $2.50. The clerk told Sara that the price of the book with all discounts was $10. Explain why the price of the book is $10 and not $2.50.

**75% off all books**

**Today only, take an additional 20% off**

2) The conversion rate of Canadian to American money is $1.37 Canadian money equals $1.00 American money. If Jerry had $26.84 of American money, how much Canadian money would that be worth?

3) There are three consecutive numbers. The sum of the first two numbers is 47 more than the third number. What are the three numbers?

4) Jane was the youngest in a group of friends whose ages totaled 109 years. Julie was twice as old as Jane and Jan was three times as old as Jane. If Jack is one year older than Jan, what is Jane's age?

5) If a slug weighs one ounce, what is the mass of the slug expressed in slugs?
(Round to the nearest thousandth.)

# Math Contest 10

1) How many triangles of any size are pointing up?

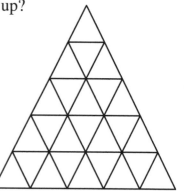

2) The price of a book after a 15% discount is $34. What was the original price of the book?

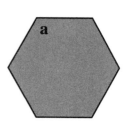

3) The sides of this hexagon are all of equal length. What is the measure of angle a?

4) Jay climbed a mountain at a speed of 2 mph. Jay's descent was at an average speed of 6 mph. What was his average speed for his entire trip up and down the mountain?

5) A painting and its frame together cost $1000. If the painting cost $900 more than the frame, what was the cost of the frame?

## Chapter 1: Language of Algebra

### Page 5

1) $n - 23$
2) $n \div 23$
3) $n$
4) $n + 23$
5) $n - 15$
6) $6n$

7) $10n$
8) $n + 7$
9) $2n + 6$
10) $\pi n$
11) $50n$
12) $4n$

### Level 1

1) Saddle $n$
   Horse $n + 900$

2) Eric $n$
   Nicki $5n$

3) Baby sister $n$
   Brianna $4n$

4) $3n$

5) $24n$

6) $4n$

7) $5n$
To find the value of any number of nickels you would multiply by 5. 12 nickels would have a value of 5 x 12. n nickels would have a value of 5 x $n$ or $5n$.

8) Smallest $n$
   Next $n + 1$
   Largest $n + 2$

9) Bob $n + 17$
   Steve $n$

10) Math $n + 2$
    Science $n$

### Level 2

1) $8n$
To find the amount of money Dave earned if he worked 7 hours, you would multiply 8 x 7. If you wanted to find out how much he would earn in 14 hours, you would multiply 8 x 14. If you wanted to know how much he earns in n hours, you would multiply 8 by n which would be $8n$.

2) $25n$

3) $n^2$ $(n \times n)$
The area of a square is found by multiplying one side by the other.

4) Smallest $n$
   Next $n + 5$
   Largest $n + 10$
To find the next consecutive multiple of 5, you would simply add 5. For example: The next multiple of 5 if you start with 145 is 145 + 5 or 150.

5) $(n - 50 + 18)$     $n - 32$

6) $65n$
In three hours a car going 65 mph goes 65 x 3 or 195 miles. In an unknown number of hours the car will go 65 x $n$ or $65n$ miles.

7) $\frac{1}{2}n + 580$
$\frac{1}{2}$ of Karen's salary plus 580

8) $n \div \pi$
If you know the circumference and want to find the diameter, you would divide the circumference by $\pi$.

9) $\frac{n}{3600}$

Because there are 3600 seconds in an hour, you can change 25,200 seconds into hours by dividing by 3600. $\frac{25,200}{3600}$ = 7 hours.

If you have an unknown number of seconds, you do the same thing, you divide by 3600 $\longrightarrow$ $\frac{n}{3600}$

10) 185 - *n*

If the hat cost $5, the coat would cost $180. (185 – 5 = 180)

If the hat cost $10, the coat would cost $175. (185 – 10 = 175)

To find the cost of the coat, you need to subtract the cost of the hat from $185. If the hat cost *n* dollars, the coat would cost 185 – *n*.

## Einstein Level

1) 8*n*

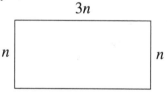

3*n* (The length is three times the width)

2) Dimes *n*
   Quarters 2*n*
   Nickels 4*n*

We call dimes *n* because there are fewer dimes than quarters or nickels. We call quarters 2*n* because there are twice as many quarters as dimes. We call nickels 4*n* because there are twice as many nickels as quarters.

3) Dimes 10*n*

The value of the dimes is 10 times the number of dimes. 10 x *n* = 10*n*

Quarters 50*n*

The value of the quarters is 25 times the number of quarters. 25 x 2*n* = 50*n*

Nickels 20*n*

The value of the nickels is 5 times the number of nickels. 5 x 4*n* = 20*n*

4) 4*n* + 202

The number of pig legs is 50 x 4 =200
The number of cow legs is 4 x *n* = 4*n*
The farmer has two legs.
    200 + 4*n* + 2  or 4*n* + 202

5) 468*n* + 2860

The bonus money in a year is $55 x 52 or $2860.

Hourly money in a week where Dan works n hours each week is 9 x *n* or 9*n*.

Hourly money in a year is the 9*n* x 52 weeks in a year or 468*n*

Total pay is 468*n* + $2860

6) $\frac{4n + 12}{4}$ (*n* + 3 is also correct)

Smallest number  *n*
Next even number  *n* + 2
Next even number  *n* + 4
Largest  *n* + 6

To find the average of four numbers , add them and divide by four.

$$\frac{n + n + 2 + n + 4 + n + 6}{4} \text{ or } \frac{4n + 12}{4}$$

7) $\frac{12n}{10}$

The amount of fencing is 12*n*. The amount of 10-foot sections therefore is 12*n* ÷ 10.

8) $75 - n$

9) $\frac{n}{\pi} \div 2$

If the circumference is known, the diameter of a circle can be found by dividing by $\pi$. If that answer is divided by two, then you will have the radius.

10) $\frac{5280}{n}$

A tire with a one-foot circumference would make 5280 revolutions in a mile. $5280 \div 1 = 5280$.

A tire with a two-foot circumference would make 2640 revolutions in a mile. $5280 \div 2 = 2640$.

A tire with a circumference of n feet would make $5280 \div n$ revolutions in a mile.

## Chapter 2: Solving Equations

### Page 13
1) $n = 25$     6) $n = 7$
2) $n = 17.5$   7) $n = 9$
3) $n = 1$      8) $n = 6$
4) $n = 5$      9) $n = 5$
5) $n = 3$      10) $n = 7$

### Page 14
1) $n = 5$      4) $n = 2$
2) $n = 2$      5) $n = 7$
3) $n = 4$      6) $n = 9.5$

### Page 15
1) 81
Equation: $3n - 7 = 236$
$n = 81$

2) $43
Scott: $n$
Jason: $n + 6$

Equation: $n + n + 6 = 92$
$n = 43$

3) $151
Mom: $n$
Sister: $n + 93$
Josh: $n + 93 - 72$ which is $n + 21$
Equation: $n + n + 93 + n + 21 = 504$
$n = 130$

4) $13.79
Baseball: $n$
Basketball: $n + 8.47$

Equation: $n + n + 8.47 = 19.11$
$n = 5.32$

The baseball cost $5.32 so the basketball cost $5.32 + $8.47 or $13.79

5) $112

Equation: $3n - 67 = 269$
$n = 112$

### Page 18
1) $n = 512$    6) $n = 84$
2) $n = 10$     7) $n = 8$
3) $n = 20$     8) $n = 50$
4) $n = 8$      9) $n = 150$
5) $n = 20$     10) $n = 15$

**Page 19**

| | |
|---|---|
| 1) $n = -11$ | 6) $n = 25$ |
| 2) $n = 11$ | 7) $n = 9$ |
| 3) $n = 25$ | 8) $n = 2$ |
| 4) $n = 25$ | 9) $n = -4$ |
| 5) $n = 4$ | 10) $n = -15.5$ |

**Page 20**

1) 17 pounds

Equation: $3n + 22 = 5n - 12$

$n = 17$

2) 1000

Equation: $5n + 6 = 6n - 994$

$n = 1000$

3) 64

Equation: $\frac{1}{2}n = 2n - 96$

$n = 64$

4) 13 inches

Equation: $2n + 3 = 3n - 2$

$n = 5$

You just found the length of a leg of the triangle is 5 inches. The problem says that you can find the length of the hypotenuse by doubling the leg length and adding three: $2 \times 5 + 3$   The hypotenuse is 13 inches.

5) $24.95

Math book: $n$

Science book: $22.95

Equation: $4n + 22.95 - 4 = 2n + 68.85$

$n = 24.95$

The 4 is subtracted on the left side of the equation because the problem says that the cost of 4 math books plus a science book is $4 more than the cost of 2 math books plus three science books. If you subtract 4, then the cost of 4 math books plus a science book will equal the cost of 2 math books plus 3 science books.

**Level 1**

1) $n = 25$

2) $n = 17$

3) $n = 11$

4) $n = 10$

5) $n = 4$

6) $n = 15$

7) $n = 3$

8) $n = 18$

9) $n = 62.5$

$\frac{n}{100} = \frac{5}{8}$ is the same as $\frac{1}{100}n = \frac{5}{8}$

$\frac{100}{1} \times \frac{1}{100}n = \frac{5}{8} \times \frac{100}{1}$

$n = \frac{500}{8}$        $n = 62.5$

10) $n = 2.5$

**Level 2**

1) $n = 4$

$\frac{2}{n} = \frac{1}{2}$   This says that 2 over some number equals $\frac{1}{2}$. That number must be 4. $\frac{2}{4} = \frac{1}{2}$

2) $n = 64$

Problem: $\frac{1}{4}n = \frac{1}{8}n + 8$

$n$'s on one side: $\frac{1}{8}n = 8$

Just one $n$: $\frac{8}{1} \times \frac{1}{8}n = \frac{8}{1} \times \frac{8}{1}$      $n = 64$

3) $n = 8$

4) $n = 16$

Problem: $15 + \frac{1}{8}n = 17$

Isolate $n$'s: $\frac{1}{8}n = 2$

Just one $n$: $\frac{8}{1} \times \frac{1}{8}n = \frac{2}{1} \times \frac{8}{1}$ $\quad n = 16$

5) $n = -3$

6) $n = 12$
Problem: $\frac{n}{2} = \frac{n}{4} + 3$ same as $\frac{1}{2}n = \frac{1}{4}n + 3$

$n$'s on one side: $\frac{1}{4}n = 3$

Just one $n$: $\frac{4}{1} \times \frac{1}{4}n = \frac{3}{1} \times \frac{4}{1}$ $\quad n = 12$

7) $n = \frac{1}{180}$

Problem: $90n = \frac{1}{2}$

Just one $n$: $\frac{90n}{90} = \frac{\frac{1}{2}}{90}$ $\quad n = \frac{1}{2} \div \frac{90}{1}$

$n = \frac{1}{180}$

8) $n = 16$
Problem: $\frac{n}{2} + \frac{n}{4} + \frac{n}{8} = 14$

$\quad\quad \frac{1}{2}n + \frac{1}{4}n + \frac{1}{8}n = 14$

Collect: $\frac{7}{8}n = 14$

Just one $n$: $\frac{8}{7} \times \frac{7}{8}n = \frac{14}{1} \times \frac{8}{7}$ $\quad n = 16$

9) $n = 2$ or $-2$

10) $n = 24$

Problem: $\frac{7}{8}n + \frac{1}{8} = 21\frac{1}{8}$

Isolate the $n$'s: $\frac{7}{8}n = 21$

Just one $n$: $\frac{8}{7} \times \frac{7}{8}n = \frac{21}{1} \times \frac{8}{7}$ $\quad n = 24$

**Einstein Level**
1) $n = 9$

2) $n = 6$
Problem: $\frac{1}{n} + \frac{2}{n} + \frac{3}{n} = 1$

This is the same as $\frac{6}{n} = 1$
(Think about it. $1+2+3 = 6$)

To make the equation true, $n$ must be equal to 6

3) $n = 11$ (-11 is acceptable)
Problem: $\quad 3n^2 + 19 = 382$

Isolate the $n^2$'s: $\quad 3n^2 = 363$

Just one $n^2$: $\frac{3n^2}{3} = \frac{363}{3}$ $\quad n^2 = 121$

Some number multiplied by itself is equal to 121. That number is 11. (-11 also works)

4) $n = 1$

Problem: $\quad 16n^3 + 4600 - n^3 = 4615$
Collect: $\quad 15n^3 + 4600 = 4615$

Isolate the $n^3$: $\quad 15n^3 = 15$

Just one $n^3$: $\frac{15n^3}{15} = \frac{15}{15}$ $\quad n^3 = 1$
$n \times n \times n = 1$ $\quad n$ must equal 1

5) $n = 16$

Problem: $\frac{1}{8}n + 35 = -\frac{1}{4}n + 41$

$n$'s on one side:  $\frac{3}{8}n + 35 = 41$

Isolate the $n$'s:  $\frac{3}{8}n = 6$

Just one $n$:  $\frac{8}{3}$ x $\frac{3}{8}n = \frac{6}{1}$ x $\frac{8}{3}$    $n = 16$

6) $n = \frac{1}{3}$
Problem:  $\frac{n}{1} + n + \frac{n}{2} + \frac{n}{3} + \frac{n}{6} = 1$

Same as:  $n + n + \frac{1}{2}n + \frac{1}{3}n + \frac{1}{6}n = 1$

Collect $n$'s:   $3n = 1$        $n = \frac{1}{3}$

7) $n = 1$  (-1 also correct)

8) $n = 9$
Problem:  $\frac{1}{n+1} + \frac{9}{10} = 1$

Isolate $n$'s:  $\frac{1}{n+1} = \frac{1}{10}$

The denominator $n + 1$ must equal 10. In order for this to happen, n must equal 9.

9) $n = 10$

Problem:     $n + \frac{n}{2} + \frac{2n}{n} + 3 = 20$
Same as:     $n + \frac{1}{2}n + 2 + 3 = 20$

Collect:    $1\frac{1}{2}n + 5 = 20$

Isolate the $n$'s:    $1\frac{1}{2}n = 15$

Just one $n$:  $\frac{2}{3}$ x $\frac{3}{2}n = \frac{15}{1}$ x $\frac{2}{3}$    $n = 10$

10) $n = 4$

Problem:    $8^{n-1} = 512$

We know that $8^3 = 512$   Because of this we

want $n - 1$ to be equal to 3. $n$ therefore must equal 4.

## Fun With Formulas: Einstein Level

1) $r = \sqrt{\dfrac{A}{\pi}}$

Problem:    $A = \pi r^2$    r = ?

Isolate $r^2$:     $r^2 = \dfrac{A}{\pi}$

If $r^2 = \dfrac{A}{\pi}$ then $r = \sqrt{\dfrac{A}{\pi}}$

2) $h = \dfrac{2A}{b_1 + b_2}$

Problem:    $A = \frac{1}{2}h(b_1 + b_2)$

Isolate $h$:    $2A = h(b_1 + b_2)$

$$\dfrac{2A}{b_1 + b_2} = h$$

3) $R = \dfrac{D}{T}$

Problem:    $D = R$ x $T$          R = ?

Isolate R:    $R = \dfrac{D}{T}$

4)    $H = \dfrac{V}{L \, x \, W}$

Problem: $V = L$ x $W$ x $H$          H = ?

Isolate $H$:    $H = \dfrac{V}{L \, x \, W}$

5)    $b = \dfrac{2A}{h}$

Problem:    $A = \frac{1}{2}bh$          b = ?

Isolate $b$:        $2A = bh$

$$b = \dfrac{2A}{h}$$

6)   $r = \sqrt[3]{\dfrac{3V}{4\pi}}$

Problem:   $V = \dfrac{4}{3}\pi r^3$        $r = ?$

Isolate $r^3$:   $\dfrac{4}{3}r^3 = \dfrac{V}{\pi}$

Just one $r^3$:   $\dfrac{3}{4} \times \dfrac{4}{3}r^3 = \dfrac{V}{\pi} \times \dfrac{3}{4}$   $r^3 = \dfrac{3V}{4\pi}$

Just $r$:        $r = \sqrt[3]{\dfrac{3V}{4\pi}}$

## Chapter 3: Using Algebra to Solve Problems

## Page 29

1) 7 years old
Nathan:  $n + 5$
Dan:  $n$

Equation: $2n + 5 = 19$      $n = 7$

2) 615 pounds
Horse: $6n + 45$
Rider: $n$

Equation:      $7n + 45 = 710$        $n = 95$
If the rider weighs 95 pounds, the horse must weigh 6 x 95 + 45 which equals 615 pounds.

3)  11 years old
Luke: $n$
Jordan: $2n$
Erin: $n - 5$ (Erin is 5 years younger than Luke)

Equation: $4n - 5 = 59$      $n = 16$
If Luke is 16 years old, then Erin must be 11 years old.

4)  585 pounds

Driver:  $n$
Truck:  $230n$
Load:  $3n + 30$

Equation:  $234n + 30 = 43{,}320$
$n = 185$   If the driver weighs 185 pounds, then the load weighs 585 pounds.

5) 13 inches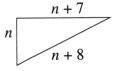

Equation:  $3n + 15 = 30$        $n = 5$
If the shortest side is 5 inches, then the longest side is 5 + 8 inches or 13 inches.

6) 3 inches;  5 inches;  8 inches
Shortest:  $n$
Middle:   $n + 2$
Longest:  $n + 5$
Equation:      $3n + 7 = 16$        $n = 3$

7)  26 girls
Boys:  $n$
Girls:  $3n + 2$

Equation: $4n + 2 = 34$      $n = 8$
If the number of boys is 8, then the number of girls is 26.

8)  87
Smallest:  $n$
Middle:   $n + 1$
Largest:   $n + 2$

Equation:  $3n + 3 = 264$        $n = 87$

9) 63 pounds
Ryan:  $n$
Steve:  $n + 18$

Equation: $2n + 18 = 144$    $n = 63$

10)  72 pounds on the earth
Stephanie: $n$
Kate: $2n$

Equation: $3n = 36$   $n = 12$

## Level 1
1)  $5
Ball: $n$
Glove: $n + 75$

Equation: $2n + 75 = 85$            $n = 5$

2)  65 pounds
Steve: $n$
Ryan: $2n$

Equation: $3n = 195$   $n = 65$

3) 5,200 pounds
Truck: $n$
Load: $n + 12,400$

Equation: $2n + 12,400 = 22,800$
                $n = 5,200$

4) 12
Equation: $4n + 36 = 7n$            $n = 12$

5) 37
Smallest: $n$
Next: $n + 1$
Next: $n + 2$
Largest: $n + 3$

Equation: $4n + 6 = 154$            $n = 37$

6) 20 years old
Daniel: $n$
Rachel: $n + 3$
Luke: $n + 6$

Equation: $3n + 9 = 51$            $n = 14$
If Daniel is 14 years old, then Luke is 20 years old.

7)  6.5 hours
Number of hours worked: $n$

Equation: $7n + 18.50 = 64$            $n = 6.5$

8) $23
Jacob: $n$
Angie: $3n$
Erin: $3n + 35$

Equation: $7n + 35 = 196$   $n = 23$

9) 36
Smallest: $n$
Largest: $3n$

Equation: $4n = 144$            $n = 36$

10) 120
Smallest: $n$
Next: $n + 15$
Next: $n + 30$
Largest: $n + 45$

Equation: $4n + 90 = 390$   $n = 75$
If the smallest number is 75, then the largest is 75 + 45 or 120.

## Level 2

1) $34.80
Price of book: $n$

Equation: $.05n = 1.74$     $n = 34.80$
Sales tax is found by changing the percent to a decimal and then multiplying by the price of the item. (5% is equal to .05)

2) 140
Smallest: $n$
Next: $n + 5$
Next: $n + 10$
Next: $n + 15$
Next: $n + 20$
Largest: $n + 25$

Equation: $6n + 75 = 765$      $n = 115$
If the smallest number is 115, then the largest is 115 + 25 or 140.

3) 256 square inches
Side: $n$

Equation: $4n = 64$   $n = 16$
The area is found by multiplying the length times the width. 16 x 16 equals 256.

4) 15 quarters
Number of quarters: $n$
Value of quarters: $25n$

Number of dimes: $2n$
Value of dimes: $20n$

Equation: $25n + 20n = 675$   $n = 15$

5) 54 feet    $n$
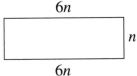

Equation: $14n = 126$     $n = 9$

6) 11.5 hours
Hours driven: $n$
Distance Jordan drove: $60n$
Distance Luke drove: $52n$

Equation: $52n + 92 = 60n$   $n = 11.5$
(If you add 92 miles to the distance Luke drove, it will equal the distance Jordan drove.)

7) 59 inches
Height: $n$

Equation: $3n = \frac{1}{2}n + 147.5$     $n = 59$

8) 119 square feet
Length of large rectangle: $3n - 8$
Width of large rectangle: $n$

Equation: $3n - 8 + 3n - 8 + n + n = 64$
(Two lengths plus two widths equal the perimeter.)
$n = 10$    If $n = 10$, then the size of the small rectangle is 7 by 17.

9) 33 hours
Nathan's pay: $8n + 33$
Marissa: $9n$

Equation: $8n + 33 = 9n$     $n = 33$
(Nathan's pay equals Marissa's pay.)

10) 6 inches
One side (Shortest side) : $n$
Second side: $n + 5$
Longest side: $n + 8$

Equation: $3n + 13 = 31$     $n = 6$

**Einstein Level**

1) 17 ducks

(Because there are 65 heads, you know that the number of animals is 65.)

Number of animals: 65

Number of cows: $n$

Number of ducks: $65 - n$

Number of cow legs: $4n$

Number of duck legs: $2(65 - n)$ or
$$130 - 2n$$

Equation: $4n + 130 - 2n = 226$    $n = 48$

The number of cow legs ($4n$) plus the number of duck legs ($130 - 2n$) must equal 226. Solving the equation, you know that $n = 48$. If there are 48 cows, then there must be 17 ducks.

2) 7 inches

Width: $n$

Length: $8n$

Area: $8n^2$ (The area is found by multiplying the width times the length.)

Equation: $8n^2 = 392$    $n = 7$

3) More than 277 minutes

Minutes talked each month: $n$

Company A cost: $.07n$

Company B cost: $.04n + 8.31$

If the Campbells spent a lot of time on the phone, then Company B would have the best deal. To find out what plan they should use we want to find out how many minutes the Campbells need to talk to make each plan cost the same.

Equation: $.07n = .04n + 8.31$

$n = 277$

The plans would cost the same if the Campbells talked for 277 minutes.

4) 28 years old

Claire: $n$

Kirsten: $4n$

Emily: $n + 6$

Zach: $n + 12$

Anna: $2n$

Equation: $9n + 18 = 81$    $n = 7$

If Claire is 7 then Kirsten must be 28.

5) 3:27

Time traveled before they meet: $n$

Distance Isaac travels:  $60n$

Distance Travis travels: $35n$

| Travis 35$n$ | → ← | Isaac 60$n$ |

You could find the total distance traveled if you add Isaac's and Travis's distances.

Equation: $35n + 60n = 327.75$

$n = 3.45$    It will take them 3.45 hours before they meet. 3.45 hours is not 3 hours and 45 minutes. 3.45 hours is 3 hours and $\frac{45}{100}$ of an hour, which is 3 hours and 27 minutes.

6) 13 dimes

Number of coins: 68

Number of quarters: $n$

Number of dimes: $68 - n$

Value of the quarters: $25n$

Value of the dimes: $10(68 - n)$  Which is the same as $680 - 10n$

If you add the value of the quarters and the

value of the dimes, you will get 1505 (Notice that the $15.05 is changed to cents. This makes the problem much easier to work with.)

Equation: $25n + 680 - 10n = 1505$
$n = 55$   If there are 55 quarters, then there must be 13 dimes.

7) $178
Amount needed: $n$
Claire's: $n - 95$
Anna's: $n - 83$

If they combined their money, they would have exactly enough for a ticket.
Claire's plus Anna's equal ticket.

Equation: $n - 95 + n - 83 = n$
$n = 178$

8) $1330.30
Cost of items without tax: $n$
Tax Zack charged $.07n$

Cost of items plus the tax Zack charged equaled $1342.85.

Equation:    $n + .07n = 1342.85$
         $1.07n = 1342.85$
         $n = 1255$
The cost of the items sold was $1255. The correct tax on this amount is .06 times 1255 or $75.30. Zack should have collected $1255 plus $75.30 tax or $1330.30.

9) 8:12
Time traveled: $n$
Distance Kate traveled: $12n$
Distance Fritz traveled: $40n$

We know that the total distance traveled before they meet will be 10.4 miles because that is the distance between home and school.

Equation: $12n + 40n = 10.4$      $n = .2$

The time traveled is .2 hours. Because we know that one tenth of an hour is 6 minutes, we know that two tenths of an hour is equal to 12 minutes.

10) 64 inches
Nancy's height: $n$
Ed's total: $\frac{1}{8}n + 32$
Steve's total: $2n - 88$

Because Ed and Steve ended up with the same number, we can set Ed's total equal to Steve's total.

Equation: $\frac{1}{8}n + 32 = 2n - 88$      $n = 64$

## Chapter 4:  Negative numbers

**Page 39**
1) -6
2) -17
3) -20
4) 20
5) $4n$
6) $16n$
7) -26
8) 0
9) 32
10) $-27n -23$

**Page 42**
1) 10
2) $5n$
3) -72.5
4) 56
5) $8n$
6) -90
7) -64
8) -1
9) $n^2$
10) $-40n$

## Level 1

1) 80° difference

2) -$34  They are in debt $34

3) 32 degrees

4) 9911 feet

5) -5 yards

6) 8

7) 0    (-8 – -8 = 0)

8) 54 degrees colder
With no wind  the air would feel like -10°. With a 30 mph wind, the air would feel like it was -64°.  -64° is 54 degrees colder than -10°

9) 24 degrees colder
10) Ryan felt colder
Scott felt like the temperature was -9° while Ryan felt like the temperature was -10°

## Level 2

1)  8:21 A.M.
There are 365 x 24 hours (8,760)  in a year. Stephanie's watch will lose 8,760 x .025 = 219 minutes in the year so her watch will be 219 minutes slow.

2) $16n^2$

3) $-4n^2$

4) 0

5) -64          -4 x -4 x -4 = -64

6) 1
-1 x -1 x -1 x -1 x -1 x 1- x -1 x -1 = 1

7) Negative number
When you are dealing with a negative number, you will notice that when the exponent is even the answer is always positive. When the exponent is odd, the answer is always negative.

8) c Not enough information
If *n* is a positive number such as 7, then -*n* is -7.  If n is a negative number such as -5, then -*n* is - (-5) which is positive.

9) -1

10) $87.50

## Einstein Level

1) 9:41
It takes the firefighter 2 minutes to make it up one step of the ladder because he goes up 4 steps in a minute and then down 3 steps in the next minute.

After 40 minutes he will be standing on the 20th rung of the ladder. In the next minute he climbs 4 steps to the top of the ladder. (He then will climb down 3 steps, but he has already reached the top of the ladder.)

2) $n = -1$
$\frac{n^3}{n^3} \times n^3$    $\frac{-1}{-1} \times -1$      1 x -1 = -1

3) $-\frac{1}{2000}$   (Remember order of operations)

$20 \div -10 \div 20 \div -10 \div -20$

Step 1: $20 \div -10 = -2$

Step 2: $-2 \div 20 = -\frac{1}{10}$

Step 3: $-\frac{1}{10} \div -10 = \frac{1}{100}$

Step 4: $\frac{1}{100} \div -20 = -\frac{1}{2000}$

4) 50

100-99+98-97.............4-3+2-1 Group numbers such as 100 and -99 and you will get an answer of 1. There are 50 such groups in this list of numbers so the answer is 50.

5) 0 (Remember order of operations)

$\frac{9}{10} \times \frac{10}{-9} = -1$ so the problem is $-1 - (-1)$, which is equal to 0.

6) -7

7) 10 (Remember order of operations)

Step 1: $8 + 6 \div (-3) + 4$

Step 2: $8 + (-2) + 4$

Step 3: $6 + 4 = 10$

8) 19,914 meters

Step 1: 29,141 + 36,198 or 65,339 feet is the difference in elevation.

Step 2: This is 784,068 inches

Step 3: Because a meter is equal to 39.372 inches, you need to divide 784,068 by 39.372 to find the number of meters in 784,068 inches.

9) When $n$ is a negative number and when $n$ is greater than 1.

(When $n$ is a fraction such as $\frac{1}{4}$, $n^2$ is smaller than $n$.)

10) -3645

$n^5 = -3,125$

$n^4 = 625$

$n^3 = -125$

$n^2 = 25$

$n = -5$

$-3,125 - (625) - (-125) - (25) - (-5) = -3,645$

## Chapter 5: The Distributive Property

**Page 51**

1) $24n - 12 = 12$      $n = 1$

2) $32n + 64 = -32$      $n = -3$

3) $-10n + 50 = -100$      $n = 15$

4) $2n + 16 = 17$      $n = .5$

5) $4n - 8 = 20$      $n = 7$

6) $-5n + 50 = 30$      $n = 4$

7) $21n - 7 = 98$      $n = 5$

8) $6n - 12 = 36$      $n = 8$

9) $-8n - 32 = -32$      $n = 0$

10) $57n + 38 = 665$      $n = 11$

**Page 54**

1) Cross-multiply: $16n = 30$    $n = 1\frac{7}{8}$

2) Cross-multiply: $4n = 18$    $n = 4\frac{1}{2}$

3) Cross-multiply: $7n + 14 = 5n - 15$          $n = -14.5$

4) Cross-multiply: $7n = 16$    $n = 2\frac{2}{7}$

5)  Cross-multiply: $40n = 81$    $n = 2\frac{1}{40}$

6)  Cross-multiply: $2n + 16 = 25$    $n = 4.5$

7)  Cross-multiply: $8n - 48 = 140$    $n = 23.5$

8)  Cross-multiply: $30n = 36$    $n = 1\frac{1}{5}$

9)  Cross-multiply: $8n = 14$    $n = 1\frac{3}{4}$

10)  Cross-multiply: $24 - 6n = 4n$    $n = 2\frac{2}{5}$

## Chapter 6: Algebra and Proportions

**Page 57**
1) $1449
Two ratios: $\dfrac{(Luke)\ 84}{(Jordan)\ 48} = \dfrac{n}{828}$
Cross-multiply: $48n = 69{,}552$
Solve: $n = 1449$

2) $11.25
Two ratios: $\dfrac{(age)\ 4}{(allowance)\ 5} = \dfrac{9}{n}$
Cross-multiply: $4n = 45$
Solve: $n = 11.25$

3) 9.9 cups
Two ratios: $\dfrac{(sugar)\ 6}{(flour)\ 7} = \dfrac{8.5}{n}$
Cross-multiply: $6n = 59.5$
Solve: $n = 9.9166$

4) 135 feet
Two ratios: $\dfrac{(stick)\ 10}{(shadow)\ 17} = \dfrac{n}{229.5}$
Cross-multiply: $17n = 2295$
Solve: $n = 135$

5) 5 feet  7.5 inches
Two ratios: $\dfrac{(stick)\ 5}{(shadow)\ 4} = \dfrac{n}{54\ inches}$
Cross-multiply: $4n = 270$
Solve: $n = 67.5$

**Page 59**
1) 15.4375 miles
Two ratios: $\dfrac{(map)\ 1\ inch}{(real)\ 3.25\ miles} = \dfrac{4.75}{n}$
Cross-multiply: $n = 15.4375$

2) 7000 feet
Two ratios: $\dfrac{(map)\ 1.2\ inches}{(real)\ 300\ feet} = \dfrac{28}{n}$
Cross-multiply: $1.2n = 8400$
Solve: $n = 7000$

3) 12.24 inches
Two ratios: $\dfrac{(map)\ 1\ inches}{(real)\ 245\ miles} = \dfrac{n}{3000}$
Cross-multiply: $245n = 3000$
Solve: $n = 12.24$

4) 6 feet  8 inches
Two ratios: $\dfrac{(height)\ 5}{(allowance)\ 6} = \dfrac{n}{8}$
Cross-multiplying: $6n = 40$
Solve: $n = 6.66666$ or $6\frac{2}{3}$

5) 13 feet  4 inches
Two ratios: $\dfrac{(model)\ 1.2\ inches}{(real)\ 1\ foot} = \dfrac{16}{n}$
Cross-multiplying: $1.2n = 16$
Solve: $n = 13.333$ or $13\frac{1}{3}$

**Page 60**
1) 77 boys
Two ratios: $\dfrac{(boys)\ 7}{(total)\ 16} = \dfrac{n}{176}$
Cross-multiplying: $16n = 1232$
Solve: $n = 77$

2) 336 boys
Two ratios: $\dfrac{(boys)\ 8}{(girls)\ 9} = \dfrac{n}{378}$
Cross-multiplying: $9n = 3024$
Solve: $n = 336$

3) 747 pounds
Two ratios: $\dfrac{(gold)\ 9}{(total)\ 23} = \dfrac{n}{1909}$

Cross-multiplying: $23n = 17,181$
Solve: $n = 747$

4) 26,913 cats
Two ratios: $\dfrac{(cats)\ 3}{(total)\ 20} = \dfrac{n}{89,710}$
Cross-multiplying: $10n = 269,130$
Solve: $n = 26,913$

5) 29.75 cups
Two ratios: $\dfrac{(lemonade)\ 7}{(whole)\ 20} = \dfrac{n}{85}$
Cross-multiplying: $20n = 595$
Solve: $n = 29.75$

## Page 62

1) 182 liters
They need 48 gallons, which equals 192 quarts. Convert 192 quarts to liters.
Two ratios: $\dfrac{(quarts)\ 1.057}{(liters)\ 1} = \dfrac{192}{n}$
Cross-multiplying: $1.057n = 192$
Solve: $n = 181.646$

2) 55 mph
Two ratios: $\dfrac{(miles)\ .621}{(kilometers)\ 1} = \dfrac{n}{88}$
Cross-multiplying: $n = 54.648$

3) 99 pounds
Two ratios: $\dfrac{(pounds)\ 2.2}{(kilograms)\ 1} = \dfrac{n}{45}$
Cross-multiplying: $n = 99$

4) 27.4 meters
90 feet is equal to 1080 inches. Now convert 1080 inches to meters.
Two ratios: $\dfrac{(inches)\ 39.372}{(meters)\ 1} = \dfrac{1080}{n}$
Cross-multiplying: $39.372n = 1080$
Solve: $n = 27.43066$

5) Yes
Two ratios: $\dfrac{(pounds)\ 2.2}{(kilograms)\ 1} = \dfrac{32,000}{n}$

Cross-multiplying: $2.2n = 32,000$
Solve: $n = 14545.45$

## Page 64

1) 0.19 miles
Two ratios: $\dfrac{(feet)\ 5280}{(mile)\ 1} = \dfrac{1000}{n}$
Cross-multiplying: $5280n = 1000$
Solve: $n = 0.1894$

2) 0.6 hours
Two ratios: $\dfrac{(hour)\ 1}{(seconds)\ 3600} = \dfrac{n}{2160}$
Cross-multiplying: $3600n = 2160$
Solve: $n = 0.6$

3) 0.31 parsecs
Two ratios: $\dfrac{(light\text{-}years)\ 3.26}{(parsec)\ 1} = \dfrac{1}{n}$
Cross-multiplying: $3.26n = 1$
Solve: $n = 0.3067$

4) 1.06 yards
Two ratios: $\dfrac{(yards)\ 1}{(inches)\ 36} = \dfrac{n}{38}$
Cross-multiplying: $36n = 38$
Solve: $n = 1.055555$

5) 0.56 gallons
Two ratios: $\dfrac{(quarts)\ 4}{(gallon)\ 1} = \dfrac{2.25}{n}$
Cross-multiplying: $4n = 2.25$
Solve: $n = 0.5625$

6) 0.09 pounds
Two ratios: $\dfrac{(pounds)\ 1}{(ounces)\ 16} = \dfrac{n}{1.5}$
Cross-multiplying: $16n = 1.5$
Solve: $n = 0.09375$

7) 0.15 hours
Two ratios: $\dfrac{(hours)\ 1}{(minutes)\ 60} = \dfrac{n}{9}$
Cross-multiplying: $60n = 9$
Solve: $n = 0.15$

8) $\frac{1}{60}$ of a mile

The car is going 60 miles in an hour. Because there are 3600 seconds in an hour, the car is going 60 miles every 3600 seconds.

Two ratios: $\frac{(miles)\ 60}{(seconds)\ 3600} = \frac{n}{1}$

Cross-multiplying: $3600n = 60$

Solve: $n = \frac{1}{60}$

9) 0.02 years

Two ratios: $\frac{(days)\ 365}{(year)\ 1} = \frac{7}{n}$

Cross-multiplying: $365n = 7$

Solve: $n = 0.019$

10) 0.001 miles

Molly is 66 inches tall. The ratio must compare miles to inches.

Two ratios: $\frac{(mile)\ 1}{(inches)\ 63,360} = \frac{n}{66}$

Cross-multiplying: $63,360n = 66$

Solve: $n = 0.001041666$

## Level 1

1) 28 girls

Two ratios: $\frac{(girls)\ 4}{(total)\ 7} = \frac{n}{49}$

Cross-multiplying: $7n = 196$

Solve: $n = 28$

2) 1.125 inches

Two ratios: $\frac{(map)\ .125}{(real)\ 12} = \frac{n}{108}$

Cross-multiplying: $12n = 13.5$

Solve: $n = 1.125$

3) 1.8 meters

Two ratios: $\frac{(inches)\ 39.372}{(meters)\ 1} = \frac{72}{n}$

Cross-multiplying: $39.372n = 72$

Solve: $n = 1.82871$

4) 97 beats per minute

If you want to know how many beats per minute, you are finding out how many beats per 60 seconds.

Two ratios: $\frac{(beats)\ 21}{(seconds)\ 13} = \frac{n}{60}$

Cross-multiplying: $13n = 1260$

Solve: $n = 96.92$

5) 0.19 yards

Two ratios: $\frac{(yard)\ 1}{(inches)\ 36} = \frac{n}{7}$

Cross-multiplying: $36n = 7$

Solve: $n = 0.1944$

6) 102.5 feet

Two ratios: $\frac{(stick)\ 10}{(shadow)\ 8} = \frac{n}{82}$

Cross-multiplying: $8n = 820$

Solve: $n = 102.5$

7) 161,031 kilometers

Two ratios: $\frac{(miles)\ .621}{(kilometers)\ 1} = \frac{100,000}{n}$

Cross-multiplying: $.621n = 100,000$

Solve: $n = 161,030.59$

8) 438 feet

Two ratios: $\frac{(flea)\ .125}{(jump)\ 9.125} = \frac{6}{n}$

Cross-multiplying: $.125n = 54.75$

Solve: $n = 438$

9) 10 seconds

Two ratios: $\frac{(feet)\ 42}{(seconds)\ 7} = \frac{60}{n}$

Cross-multiplying: $42n = 420$

Solve: $n = 10$

10) 840 pounds

Two ratios: $\frac{(gold)\ 8}{(silver)\ 7} = \frac{960}{n}$

Cross-multiplying: $8n = 6720$

Solve: $n = 840$

## Level 2

**1) 106 students**

Two ratios: $\dfrac{(flu)\ 2}{(students)\ 9} = \dfrac{n}{477}$

Cross-multiplying: $9n = 954$

Solve: $n = 106$

**2) 131,778 births**

Two ratios: $\dfrac{(births)\ 9}{(people)\ 1000} = \dfrac{n}{14,642,000}$

Cross-multiplying:

$1000n = 131,778,000$

Solve: $n = 131,778$

**3) 0.0055555 hours**

Two ratios: $\dfrac{(hour)\ 1}{(seconds)\ 3600} = \dfrac{n}{20}$

Cross-multiplying: $3600n = 20$

Solve: $n = 0.00555555$

**4) 156.25 miles**

Two ratios: $\dfrac{(globe)\ 32}{(real)\ 25,000} = \dfrac{.2}{n}$

Cross-multiplying: $32n = 5000$

Solve: $n = 156.25$

**5) 39,950 smokers**

Two ratios: $\dfrac{(smokers)\ 85}{(total)\ 100} = \dfrac{n}{47,000}$

Cross-multiplying: $100n = 3,995,000$

Solve: $n = 39,950$

**6) 1326.5 miles**

Two ratios: $\dfrac{(broken\ odometer)\ 6}{(real\ miles)\ 7} = \dfrac{1137}{n}$

Cross-multiplying: $6n = 7959$

Solve: $n = 1326.5$

**7) 2:30 P.M.**

The broken clock has gone 140 minutes when it is 2:20.

Two ratios: $\dfrac{(broken)\ 56}{(normal)\ 60} = \dfrac{140}{n}$

Cross-multiplying: $56n = 8400$

Solve: $n = 150$ The normal clock has gone 150 minutes in the time it took the broken clock to go 140 minutes.

**8) 19 seconds**

The dinosaur will gain 52 feet per second.

Two ratios: $\dfrac{(second)\ 1}{(feet\ gained)\ 52} = \dfrac{n}{988}$

Cross-multiplying: $52n = 988$

Solve: $n = 19$

**9) 17.5 feet**

Two ratios: $\dfrac{3.4}{5} = \dfrac{11.9}{n}$

Cross-multiplying: $3.4n = 59.5$

Solve: $n = 17.5$

**10) 40 mg.**

Two ratios: $\dfrac{(medicine)\ 28}{(weight)\ 140} = \dfrac{n}{200}$

Cross-multiplying: $140n = 5600$

Solve: $n = 40$

## Einstein Level

**1) $16\frac{2}{3}$ yards behind**

When Anna crossed the 60-yard finish line, Kirsten only ran 50 yards. We are trying to find out how far Kirsten would run when Anna crosses the 100-yard finish line.

Two ratios: $\dfrac{(Anna)\ 60}{(Kirsten)\ 50} = \dfrac{100}{n}$

Cross-multiplying: $60n = 5000$

Solve: $n = 83.3333$ or $83\frac{1}{3}$ Kirsten would run $83\frac{1}{3}$ yards, therefore she would be $16\frac{2}{3}$ yards behind.

**2) 32 inches**

We are trying to find out how far the second place finisher ran when the winner crossed the finish line. We know he went 100 yards in 10.04 seconds. We need to find how far he went in 9.95 seconds. Because we want the answer in inches, we will change yards to inches.

Two ratios: $\dfrac{(inches)\ 3600}{(seconds)\ 10.04} = \dfrac{n}{9.95}$

Cross-multiplying: $10.04n = 35{,}820$

Solve: $n = 3{,}567.73$

The second place finisher ran 3,568 inches when the winner crossed the finish line. He was therefore 32 inches behind the winner.

3) 6:00 P.M.

Two ratios: $\dfrac{(broken)\ 53}{(normal)\ 60} = \dfrac{318}{n}$

Cross-multiplying: $53n = 19{,}080$

Solve: $n = 360$ The normal clock went 360 minutes or 6 hours.

4) 1.3 cubic yards

The first thing we need to find is how many yards are in one meter. Because there are 39. 372 inches in a meter, we can change this to yards by dividing by 36.

$39.372 \div 36 = 1.0937$ yards in a meter. To find the volume of a cubic meter expressed in yards, we simply multiply the length times the width times the height:

$1.0937 \times 1.0937 \times 1.0937 = 1.308$

5) 9.16666 miles

Two ratios: $\dfrac{24}{22} = \dfrac{10}{n}$

Cross-multiplying: $24n = 220$

Solve: $n = 9.16666$

6) 135 cents or $1.35

Two ratios: $\dfrac{(Canadian)\ 100}{(American)\ 74} = \dfrac{n}{100}$

Cross-multiplying: $74n = 10{,}000$

Solve: $n = 135.135$

7) $44.98

Two ratios: $\dfrac{.35}{.40} = \dfrac{n}{51.40}$

Cross-multiplying: $.40n = 17.99$

Solve: $n = 44.975$

8) 10.8 inches; 9.6 ounces; 42 seconds

Two ratios: $\dfrac{(inches)\ 12}{(foot)\ 1} = \dfrac{n}{.9}$

Cross-multiplying: $n = 10.8$

Two ratios: $\dfrac{(ounces)\ 16}{(pound)\ 1} = \dfrac{n}{.6}$

Cross-multiplying: $n = 9.6$

Two ratios: $\dfrac{(minutes)\ 1}{(seconds)\ 60} = \dfrac{.7}{n}$

Cross-multiplying: $n = 42$

9) 44 feet

You first need to find out how tall Meagan is.

Meagan: $n$

Mark: $n + 5$

Two ratios: $\dfrac{(Meagan)\ n}{(shadow)\ 127.5"} = \dfrac{(Mark)\ n + 5}{(shadow)\ 140"}$

Cross-multiplying: $140n = 127.5n + 637.5$

Solve: $n = 51$          Meagan is 51" tall

Now you can find the height of the tree.

Two ratios: $\dfrac{(Meagan)\ 51}{(shadow)\ 127.5} = \dfrac{(tree)\ n}{(shadow)\ 1320"}$

Cross-multiplying: $127.5n = 67{,}320$

Solve: $n = 528$ inches or 44 feet

10) $\frac{1}{17}$ pound

Two ratios: $\dfrac{(gold)\ 8}{(total)\ 17} = \dfrac{n}{.125\ pounds}$

Cross-multiplying: $17n = 1$

Solve: $n = \frac{1}{17}$

## Chapter 7: Algebra and Percents

**Page 73**

| | |
|---|---|
| 1) 0.75 | 6) 0.05 |
| 2) 0.07 | 7) 0.12 |
| 3) 1 | 8) 0.00008 |
| 4) 0.005 | 9) 10 |
| 5) 2.5 | 10) 0.95 |

## Page 73

| | |
|---|---|
| 1) 7% | 6) .01% |
| 2) 70% | 7) 4500% |
| 3) 700% | 8) 3% |
| 4) 12% | 9) 100% |
| 5) 1.2% | 10) 920% |

## Page 74

| | |
|---|---|
| 1) 37.5% | 6) 250% |
| 2) 75% | 7) 362.5% |
| 3) 6.25% | 8) 83.33% |
| 4) 20% | 9) 100% |
| 5) 33.33% | 10) 80% |

## Page 75

| | |
|---|---|
| 1) $\frac{1}{20}$ | 6) $\frac{1}{125}$ |
| 2) $\frac{2}{5}$ | 7) 1 |
| 3) $\frac{3}{4}$ | 8) $2\frac{1}{4}$ |
| 4) $\frac{1}{50}$ | 9) $\frac{9}{10}$ |
| 5) $\frac{7}{50}$ | 10) $\frac{1}{100}$ |

## Page 76

1) $56
.3 x 80 = 24  Discount is $24

2) $9.75
.15 x 65 = 9.75

3) $38.40
.04 x 960 = 38.4

4) $37,836
.051 x 36,000 = 1,836 raise

5) Store B
Store A: .4 x $250 = $100 discount. The new price is $150.

Store B: .15 x $175 = $26.25 discount. The new price is $148.75

6) 102 students
.18 x 568 = 102.24

7) $12.95
Iowa sales tax: .06 x $1295 = $77.70
Illinois sales tax: .07 x $1295 = $90.65

8) $13,050
.42 x 22,500 = $9450 loss

9) $286.25
.229 x $1250 = $286.25

10) 40 cents
.005 x 80 = 0.40  or 40 cents

## Page 78

1) 12.5%
Compare: $\frac{2}{16}$ = .125 = 12.5%

2) 33.33% or $33\frac{1}{3}$%
Compare: $\frac{1}{3}$ = .3333 = 33.33%

3) 66.66% or $66\frac{2}{3}$%
Compare: $\frac{28,000}{42,000}$ = .6666 = 66.66%

4) 300%
Compare: $\frac{3}{1}$ = 3 = 300%

5) 100%
Scott's room: 120 square feet
Dan's room: 120 square feet
Compare: $\frac{120}{120}$ = 1 = 100%

6) 36%

Compare: $\frac{25}{70}$ = .35714 = 35.714%

7) 30%

Compare: $\frac{540}{1800}$ = .3 = 30%

8) 25%

Compare: $\frac{1}{4}$ = .25 = 25%

9) 1%

Compare: $\frac{1\ Centimeter}{100\ centimeters\ in\ a\ meter}$ = .01 = 1%

10) .1%

Compare: $\frac{1\ Meter}{1000\ meters\ in\ a\ kilometer}$ = .001 = .1%

## Page 80

1) 25% increase

Make fraction: $\frac{(increase)\ 2}{(original)\ 8}$ = .25

Change to percent: .25 = 25%

2) $83\frac{1}{3}$% decrease

Make fraction: $\frac{(decrease)\ 150}{(original)\ 180}$ = .8333

Change to percent: .8333 = $83\frac{1}{3}$%

3) 20%

Make fraction: $\frac{(increase)\ 3}{(original)\ 15}$ = .2

Change to percent: .2 = 20%

4) $96\frac{2}{3}$%

Make fraction: $\frac{(decrease)\ 290}{(original)\ 300}$ = .9666

Change to percent: .9666 = $96\frac{2}{3}$%

5) 220%

Make fraction: $\frac{(increase)\ 110}{(original)\ 50}$ = 2.2

Change to percent: 2.2 = 220%

6) 35.3%

Make fraction: $\frac{(increase)\ 24}{(original)\ 68}$ = .35294

Change to percent: .35294 = 35.3%

7) 40%

Make fraction: $\frac{(decrease)\ 50}{(original)\ 125}$ = .4

Change to percent: .4 = 40%

8) 999,900%

Make fraction: $\frac{(increase)\ 49,995}{(original)\ 5}$ = 9,999

Change to percent: 9,999 = 999,900%

9) 99.17%

Make fraction: $\frac{(decrease)\ 29.75}{(original)\ 30}$ = .99166

Change to percent: .9916 = 99.17%

10) 1%

Make fraction: $\frac{(decrease)\ .1}{(original)\ 10}$ = .01

Change to percent: .01 = 1%

## Page 82

1) $528

2) 825

Some number: $n$

Equation: $.15n = 123.75$

Solve: $n = 825$

3) 175 pounds

Father's weight: $n$

Equation: $.42n = 73.5$

Solve: $n = 175$

4) $9.90

Shoes: $n$

Socks: $.22n$

Equation: $n + .22n = 54.90$

Solve: $n = 45$          Shoes cost $45

5) $220

Equation: $.07n = 15.4$

Solve: $n = 220$

## Page 83
1) $36

2) $29.20
Cost of Tree: $n$
Discount: $.95n$ (95% of $n$)
Tree minus discount: $n - .95n = .05n$
Equation: $.05n = 1.46$
Solve: $n = 29.2$

3) $918
Money at start: $n$
Interest earned: $.07n$ (7% of $n$)
Money year later: $n + .07n$
Equation: $n + .07n = 982.26$
Solve: $n = 918$

4) $27,000
Car without tax: $n$
Tax: $.05n$ (5% of $n$)
Equation: $n + .05n = 28,350$
Solve: $n = 27,000$

5) $28,500
Original salary: $n$
Raise: $.22n$ (22% of $n$)
Equation: $n + .22n = 34,770$
Solve: $n = 28,500$

## Page 85
1) $8

2) 64 square feet
Original area: $n$
New area: 144
Amount of increase: $144 - n$
Equation: $\frac{(increase)\ 144 - n}{(original)\ n} = \frac{125}{100}$
Cross-multiply: $125n = 14,400 - 100n$
Solve: $n = 64$

3) $68.50
Original rates: $n$
New rate: 117.82
Increase: $117.82 - n$
Equation: $\frac{(increase)\ 117.82 - n}{(original)\ n} = \frac{72}{100}$
Cross-multiply: $72n = 11,782 - 100n$
Solve: $n = 68.5$

4) 72 square feet
Original picture: $n$
New size: 234
Increase: $234 - n$
Equation: $\frac{(increase)\ 234 - n}{(original)\ n} = \frac{225}{100}$
Cross-multiply: $225n = 23,400 - 100n$
Solve: $n = 72$

5) 99.5%
Original: 200
New: 1
Equation: $\frac{(decrease)\ 199}{(original)\ 200} = .995 = 99.5\%$

## Level 1
1) $185
Bike: $n$
Tax: $.06n$ which is $11.10
Equation: $.06n = 11.10$
Solve: $n = 185$

2) Saturday
Friday discount: $35
Saturday discount: $.15 \times 245 = \$36.75$

3) $672
Marissa's savings: $n$
Interest: $.03n$ or $20.16
Equation: $.03n = 20.16$
Solve: $n = 672$

4) 932
Equation: $.176n = 164.032$
Solve: $n = 932$

5) $96
Compare: $\dfrac{(Rick)\ 78.72}{(Ed)\ n} = \dfrac{82}{100}$
Cross-multiply: $82n = 7872$
Solve: $n = 96$

6) $142
April bill: $n$
May bill: $.32n$ or $45.44
Equation: $.32n = 45.44$
Solve: $n = 142$

7) Nathan weighs 81 pounds
Dad's weight: $n$
Nathan: $.5n$  (50% of n)
Equation: $n + .5n = 243$
Solve: $n = 162$ If Nathan's dad weighs 162 pounds, then Nathan weighs 81 pounds.

8) 190 pounds
Tom can lift: $n$
Brad can lift: $.85n$ (85% of $n$)
Equation: $.85n = 161.5$
Solve: $n = 190$

9) $12,650
Old salary: $n$
Raise: $.15n$  ($1650)
Equation: $.15n = 1650$
Solve: $n = 11,000$
Larry's new salary is his original salary of $11,000 plus his raise of $1650.

10) $895
Money spent: $n$
Sales tax: $.09n$

Equation: $.09n = 80.55$
Solve: $n = 895$

**Level 2**
1) $378
Cost of mower: $n$
Tax: $.05n$
Equation: $n + .05n = 396.90$
Solve: $n = 378$

2) $278
Original cost: $n$
Discount: $.35n$  (35% of $n$)
Equation: $n - .35n = 180.70$
Solve: $n = 278$

3) 5 horsepower
Brand A engine size: $n$
Brand B engine size: $n + .4n$  (40% $n$)
Equation: $n + .4n = 7$
Solve: $n = 5$

4) 20 inches
Baby size: $n$
Man: 350% of $n$
Equation: $3.5n = 70$ inches
Solve: $n = 20$

5) 256 square feet
Area of Mississippi room: $n$
Area of Iowa room: $56.25\%n$  (12 x 12)
Equation: $.5625n = 144$
Solve: $n = 256$

6) 3%
Interest rate: $n$
(The interest rate times 1181 must equal 35.43)
Equation: $n \times 1181 = 35.43$
Solve: $n = .03$ or 3%

7) 22.9%

Interest rate: $n$

(The interest rate times 27,000 must equal 6,183)

Equation: $n$ x 27,000 = 6,183

Solve: $n$ = .229 or 22.9%

8) 113 correct problems

Compare: $\dfrac{(right)\ n}{(total)\ 138} = \dfrac{82}{100}$

Cross-multiply: $100n = 11{,}316$

Solve: $n = 113.16$

9) 90 inches

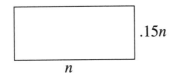

Equation: $n + n + .15n + 15n = 207$

Solve: $n = 90$

10) $187.50

Horse: $n$

Saddle: .15$n$   (15%n)

Equation: $n + .15n = 1437.50$

Solve: $n = 1250$

If the horse cost $1250, then the saddle cost 15% of $1250 or $187.50

## Einstein Level

1) $37.30

We want to first find out what the sales total was for the day without sales tax.

Amount of sales without tax: $n$

Sales tax collected at 5% rate: .05$n$

Equation: $n + .05n = 1958.25$

Solve: $n = 1865$   Sales were $1865

The amount of sales tax Mark should have collected is 7% of $1865.

.07 x $1865 = 130.55

The amount of sales tax Mark did collect was 5% of $1865.

.05 x $1865 = 93.25

Mark owes his boss $37.30

2) $1300

Original price: $n$

Discount: .45$n$      (45% of $n$)

New price: $n - .45n$ which equals .55$n$

Sales tax on the new price: .08 x .55$n$

New price plus sales tax = $772.20

Equation: .55$n$ + (.08n x.55$n$)=772.20

Solve: .55$n$ + .044$n$ = 772.20

.594$n$ = 772.20

$n = 1300$

3) 35%

Total bridge: $n$

Andy's share: .5$n$

Todd's share: .5$n$

Amount Andy finished: .85 x .5$n$ or .425$n$

Amount Todd finished: .45 x .5$n$ or .225$n$

The amount of bridge finished was .425$n$ + .225$n$ or .65$n$, which equals 65%. 35% remains to be painted.

4) 72 inches

Sue's height: $n$

Donna's height: .9375n

Dave's height: 80% of .9375$n$

Dave's height: 54 inches

Equation:    .80 x .9375$n$ = 54

.75$n$ = 54

Solve: $n = 72$

5) 25 cents

Price in 1965: $n$

Cost today: $1.20

Increase: $1.20 – n$

Make fraction: $\dfrac{(increase)\ 1.20 - n}{(original)\ n} = \dfrac{380}{100}$

Cross-multiply: $380n = 120 - 100n$

Solve: $n = .25$ or 25 cents

6) 94%

7th test: $n$

To find the average of seven tests, you need to add all seven tests and then divide by seven. This average must be equal to 90.

$$\frac{83 + 92 + 79 + 98 + 89 + 95 + n}{7} = \frac{90}{1}$$

Collect: $\dfrac{536 + n}{7} = \dfrac{90}{1}$

Cross-multiply: $536 + n = 630$

Solve: $n = 94$

7) 100°

Angle A: $n$

Angle B: $.45n$        (45% of $n$)

Angle C: $.35n$        (35% of $n$)

Because the interior angles of a triangle add up to 180°, we can write the following equation.

Equation: $n + .45n + .35n = 180$

Solve: $n = 100$

8) 60 inches

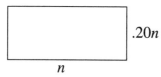

Equation:     $n \times .20n = 720$

$.20n^2 = 720$

$n^2 = 3600$

Solve: $n = 60$

9) 160 pigs

Pigs: $n$

Cows: $.3n$              (30% of $n$)

Horses: $.125n$         (12.5% of $n$)

Sheep: $.125 \times .3n$   (12.5% of cows)

Equation:

$n + .3n + .125n + (.125 \times .3n) = 234$

Solve:

$n + .3n + .125n + .0375n = 234$

$1.4625n = 234$

$n = 160$

10) 32% remains to be completed

Entire job: $n$

Mark's job: $.25n$

Mike's job: $.25n$

Janelle's job: $.25n$

Debra's job: $.25n$

If Mark completed unloading 64% of his truck, then he has 36% of his job remaining $(.36 \times .25n)$. If Mike finished unloading 56% of his truck, then he has 44% of his job remaining.
$(.44 \times .25n)$

Mark remaining: $.36 \times .25n = .09n$

Mike remaining: $.44 \times .25n = .11n$

Janelle remaining: $.20 \times .25n = .05n$

Debra remaining: $.28 \times .25n = .07n$

Total remaining:

$.09n + .11n + .05n + .07n = .32n$

32% remains to be completed.

## Chapter 8: Exponents, Radicals, and Scientific Notation

### Page 95
1) $6^3$
2) 32
3) $10^6$
4) 512
5) 125
6) $10^5$
7) 1
8) 1024
9) $3^2$
10) 36

### Page 97
1) $\frac{1}{10,000}$
2) .1
3) $10^{-4}$
4) $\frac{1}{64}$
5) $\frac{1}{n^x}$
6) $10^2$
7) $10^{-2}$
8) $2^{-2}$
9) $10^{-7}$
10) $5^{-2}$

### Page 99
1) 10
2) 5
3) 1
4) 3
5) 1,000
6) 2
7) 13
8) 1
9) 10
10) $n = 6$

11) 15 feet
12) 15 years old
13) 3 inches
14) 1 inch
15) $\frac{1}{2}$ inch

### Page 100
1) $8.877 \times 10^4$
2) $3.6 \times 10^3$
3) $6.696 \times 10^8$
4) $7.2 \times 10^2$
5) $8 \times 10^5$

### Page 101
1) $9.46 \times 10^{-1}$
2) $1 \times 10^{-6}$
3) $6 \times 10^{-2}$
4) .00000001
5) $1.7 \times 10^{-24}$

### Level 1
1) $9.3 \times 10^7$
2) 100 decimeters
3) $n^3$
4) $8.0 \times 10^5$
5) $n = 4$
6) $10^6$ (There are others)
7) 11
8) Multiply 5 x 2 instead of 5 x 5
9) 6,561
10) Both the same

### Level 2
1) 17 inches
2) $x = 4$
3) 7 inches
Equation: $153.86 = \pi r^2$

$$\frac{153.86}{3.14} = r^2$$
$$r^2 = 49$$
$$r = 7$$

4) $10^{-4}$
5) $\frac{1}{2}$ ($\frac{1}{2} \times \frac{1}{2} = \frac{1}{4}$)
6) $4 \times 10^{-3}$
7) When you have the same base and you are multiplying exponents, you simply add the exponents.
8) $8.0 \times 10^3$ $\qquad$ $2.5 \times 10^4$
9) $7.3 \times 10^8$
10) 10

**Einstein Level**

1) $1.86 \times 10^5 \times 3.1536 \times 10^7 =$
$5.865696 \times 10^{12}$
This equals 5,865,696,000,000 miles

2) 29th hour

3) 586,569,600,000,000,000 miles

4) 9,370,000,000 grains of sand

A cubic meter of sand contains
100 x 100 x 100 or 1,000,000 cubic centimeters of sand.

$9.37 \times 10^3 \times 1,000,000 =$
$9.37 \times 10^3 \times 10^6 = 9.37 \times 10^9$ which equals 9,370,000,000 grains of sand.

5) No, $3^2$ does not equal $2^3$. There are many other examples where this rule does not work.

6) $10^{86}$ ($10^{86} \times 10 = 10^{87}$)

7) $n = 7$
$5^5 = 3125$     The exponent $n - 2$ must equal 5. $n$ must be equal to 7.

8) $\frac{1}{4}$ inch

9) 10th of August

10) $n = 2.5$
$2.5 \times 2.5 \times 2.5 = 15.625$

## Chapter 9: Pythagorean Theorem

### Level 1

1) 24 units
$6^2 + 8^2 = c^2$

$36 + 64 = c^2$
$100 = c^2$
$c = 10$  Perimeter equals $6 + 8 + 10$

2) 6.4 units
$4^2 + 5^2 = c^2$
$16 + 25 = c^2$
$41 = c^2$
$c = 6.4$

3) 4 miles shorter
$12^2 + 5^2 = c^2$
$144 + 25 = c^2$
$169 = c^2$
$c = 13$    Distance AB equals 13 miles

4) $53.40
$10^2 + 24^2 = c^2$
$100 + 576 = c^2$
$676 = c^2$
$c = 26$ feet    Perimeter equals 60 feet
$60 \times \$.89 = \$53.40$

5) 24 feet
$26^2 - 10^2 = b^2$
$576 = b^2$
$b = 24$ feet

6) 39 feet
$36^2 + 15^2 = c^2$
$1296 + 225 = c^2$
$1521 = c^2$
$c = 39$

7) Yes
$9^2 + 40^2 = 41^2$ so these measurements do make up a right triangle.

8) 25 miles

$15^2 + 20^2 = c^2$

$225 + 400 = c^2$

$625 = c^2$

$c = 25$

9) 12.8 inches

The longest straight line would be a diagonal from corner to corner.

$8^2 + 10^2 = c^2$

$64 + 100 = c^2$

$164 = c^2$

$c = 12.8$

10) $\frac{5}{12}$ yards

$\left(\frac{1}{4}\right)^2 + \left(\frac{1}{3}\right)^2 = c^2$

$\frac{1}{16} + \frac{1}{9} = c^2$

$\frac{9}{144} + \frac{16}{144} = c^2$

$\frac{25}{144} = c^2$

$c = \frac{5}{12}$

## Level 2

1) 5 feet

Half of the triangle is shown below:

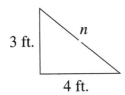

$3^2 + 4^2 = n^2$

$n = 5$

2) 36 feet

The 45 feet is the hypotenuse

$45^2 - 27^2 = b^2$

$2025 - 729 = b^2$

$1296 = b^2$

$b = 36$

3) 48 feet

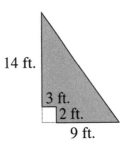

With the dotted lines drawn in, it is easy to see that this is a right triangle with legs of 12 and 16 feet. Using the Pythagorean Theorem, you will find that the hypotenuse is 20 feet. The perimeter is therefore 20 + 14 + 3 + 2 + 9 which equals 48 feet.

4) $2694.40

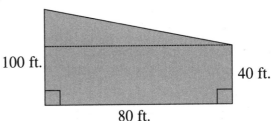

With the dotted line drawn, it is easy to see that there is a right triangle at the top of the figure. The legs are 80 feet and 60 feet. (Don't let the fact that the figure isn't drawn to scale confuse you. The small leg of the right triangle is really 60 feet.)

Using the Pythagorean Theorem, the hypotenuse turns out to be 100 feet long. The perimeter of the garden is 320 feet. Cost equals: 320 x $8.42

5) $\sqrt{32}$ feet

If the circumference of the circle is 25.12 feet, then the diameter of the circle is 25.12 ÷ 3.14 which equals 8 feet.

If the diameter of the circle is 8 feet, then AC and CB are each equal to 4 feet.

$4^2 + 4^2 = c^2$

$32 = c^2$

$c = \sqrt{32}$

6) Yes

Does $15^2 + (\sqrt{31})^2 = 16^2$?

Does $225 + 31 = 256$? Yes it does, so these measurements are from a right triangle.

7) 41 miles

$9^2 + 40^2 = c^2$

$81 + 1600 = c^2$

$c = 41$

8) $\sqrt{31}$ feet

$16^2 - 15^2 = a^2$

$31 = a^2$

$a = \sqrt{31}$

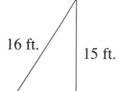

9) 128 feet

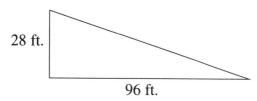

Using the Pythagorean Theorem, you will find that the hypotenuse is 100 feet. The original height of the tree is 100 feet plus 28 feet.

10) 12 inches

If a square has an area of 72 square inches, then the length of each side must be $\sqrt{72}$ feet.

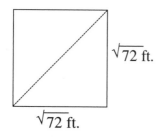

Using the Pythagorean Theorem:

$\left(\sqrt{72}\right)^2 + \left(\sqrt{72}\right)^2 = c^2$

$72 + 72 = c^2$

$c = 12$

**Einstein Level**

1) 12 feet

The new right triangle after the ladder slipped is shown below.

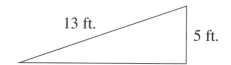

Using the Pythagorean Theorem, you will find that the missing leg is 12 feet.

2) 36 feet

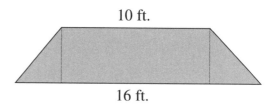

The right triangles on each end of the trapezoid have legs of 3 feet and 4 feet.

Using the Pythagorean Theorem, you will find that the hypotenuse of each triangle is 5 feet. The perimeter is therefore $10 + 16 + 5 + 5$ or 36 feet.

3) $17\frac{1}{3}$ seconds

Using the Pythagorean Theorem, you will find that the hypotenuse (ladder) is 156 feet long. If the firefighter climbs at the rate of 9 feet per second, it will take her $17\frac{1}{3}$ seconds to climb to the top of the ladder.

4) $\sqrt{75}$ inches or $5\sqrt{3}$ inches

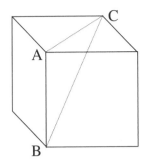

Triangle ABC has the following measurements:
Leg AB is 5 inches
Leg AC is √50 inches

Using the Pythagorean Theorem, hypotenuse BC has a length of √75 inches.

5) 48 square feet

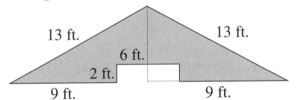

The triangle made by the dotted lines has legs of 5 inches and 12 inches. (Pythagorean Theorem) The area of the triangle is therefore 30 square feet. The area of the identical triangle on the left is also 30 square feet. The area of the shaded part is 60 square feet minus the area of the 2 foot by 6 foot rectangle.

6) 16 square inches
If a square has a diagonal of √32, then each side must be 4 inches. (Check this using the Pythagorean Theorem.)

7) 63.64 feet per second
The distance from home to second base is found by using the Pythagorean Theorem.
$90^2 + 90^2 = c^2$
$8100 + 8100 = c^2$

$16{,}200 = c^2$
$c = 127.279$
If the ball takes 2 seconds to get to second base, then it is traveling at a speed of 63.64 feet per second.

8) 35 feet

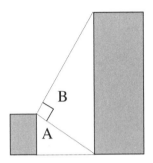

The hypotenuse of triangle A can be found using the Pythagorean Theorem.

$12^2 + 16^2 = c^2$
$400 = c^2$
$c = 20$ feet

16 ft.

12 ft.

Now the missing side of triangle B can be found using the Pythagorean Theorem.

$25^2 - 20^2 = b^2$
$625 - 400 = b^2$
$225 = b^2$
$b = 15$

25 ft.

20 ft.

9) 198 square inches

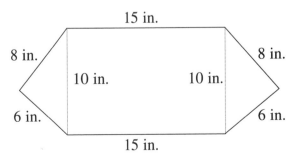

The hypotenuse of each triangle is equal to 10 inches (Pythagorean Theorem)

The area of each triangle is 24 square inches, while the area of the rectangle is 150 square inches.

10)  41 feet

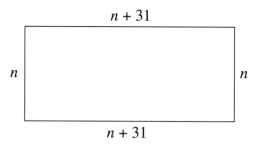

Find $n$: $n + n + n + n + 31 + 31 = 98$
Solve: $n = 9$ feet

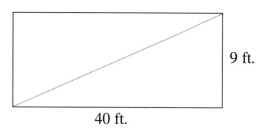

9 ft.

40 ft.

The diagonal can be found using the Pythagorean Theorem.
$c^2 = 40^2 + 9^2$
$c^2 = 1681$
$c = 41$

## Chapter 10: Geometry and Algebra

## Page 118

1) 55°  60°  65°
Smallest angle: $n$
Middle angle: $n + 5$
Largest angle: $n + 10$
Equation: $n + n + 5 + n + 10 = 180$
Solve: $n = 55$

2) 121 feet
Each side of garden: $n$
Equation: $n + n + n + n = 484$
Solve: $n = 121$

3) 11 feet by 42 feet

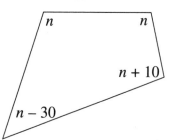

3n + 9

Equation: $3n + 9 + 3n + 9 + n + n = 106$
Solve: $n = 11$

4) 95°  95°  105°  65°

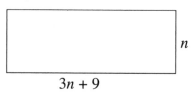

The angle measurements in a four-sided room add up to 360°.

Equation: $n + n + n - 30 + n + 10 = 360$
Solve: $n = 95$

5) 30°  60°  90°
Smallest: $n$
Middle: $2n$
Largest: $3n$
Equation: $n + 2n + 3n = 180$
Solve: $n = 30$

## Page 119

1) 8 feet
Formula: $C = \pi D$
Equation: $25.12 = 3.14 \times D$
Solve: $D = 8$

2) 42 inches
Formula: $A = \frac{1}{2}bh$
Equation: $315 = \frac{1}{2} \times 15 \times h$
Solve: $315 = 7.5h$
$\quad\quad h = 42$

3) Diameter equals 12 feet
Area of room:
$282.60 \div 2.50 = 113.04$ square feet

Formula: $A = \pi r^2$
Equation: $113.04 = 3.14 \times r^2$
Solve: $r^2 = \frac{113.04}{3.14}$
$r^2 = 36$
radius = 6 feet

4) Height equals 8 feet
Equation: $12 \times 12 \times h = 1152$
Solve: $144h = 1152$
$\quad\quad h = 8$

5) Radius equals 8 inches
Formula: $V = \pi r^2 h$
Equation: $3014.4 = 3.14 \times r^2 \times 15$
Solve: $3014.4 = 47.1r^2$
$\quad\quad r^2 = \frac{3014.4}{47.1}$
$\quad\quad r^2 = 64$
$\quad\quad\quad r = 8$

# Level 1
1) 4 units
Equation: $4n = n^2$
Solve: $\frac{4n}{n} = \frac{n^2}{n}$
$n = 4$

2) 11 inches
Width: $n$
Length: $n + 7$
Equation: $n + n + 7 + n + n + 7 = 58$
Solve: $n = 11$

3) 34°　56°
Smaller acute angle: $n$
Larger acute angle: $n + 22$
Equation: $n + n + 22 + 90 = 180$
Solve: $n = 34$

4) 14 inches
Side of triangle: $n$
Side of square: $n$
Perimeter of triangle: $3n$
Perimeter of square: $4n$
Equation: $7n = 98$
Solve: $n = 14$

5) 2 miles
Circumference of circle: 6.28
Formula: $C = \pi D$
Equation: $6.28 = 3.14 \times D$
Solve: $D = \frac{6.28}{3.14}$
$\quad\quad D = 2$

6) 3363 rotations
Inches in 5 miles: 316,800
Inches traveled each rotation:
$3.14 \times 30 = 94.2$

If the tire goes 94.2 inches in one rotation,
then it will need to turn
$316,800 \div 94.2$ to go 5 miles.

7) 20°
Smallest angle: $n$
Middle: $2n$
Largest: $6n$
Equation: $n + 2n + 6n = 180$
Solve: $9n = 180$
$\quad\quad n = 20$

8) 8 inches
Width: $n$
Length: $4n$

Equation: $4n^2 = 256$

Solve:    $n^2 = 64$

$n = 8$

9) 57 feet

Circumference must be 45 x 4 = 180 ft.

Formula: $C = \pi D$

Equation: $180 = 3.14 \times D$

Solve: D = 57 feet

10)  21 inches

Smallest side: $n$

Middle side: $n + 3$

Longest side: $n + 10$

Equation: $n + n + 3 + n + 10 = 46$

Solve: $n = 11$

## Level 2

1) 37°

Angle d: $n$

Angle b: $2n$

Angle a: $2n + 10$

Angle c: $2n + 10$

Angle e: $2n + 7$

Equation: $9n + 27 = 360$

Solve: $n = 37$

2) 15 inches

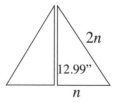

Equation: $12.99 + n + 2n = 35.49$ (The perimeter is 35.49 inches)

Solve: $n = 7.5$

3) 37.5°

Angle b: $n$

Angle a: $n + 15$

(Angles a and b add up to 90°)

Equation: $2n + 15 = 90$

Solve: $n = 37.5$

Angle d is equal to angle b so d = 37.5°

4) 60°

Obtuse angles: $2n$

Acute angles: $n$

The interior angles add up to 360°

Equation: $2n + n + 2n + n = 360$

Solve: $6n = 360$

$n = 60$

5) 11.775 square inches

The area of the circle is 78.5 square inches.

The supplies part of the graph is 15% of 78.5 or 11.775 square inches.

6) 45°

Smallest angle: $n$

Next: $n + 30$

Next: $n + 60$

Largest: $n + 90$

Equation: $4n + 180 = 360$

Solve: $n = 45$

7) 24 feet

Base: $n$

Height: $n$

Equation: $\frac{1}{2}n \times n = 288$

Solve: $\frac{1}{2}n^2 = 288$

$n^2 = 576$

$n = 24$

8) 27.5°

Equation: $6x + 15 = 180$

Solve: $x = 27.5$

9) 8 feet

Equation: $5n^2 = 320$

Solve:  $n^2 = 64$        $n = 8$

10) 100°
Smallest angle: $n$
Middle: $7n$
Largest: $10n$
Equation: $18n = 180$
Solve: $n = 10$

**Einstein Level**
1) 28 inches

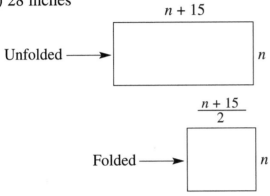

Unfolded ——→   $n + 15$   $n$

Folded ——→   $\dfrac{n + 15}{2}$   $n$

Equation: $\dfrac{n + 15}{2} + \dfrac{n + 15}{2} + n + n = 54$
Solve: $n + 15 + n + n = 54$
$\qquad 3n + 15 = 54$
$\qquad n = 13 \qquad$ Length $= 13 + 15$

2) 21 inches
Width: $n$
Length: $n + 3$
Equation: $4n + 6 = 22$ (perimeter)
Solve: $n = 4$

Width: 4 inches
Length: 7 inches

Length tripled is 21 inches

3) $n = 36°$
Equation: $4n + 36 = 180$
Solve: $n = 36$

4) $.215n^2$
The shaded part is found by subtracting the
area of the circle from the area of the square.

The radius of the circle is equal to $\frac{1}{2}n$
Area of square: $n^2$
Area of circle: $\qquad 3.14 \times \left(\frac{1}{2}n\right)^2$
$\qquad\qquad\qquad 3.14 \times \frac{1}{4}n^2$
$\qquad\qquad\qquad .785n^2$

Subtracting: $n^2 - .785n^2 = .215n^2$

5) 72°
If you find the size of angle c, then d is easy
to find because d + c = 180°

Angle a: $n$
Angle b: $n$
Angle c: $3n$
Equation: $5n = 180$
Solve: $n = 36 \qquad\qquad$ Angle c $= 108°$

Angle d must equal 72°

6) There are 360° in a circle. You can find out
how many $7\frac{1}{2}°$ segments there are in 360°
by dividing. $360 \div 7\frac{1}{2}° = 48$ Each $7\frac{1}{2}°$ seg-
ment is equal to 500 miles, so 48 segments
means the circumference of the earth is
24,000 miles.

7) 81 square inches
Diameter $= 56.52 \div \pi$
Diameter $= 18$ inches.
The base of the triangle is 18 inches, while
the height is equal to the radius of the circle
which is 9 inches.

Area of the shaded triangle is equal to
$\frac{1}{2} \times 18 \times 9$ or 81 square inches.

8) 5 inches
The area of the eight pancakes would be
$8 \times \pi \times r^2$ which equals $8 \times 3.14 \times 25$ or 628
square inches.

If Nana is to make 32 pancakes, the area of each pancake would be 628 ÷ 32 or 19.625 square inches.

We need to set up an equation with the new area in it.
Formula: $A = \pi r^2$
Equation $19.625 = 3.14 \times r^2$
Solve: $r^2 = \dfrac{19.625}{3.14}$
$r^2 = 6.25$
$r = 2.5$
Nana should make pancakes with a diameter of 5 inches.

9) 0.2 inches
Area of the mirror: $\pi \times 100^2$ which equals 31,400 square inches.

Area of Eric's eye is 31,400 ÷ 1,000,000 or 0.0314 square inches.

Formula: $A = \pi r^2$
Equation: $0.0314 = 3.14 \times r^2$
Solve: $r^2 = \dfrac{0.0314}{3.14}$
$r^2 = 0.01$
$r = 0.1$
The diameter of Eric's eye is 0.2 inches

10) 30 feet
The 12 packets seeded 12 x 235.5 or 2826 square feet of lawn. Because this was a circular area, we use the formula for area of a circle.

Formula: $A = \pi r^2$
Equation: $2826 = 3.14 \times r^2$
Solve: $r^2 = \dfrac{2826}{3.14}$
$r^2 = 900$
$r = 30$

The chain was 30 feet

# Chapter 11: Algebra and Levers

## Level 1
1) 8 feet from the fulcrum
Formula:
weight x distance from fulcrum = weight x distance from fulcrum

Equation: $40 \times 10 = 50 \times n$
Solve: $400 = 50n$
$n = 8$

2) 3.2 feet from the fulcrum
Formula:
weight x distance from fulcrum = weight x distance from fulcrum
Equation: $60 \times 4 = 75 \times n$
Solve: $240 = 75n$
$n = 3.2$ feet

3) 42 pounds
Formula:
weight x distance from fulcrum = weight x distance from fulcrum

Equation: $84 \times 4 = n \times 7$
Solve: $336 = 7n$
$n = 48$
The amount of weight at that spot should be 48 pounds. Because the box weighs 6 pounds, the friend should weigh 42 pounds.

4) $5\frac{1}{3}$ feet from the fulcrum
Formula:
weight x distance from fulcrum = weight x distance from fulcrum

Equation: $48 \times 8 = 72 \times n$
Solve: $384 = 72n$
$n = 5.3333$ feet

5) $1\frac{1}{3}$ pounds
Formula:
weight x distance from fulcrum = weight x distance from fulcrum

Equation: 4 x 6 = $n$ x 18
Solve: 24 = 18$n$
$n = 1\frac{1}{3}$

6) Right side
If the board was balanced, then
115 x 6 would equal 80 x 9.
(Mike)        (Eric)
690 < 720 so the right side would go down.

7) $7\frac{1}{3}$ feet
Formula:
weight x distance from fulcrum = weight x distance from fulcrum
Equation: 110 x 8 = 120 x $n$
Solve: 880 = 120$n$
$n = 7.3333$

8) 500 pounds
Formula:
weight x distance from fulcrum = weight x distance from fulcrum

Equation: 2000 x 3 = n x 12
Solve: 6000 = 12$n$
$n = 500$

9) $6\frac{1}{4}$ feet
Formula:
weight x distance from fulcrum = weight x distance from fulcrum

Equation: 50 x 10 = 80 x $n$
Solve: 500 = 80$n$
$n = 6.25$

10) Yes, if a long enough lever was used.

## Level 2

1) 8 feet from the child
Child's distance from fulcrum: $n$
Mother's distance from fulcrum: $12 - n$

Formula:
weight x distance from fulcrum = weight x distance from fulcrum

Equation: 50 x $n$ = 100 x $(12 - n)$
Solve: 50$n$ = 1200 - 100$n$
150$n$ = 1200
$n = 8$

2) 6 feet
Equation: 60 x 8 = 80 x $n$
Solve: 480 = 80$n$
$n = 6$

3) $33\frac{1}{3}$ pounds
Equation: 50 x 4 = $n$ x 6
Solve: 200 = 6$n$
$n = 33.333$

4) $5\frac{1}{3}$ feet
Equation: 80 x 8 = 120 x $n$
Solve: 640 = 120$n$
$n = 5.333$

5) 12 pounds
Equation: 60 x 2 = $n$ x 10
Solve: 120 = 10$n$
$n = 12$

6) 62.5 pounds of force
Equation: 1000 x 1 = $n$ x 16
Solve: 1000 = 16$n$
$n = 62.5$

7) 50 pounds of force
Equation: 1250 x .5 = $n$ x 12.5
Solve: 625 = 12.5$n$
$n$ = 50

8) 2.5 feet from the fulcrum
Equation: 50 x 50 = 1000 x $n$
Solve: 2500 = 1000$n$
$n$ = 2.5

9) The car would tip to the left because as the gas is used, the side with the gas tank becomes lighter.

10) 3.6 feet from the fulcrum
Equation: 72.25 x 6 = 120.375 x $n$
Solve: 433.5 = 120.375$n$
$n$ = 3.6

**Einstein Level**
1) 125 pounds
Equation: 500 x 2 = $n$ x 8
Solve: 1000 = 8$n$
$n$ = 125

2) $26\frac{2}{3}$ feet from the fulcrum
Equation: 200 x 12 = 90 x $n$
Solve: 2400 = 90$n$
$n$ = 26.666

3) 1 foot from the fulcrum
Equation:    (150 x 8) + (80 x $n$) =
            (100 x 8) + (120 x 4)
Solve: 1200 + 80$n$ = 800 + 480
       80$n$ = 80
       $n$ = 1

4) $3\frac{1}{8}$ feet from the fulcrum
Equation:
150 x 5 = (100 x 5) + ( 80 x $n$)
Solve: 750 = 500 + 80$n$
       80$n$ = 250
       $n$ = 3.125

5) $26\frac{6}{19}$ feet
Equation: 500 x 2 = $n$ x 38
Solve: 1000 = 38$n$
       $n$ = $26\frac{6}{19}$ feet

6) $166\frac{2}{3}$ pounds
Equation: 2000 x 2 = $n$ x 24
Solve: 4000 = 24$n$
       $n$ = 166.666

7) She could slide her hand to the bottom of the wrench. She also could put a pipe over the handle to make the handle longer. If Kristin bought a longer wrench, she would be able to apply more force.

8) 1650 pounds of force
Equation: 150 x 11 = $n$ x 1
Solve: 1650 = $n$

9) The shovel was being used as a lever. The ground is serving as a fulcrum.

10) $1133\frac{1}{3}$ pounds of force.
Equation: 200 x 8.5 = $n$ x 1.5
Solve: 1700 = 1.5$n$
       $n$ = 1133.33

This amount of force is present when the 200-pound man is just standing. If he jumps, the force will increase significantly.

**Chapter 12: Algebra and Money**

**Page 141**
1) 20$d$ + .20$m$

2) $302
Equation: (20 x 7) + (810 x .20)
Solve: 140 + 162 = 302

3) Over 75 checks
Number of checks: $n$
Bank A charge: $5 + .2n$
Bank B charge: 20

If we set Bank A's charge equal to Bank B's, then we will know the number of checks when both charges are the same.

Equation: $5 + .2n = 20$
Solve: $.2n = 15$
$\quad\quad n = 75$

## Page 144
1) 9 quarters
Number of dimes: $3n$
Number of quarters: $n$

Value of dimes: 10 x $3n$ or $30n$
Value of quarters: 25 x $n$ or $25n$

Equation: $30n + 25n = 495$
Solve: $55n = 495$
$\quad\quad n = 9$

2) 28 nickels
Number of nickels: $7n$
Number of dimes: $3n$
Number of quarters: $n$

Value of nickels: 5 x $7n$ or $35n$
Value of dimes: 10 x $3n$ or $30n$
Value of quarters: 25 x $n$ or $25n$

Equation: $35n + 30n + 25n = 360$
Solve: $90n = 360$
$\quad\quad n = 4$

3) 2 quarters
Number of nickels: $n$
Number of quarters: $28 - n$

Value of nickels: 5 x $n$ or $5n$
Value of quarters:
$25(28 - n)$ or $700 - 25n$

Equation: $5n + 700 - 25n = 180$
Solve: $-20n = -520$
$\quad\quad 20n = 520$
$\quad\quad n = 26$

## Level 1
1) $29.95d + .08m$

2) $25n$

3) $35 + .03n$

4) $25 - n$

5) 17 nickels
Number of nickels: $n$
Number of dimes: $2n$

Value of nickels: 5 x $n$ or $5n$
Value of dimes: 10 x $2n = 20n$

Equation: $5n + 20n = 425$
Solve: $25n = 425$
$\quad\quad n = 17$

6) $39.50
Equation: $35 + (.03 \times 150) = 35 + 4.50$

7) 15  $5 bills
Number of $5 bills: $n$
Number of $10 bills: $2n$

Value of $5 bills: $5n$
Value of $10 bills: $20n$

Equation: $5n + 20n = 375$
Solve: $25n = 375$
$\quad\quad n = 15$

8) $500n$

9) 22 nickels

Number of nickels: $2n$
Number of dimes: $n$
Number of quarters: $n$

Value of nickels: 5 x 2n or 10n
Value of dimes: 10 x *n* or 10n
Value of quarters: 25 x *n* or 25n

Equation: $10n + 10n + 25n = 495$
Solve: $45n = 495$
$n = 11$

10) $15d + 12.50n$

## Level 2

1) $25(20 - n)$ or $500 - 25n$

2) 93 bars of soap
Because we want to know how many bars must be sold to make "0" profit, we will write our equation with profit listed as 0.
Equation: $0 = 1.75n - 162.75$
Solve: $1.75n = 162.75$
$n = 93$

3) 293 bars of soap
We will set our profit at $350.
Equation: $350 = 1.75n - 162.75$
Solve: $1.75n = 512.75$
$n = 293$

4) 14 nickels
Number of nickels: *n*
Number of quarters: $25 - n$

Value of nickels: 5 x *n* or 5n
Value of quarters:
25 x $(25 - n)$ or $625 - 25n$

Equation: $5n + 625 - 25n = 345$
Solve: $20n = 280$
$n = 14$

5) 51 refrigerators were sold

Number of refrigerators: 3n
Number of washing machines: *n*

Value of refrigerators:
800 x 3n or 2400n
Value of washing machines:
300 x *n* or 300n

Equation: $2400n + 300n = 45,900$
Solve: $2700n = 45,900$
$n = 17$

6) Loss of $22.50
Daily profit:
$-.025(10)^2 + (12 \times 10) - 140$

$-2.5 + 120 - 140$ or $-22.50$

7) 20 quarters
Number of pennies: *n*
Number of nickels: 2n
Number of dimes: 3n
Number of quarters: 4n

Value of pennies: 1 x *n* or *n*
Value of nickels: 5 x 2n or 10n
Value of dimes: 10 x 3n or 30n
Value of quarters: 25 x 4n or 100n

Equation: $n + 10n + 30n + 100n = 705$
Solve: $141n = 705$
$n = 5$

8) 13    5-cent stamps
Number of 20-cent stamps: 2n
Number of 34-cent stamps: *n*
Number of 5-cent stamps: $n + 6$

Value of 20-cent stamps: 40n
Value of 34-cent stamps: 34n
Value of 5-cent stamps: $5(n + 6)$

Equation: $40n + 34n + 5n + 30 = 583$
$79n = 553$    $n = 7$

9) Profit = $12n - 7500$

Each CD they sell they take in $12, but they have to subtract the $7500 that it cost them to make the CDs. If they sell n CDs, then they make (12 x $n$) – 7500 profit.

10) 49 nickels
Number of nickels: $n$
Number of dimes: $n + 5$
Number of quarters: $n + 10$

Value of nickels: 5 x $n$ or $5n$
Value of dimes: $10(n + 5)$ or $10n + 50$
Value of quarters: $25(n + 10)$ or $25n + 250$

Equation:
$5n + 10n + 50 + 25n + 250 = 2260$
Solve: $40n + 300 = 2260$
$n = 49$

### Einstein Level
1) Over 300 minutes
Charge Company A: $.03n + 18$
Charge Company B: $.09n$

If you make an equation to find when the charges are equal, then you can find the best deal.

Equation: $.03n + 18 = .09n$
Solve: $.06n = 18$
$n = 300$

2) 3 nickels
Number of nickels: $n - 4$
Number of dimes: $n + 6$
Number of quarters: $n$

Value of Nickels: $5(n - 4)$ or $5n - 20$
Value of dimes: $10(n + 6)$ or $10n + 60$
Value of Quarters: $25n$

Equation:
$5n - 20 + 10n + 60 + 25n = 320$
Solve: $40n + 40 = 320$
$n = 7$

3) 12 $50 bills
Number of $1 bills: $3n$
Number of $5 bills: $3n$
Number of $10 bills: $2n$
Number of $20 bills: $2n$
Number of $50 bills: $n$

Value of $1 bills: $3n$
Value of $5 bills: 5 x $3n$ or $15n$
Value of $10 bills: 10 x $2n$ or $20n$
Value of $20 bills: 20 x $2n$ or $40n$
Value of $50 bills: $50n$

Equation:
$3n + 15n + 20n + 40n + 50n = 1536$
Solve: $128n = 1536$
$n = 12$

4) Over $333\frac{1}{3}$ miles
Lemon Company: $39.95 + .12n$
Kiwi Company: $79.95$

If you make an equation to find when the charges are equal, then you can find the best deal.

Equation: $39.95 + .12n = 79.95$
Solve: $n = 333.33$

5) Profit = $900n - 1700$

Money taken in each day: $45n$
Money in a month: $20(45n)$ or $900n$
Expenses: $1700$

Equation: $900n - 1700 = $ profit

6) 12 dimes
Number of nickels: $40 - 2n$
Number of dimes: $n$
Number of quarters: $n$

Value of nickels: $5(40 - 2n)$ or $200 - 10n$
Value of dimes: $10n$
Value of quarters: $25n$

Equation:
$200 - 10n + 10n + 25n = 500$
Solve: $25n = 300$
$n = 12$

7) Profit = .18n - 2.00
Profit per customer: $.18
The profit for 7 customers would be .18 x 7. The profit for n customers would be .18 x n or .18n. You then must subtract Linus's $2 expense for renting Lucy's yard.

8) $3500
Amount of money Bank A: $n$
Amount of money Bank B: $10,000 - n$

Interest Bank A: .08 x $n$ or $.08n$
Interest Bank B: .07 x $(10,000 - n)$ or $700 - .07n$

Equation: $.08n + 700 - .07n = 735$
Solve: $.01n = 35$
$n = 3500$

9) Profit = $13n - 7514$
The amount of money Maria makes from each CD is $13, but she has to pay for her studio time of $7514.

10) 144.5 days
Maria will earn $52 per day, so it will take her $7514 \div 52$ or 144.5 days before she starts to make a profit.

# Chapter 13:
# Algebra and Physics D = R x T

## Page 154
1) 12.5 mph
Distance = Rate x Time
Equation: $6.25 = n$ x $.5$
Solve: $n = 12.5$

2) 669,600,000 mph
Distance = Rate x Time
Equation: $167,400,000 = n$ x $.25$
Solve: $n = 669,600,000$

3) 6.2 hours  (6 hours and 12 minutes)
Distance = Rate x Time
Equation: $396.8 = 64$ x $n$
Solve: $n = 6.2$

4) 7:45
Distance = Rate x Time
Equation: $15 = 60$ x $n$
Solve: $n = .25$
It takes Sara .25 hours or 15 minutes to drive to work.

5) 60 miles
Distance = Rate x Time
Equation: $n = 18$ x $3\frac{1}{3}$
Solve: $n = 60$

## Page 156
1) 7.5 mph
Distance = Rate x Time
Equation: $1 = n$ x $\frac{8}{60}$
Solve: $1 = n$ x $.133333$
$n = 7.5$

2) 720 mph
Equation: $1 = n$ x $\frac{5}{3600}$
(3600 seconds in an hour)
Solve: $1 = .001388888n$
$n = 720$

3) .5 mph or $\frac{1}{2}$ mph

Equation: $\frac{440}{1760} = n \times .5$

(There are 1760 yards in a mile.)

Solve: $.25 = .5n$

$n = .5$

4) $\frac{1}{3600}$

(There are 3600 seconds in one hour.)

5) $\frac{1}{5280}$

(There are 5280 feet in one mile.)

## Level 1

1) 7 hours  20 minutes

Equation: $22 = 3 \times n$

Solve: $n = 7.33$

2) 55 mph

Equation: $770 = n \times 14$

Solve: $n = 55$

3) 449.5 miles

Equation: $n = 58 \times 7.75$

Solve: $n = 449.5$

4) $2\frac{2}{3}$ mph

Equation: $12 = n \times 4.5$

Solve: $n = 2.6666$

5) 2.5 miles

Phil's equation: $n = 65 \times .5$

Denzel's equation: $n = 60 \times .5$

Phil's distance: 32.5 miles

Denzel's distance: 30 miles

6) 357.5 miles

Equation: $n = 55 \times 6.5$

Solve: $n = 357.5$

7) 11 hours

Boston to Cleveland: 642 miles

Equation: $642 = 58 \times n$

Solve: $n = 11.069$

8) $58\frac{1}{3}$ mph

Detroit to Washington D.C.: 525 miles

Equation: $525 = n \times 9$

Solve: $n = 58.333$

9) $49\frac{1}{6}$ hours or 49 hours 10 minutes

Dallas to Cleveland: 1180 miles

Equation to Cleveland: $1180 = 60 \times n$

Solve: $n = 19.666$  It took Jose $19\frac{2}{3}$ hours on his trip to Cleveland.

Equation return trip: $1180 = 40 \times n$

Solve: $n = 29.5$

It took Jose $29\frac{1}{2}$ hours on his return trip.

10) 12 hours

Round trip distance: 732 miles

Equation: $732 = 61 \times n$

Solve: $n = 12$

## Level 2

1) 12:00 noon

Time traveled: $n$

Distance traveled by first train: $60n$

Distance traveled by second train: $45n$

The total distance they are apart is 472.5 miles.

Equation: $60n + 45n = 472.5$

Solve: $n = 4.5$ hours

2) 3500 mph

Time: 143 hours

Equation: $500,000 = n \times 143$

Solve: $n = 3496.5034$

3) Sunday at 2:00 P.M.

You must first determine how many hours the trip will take.

Equation: $2970 = 55 \times n$

Solve: $n = 54$ hours

Because Kate is traveling 8 hours per day, she will travel 6 days with 6 hours left over.

4) 48 minutes
Equation: $2 = 2.5 \times n$
Solve: $n = .8$ hours
.8 hours is equal to 48 minutes

5) $1\frac{1}{6}$ miles
Equation: $n = 70 \times \frac{1}{60}$
Solve: $n = 1\frac{1}{6}$

6) 10:45 A.M.
Equation: $2380 = 560 \times n$
Solve: $n = 4.25$ hours

It will be 12:45 Chicago time when Jill arrives in San Fransisco. San Fransisco is 2 hours behind Chicago time.

7) 48 seconds
Equation: $1 = 75 \times n$
Solve: $n = .013333$ hours which is equal to 48 seconds.
Two ratios: $\frac{1 \ hour}{3600 \ seconds} = \frac{.013333 \ hours}{n \ seconds}$
Cross-multiply: $n = 48$

8) 4:45
Equation: $3.75 = 15 \times n$
Solve: $n = .25$ hours

9) 1625 mph
Equation: $325 = n \times \frac{12}{60}$
Solve: $325 = .2n$
$\qquad n = 1625$

10) 12 hours
Speed downriver: 2 mph + 1 mph = 3 mph
Speed upstream: 2 mph - 1 mph = 1 mph

You need to find the distance each way.
Equation: $n = 3 \ mph \times 3 \ hours$
Solve: $n = 9$ miles

Time downstream: 3 hours
Time upstream: $9 = 1 \times n$  $n = 9$ hours

**Einstein Level**
1) 15 mph
Equation: $1 = n \times \frac{4}{60}$
Solve: $n = 15$ mph

2) 2.25 seconds
660 feet $= \frac{660}{5280}$ miles
Equation: $\frac{660}{5280} = 200 \times n$
Solve: $.125 = 200n$
$\qquad n = .000625$ hours

Because there are 3600 seconds in an hour, you can change .000625 hours into seconds by multiplying by 3600.
$3600 \times .000625 = 2.25$

3) 20.45 mph
Remember that when you use the equation $D = R \times T$, that distances should be in miles and time in hours.
100 yards $= \frac{100}{1760}$ miles
10 seconds $= \frac{10}{3600}$ hours

Equation: $\frac{100}{1760} = n \times \frac{10}{3600}$
Solve: $\frac{100}{1760} = \frac{10n}{3600}$
Cross-multiply: $17,600n = 360,000$
$\qquad n = 20.4545$

4) 17 seconds
Equation: $\frac{100}{1760} = 12 \times n$
Solve: $\frac{12n}{1} = \frac{100}{1760}$
Cross-multiply: $21,120n = 100$
$\qquad n = .0047$ hours

Because there are 3600 seconds in an hour, you can change .0047 hours into seconds by multiplying by 3600.

.0047 x 3600 = 16.92

5) 450 mph

2 seconds = $\frac{2}{3600}$ hours

Equation: $.25 = n$ x $\frac{2}{3600}$

Solve: $.25 = .00055555n$

$n = 450$

6) 750 mph

Remember that when you use the equation D = R x T, that distances should be in miles and time in hours.

1100 feet = $\frac{1100}{5280}$ miles

1 second = $\frac{1}{3600}$ hours

Equation: $\frac{1100}{5280} = n$ x $\frac{1}{3600}$

Solve: $\frac{1100}{5280} = \frac{n}{3600}$

Cross-multiply: $5280n = 3,960,000$

$n = 750$

7) 1.4 miles

You must first find out how much time went by when Kevin crosses the finish line.

Equation: $6.3 = 9$ x $n$

Solve: $n = .7$ hours

Now you need to find how much distance Warren traveled at the time Kevin crossed the finish line. Once you have that information, it is very easy to find out how far behind Warren was.

Equation: $n = 7$ x $.7$ hours

Solve: $n = 4.9$ miles

When Kevin ran 6.3 miles, Warren ran 4.9 miles. Warren was 1.4 miles behind Kevin.

8) 22.5 seconds

Equation: $.25 = 40$ x $n$

Solve: $n = .00625$ hours

Because there are 3600 seconds in an hour, you can change .00625 hours into seconds by multiplying by 3600.

3600 x .00625 = 22.5 seconds

9) .25 miles from the dinosaur

We can determine how close the cheetah is to the dinosaur by finding out how far they each are from the starting point after one minute. (One minute is equal to $\frac{1}{60}$ of an hour.)

Dinosaur: $n = 55$ x $\frac{1}{60}$

Solve: $n = \frac{11}{12}$ miles

Because the dinosaur had a $\frac{1}{2}$-mile head start, you need to add $\frac{1}{2}+\frac{11}{12}$ which equals $1\frac{5}{12}$ miles from the start.

Cheetah: $n = 70$ x $\frac{1}{60}$

Solve: $n = 1\frac{1}{6}$ miles from the start.

The Cheetah is $\frac{3}{12}$ miles from the dinosaur.

10) 37.5 mph

Equation: $.25 = n$ x $\frac{24}{3600}$

Solve: $n = 37.5$

## Chapter 14:
## A Different Kind of Average Speed

### Level 1

1) $1\frac{2}{3}$ mph

Block of time: 5

| 1 | 1 | 1 | 1 | 1 | 5 |
|---|---|---|---|---|---|

$\frac{1 + 1 + 1 + 1 + 1 + 5}{6\ blocks\ of\ time} = \frac{10}{6} = 1.66$

2) 20 mph

Block of time: 60

| 12 | 12 | 12 | 12 | 12 | | 60 |

$$\frac{12 + 12 + 12 + 12 + 12 + 60}{6 \text{ blocks of time}} = \frac{120}{6} = 20$$

3) $10\frac{2}{3}$ mph
Block of time: 48

| 6 | 6 | 6 | 6 | 6 | 6 | 6 | 6 | | 48 |

$$\frac{6 + 6 + 6 + 6 + 6 + 6 + 6 + 6 + 48}{9 \text{ blocks of time}} = 10.66$$

4) 12 mph

Block of time: 30    Because 10 doesn't fit into 15 evenly, you need to come up with a new block of time that both numbers will fit into.

| 10 | 10 | 10 | | 15 | 15 |

$$\frac{10 + 10 + 10 + 15 + 15}{5 \text{ blocks of time}} = 12$$

5) 16 mph
Block of time: 48

| 12 | 12 | 12 | 12 | | 12 | 12 | 12 | 12 | 48 |

Because Anty went two thirds of the way to school at 12 mph, the traveling is broken into three sections as shown above.

$$\frac{12 + 12 + 12 + 12 + 12 + 12 + 12 + 12 + 48}{9 \text{ blocks of time}} = 16$$

## Level 2

1) 48 mph
Block of time: 120

| 40 | 40 | 40 | | 60 | 60 |

$$\frac{40 + 40 + 40 + 60 + 60}{5 \text{ blocks of time}} = 48$$

2) 1.56 mph
Block of time: 7

| 1 | 1 | 1 | 1 | 1 | 1 | 1 | | 3.5 | 3.5 |

$$\frac{1 + 1 + 1 + 1 + 1 + 1 + 1 + 3.5 + 3.5}{9 \text{ blocks of time}} = 1.555$$

3) $1\frac{2}{3}$ mph

Because of the current, Luke paddled downstream at 5 mph and upstream at 1 mph.
Block of time: 5

| 1 | 1 | 1 | 1 | 1 | | 5 |

$$\frac{1 + 1 + 1 + 1 + 1 + 5}{6 \text{ blocks of time}} = 1\frac{2}{3}$$

4) $10\frac{2}{3}$ mph

Sara's trip needs to be broken into fourths.
Block of time: 40

| 5 | 5 | 5 | 5 | 5 | 5 | 5 | 5 | 8 | 8 | 8 | 8 | 8 |

| 40 | 40 |

$$\frac{(8 \times 5) + (5 \times 8) + 40 + 40}{15 \text{ blocks of time}} = 10.666$$

5) 2.8 mph
Block of time: 7

| 7 | | 1.75 | 1.75 | 1.75 | 1.75 |

$$\frac{7 + 1.75 + 1.75 + 1.75 + 1.75}{5 \text{ blocks of time}} = 2.8$$

## Einstein Level

1) 7 mph
Block of time: 48
The trip needs to be broken into fourths.

16 x | 3 |    8 x | 6 |    | 16 | 16 | 16 | | 48 |

$$\frac{48 + 48 + 48 + 48}{28 \text{ blocks of time}} = 6.857$$

2) 80 mph
You must first find how long it took Kate to go the 16 miles (1/4 of the trip)
Equation: $16 = 40 \times n$
Solve: $n = .4$ hours

For Kate to arrive at 12:00 she must go the remaining 48 miles in .6 hours.
Equation: $48 = n \times .6$
Solve: $n = 80$

3) 180 mph
Nancy's trip needs to be broken into fifths because she went 100 miles at one speed and then 400 miles at another speed.
Block of time: 360

| 60 | 60 | 60 | 60 | 60 | 60 |
|----|----|----|----|----|----|

| 360 | 360 | 360 | 360 |
|-----|-----|-----|-----|

$$\frac{(6 \times 60) + (4 \times 360)}{10 \; blocks \; of \; time} = 180$$

4) 50 mph
If you can find how long the trip took, then it is easy to find the average speed because you will know the distance and the time.

Distance = Rate x Time

Distance first part of trip:
$55 \times 16 = 880$ miles
There are now $1800 - 880$ or 920 miles remaining for the second part of the trip which is done at a speed of 46 mph.

Time for second part of trip:
$920 = 46 \times n$
Solve: $n = 20$ hours

The trip took $16 + 20$ or 36 hours

Equation: $1800 = n \times 36$
Solve: $n = 50$

5) $1\frac{5}{7}$ mph
Block of time: 6

| 2 | 2 | 2 |   | 1.5 | 1.5 | 1.5 | 1.5 |
|---|---|---|---|-----|-----|-----|-----|

$$\frac{2 + 2 + 2 + 1.5 + 1.5 + 1.5 + 1.5}{7 \; blocks \; of \; time} = 1\frac{5}{7}$$

## Chapter 15: Physics and Algebra
## D = R x T (advanced)

### Level 1
1) 6 hours

|         | Rate   | Time  | Distance |
|---------|--------|-------|----------|
| Ryan    | 12 mph | $n$   | $12n$    |
| Brother | 8 mph  | $n + 3$ | $8(n + 3)$ |

Because the distances are equal to each other, you can make an equation setting each distance equal to the other.
Equation: $12n = 8(n + 3)$
Solve: $12n = 8n + 24$
$n = 6$

2) 3:12
Because they travel for the same amount of time, you can call both times $n$.

|        | Rate   | Time | Distance |
|--------|--------|------|----------|
| Steph  | 10 mph | $n$  | $10n$    |
| Mother | 40 mph | $n$  | $40n$    |

When you add the distance Stephanie travels to the distance her mother travels, you will get 10 miles.

Equation: $10n + 40n = 10$
Solve: $n = .2$ hours or 12 minutes

3) 1.25 hours

|  | Rate | Time | Distance |
|------|------|------|----------|
| Kate | 13 mph | $n$ | $13n$ |
| Erin | 5 mph | $n + 2$ | $5(n + 2)$ |

When Kate catches Erin, they will have both traveled the same distance.
Equation: $13n = 5(n + 2)$
Solve: $13n = 5n + 10$
　　　$n = 1.25$ hours

4) 12.5 hours

|  | Rate | Time | Distance |
|------|------|------|----------|
| Joey | 22 mph | $n$ | $22n$ |
| Josh | 26 mph | $n$ | $26n$ |

Because Joey and Josh will be traveling for the same amount of time, you can call each of their times $n$.

When you add up their distances, it will equal 600 miles.
Equation: $22n + 26n = 600$
Solve: $48n = 600$
　　　$n = 12.5$ hours

5) $2\frac{6}{7}$ hours

|  | Rate | Time | Distance |
|------|------|------|----------|
| Dan | 3 mph | $n$ | $3n$ |
| Luke | 4 mph | $n$ | $4n$ |

Because they will both be running the same amount of time, you can call each time $n$. The question wants to know when their total mileage equals 20 miles.

Equation: $3n + 4n = 20$
Solve: $7n = 20$
　　　$n = 2\frac{6}{7}$ hours

## Level 2
1) 5 hours

|  | Rate | Time | Distance |
|--------|------|------|----------|
| Steve | 6 mph | $n$ | $6n$ |
| Jordan | 7 mph | $n$ | $7n$ |

Because Steve and Jordan will be riding for the same amount of time, you can call each of their times $n$.

Because he is 5 miles behind, the distance Jordan needs to travel is 5 miles more than the distance Steve will travel. The equation will show that.
Jordan's distance = Steve's distance +5
Equation: $7n = 6n + 5$
Solve: $n = 5$

2) 2.1 hours  or  2 hours 6 minutes

|  | Rate | Time | Distance |
|---------|--------|------|----------|
| Boat | 17 mph | $n$ | $17n$ |
| Coast G | 42 mph | $n$ | $42n$ |

Because the sailboat and the Coast Guard cutter will be traveling for the same amount of time, you can call each of their times $n$.

When you add the distances they travel, you will get 123.9 miles. The equation will show that.

Equation: $17n + 42n = 123.9$
Solve: $59n = 123.9$
$n = 2.1$ hours

3) 22.5 minutes

|       | Rate   | Time | Distance |
|-------|--------|------|----------|
| Megan | 12 mph | $n$  | $12n$    |
| Kate  | 16 mph | $n$  | $16n$    |

Because Megan and Kate will be traveling for the same amount of time, you can call each of their times $n$.

We want to know when Kate's distance minus Megan's distance equals 1.5 miles.
Equation: $16n - 12n = 1.5$
Solve: $4n = 1.5$
$n = .375$ hours

Remember, you can change .375 hours to minutes simply by multiplying by 60.
.375 x 60 = 22.5

4) .1 hours or 6 minutes

|        | Rate    | Time | Distance |
|--------|---------|------|----------|
| Driver | 80 mph  | $n$  | $80n$    |
| Police | 100 mph | $n$  | $100n$   |

The times will be the same, so each time will be called $n$.

The patrolman's distance traveled will be 2 miles more than the driver's distance. The equation will show that.

Police's distance = Driver's distance + 2
Equation: $100n = 80n + 2$
Solve: $20n = 2$
$n = .1$ hours

Remember, you can change .1 hours to minutes simply by multiplying by 60.
.1 x 60 = 6 minutes

5) Sister by 5 minutes

|        | Rate   | Time | Distance |
|--------|--------|------|----------|
| Josh   | 8 mph  | $t$  | $8t$     |
| Sister | 15 mph | $n$  | $15n$    |

We can find the amount of time it took each of the children to finish the race by making equations setting the distance equal to 10 miles.

Josh's equation: $8t = 10$ miles
Solve: $t = 1.25$ hours   (1 hour 15 min.)

Sister's equation: $15n = 10$ miles
Solve: $n = .66$ hours   (40 minutes)

Even with a half hour head start, Josh still lost the race by 5 minutes.

## Einstein Level
1) 15 mph

|        | Rate    | Time | Distance   |
|--------|---------|------|------------|
| School | $n$     | 2    | $2n$       |
| Home   | $n - 5$ | 3    | $3(n - 5)$ |

Steve's speed going home was 5 mph slower than his speed going to school. Therefore his speed home is expressed as $n - 5$.

Because the distances to school and back home are equal, the equation will show that.
Equation: $2n = 3(n - 5)$
Solve: $2n = 3n - 15$
$n = 15$ mph

2) 30 seconds

|  | Rate | Time | Distance |
|---|---|---|---|
| Horse | 26 mph | $n$ | $26n$ |
| Chicken | 4 mph | $n$ | $4n$ |

The horse and the chicken's times will both be called n. When they meet, the total distance would be .25 miles, so the equation will show that.
Equation: $26n + 4n = .25$
Solve: $30n = .25$
$n = .008333$ hours
Hours can be changed into seconds by multiplying by 3600.
$.0083333 \times 3600 = 30$ seconds

3) 3 minutes

|  | Rate | Time | Distance |
|---|---|---|---|
| Turtle | 2 mph | $n$ | $2n$ |
| Rabbit | 8 mph | $n$ | $8n$ |

The times are the same so they will be called n. The distances run will add up to .5 miles because they are going to meet twice.
Equation: $2n + 8n = .5$
Solve: $10n = .5$
$n = .05$ hours
$.05 \times 60 = 3$ minutes

4) 2:24 P.M.

|  | Rate | Time | Distance |
|---|---|---|---|
| East | 420 mph | $n$ | $420n$ |
| West | $413\frac{1}{3}$ mph | $n$ | $413\frac{1}{3}n$ |

The times are the same so they will be called $n$. The equation will add the distances traveled and set this equal to 2000 miles because the problem wants to know the time when they are 2000 miles apart.
Equation: $420n + 413\frac{1}{3}n = 2000$
Solve: $833\frac{1}{3}n = 2000$
$n = 2.4$ hours
.4 hours equals .4 x 60 or 24 minutes
The planes are 2000 miles apart in 2 hours 24 minutes.

5) 4 miles

|  | Rate | Time | Distance |
|---|---|---|---|
| Dan | 4 mph | 4 hours | 16 miles |
| Luke | 5 mph | $n$ | $5n$ |

We first need to find out how long it took Luke to cross the finish line.
Equation: $5n = 20$
Solve: $n = 4$ hours

We then put in the 4 hours into Dan's time and simply multiply to find that Dan has run 16 miles in the 4 hours. He is 4 miles behind when Luke crosses the finish line.

## Chapter 16: Algebra and Work
## Distance = Rate x Time

### Level 1

1) 1 hour  20 minutes
Armando's rate: 1/4 fence per hour
Sister's rate: 1/2 fence per hour

Armando's work: $\frac{1}{4}t$
Sister's work: $\frac{1}{2}t$
Equation: 1 fence $= \frac{1}{4}t + \frac{1}{2}t$
Solve: $1 = \frac{3}{4}t$    $t = 1\frac{1}{3}$ hours

2) 2 hours
Large drain's rate: 1/3 pool per hour
Small drain's rate: 1/6 pool per hour

Large drain's work: $\frac{1}{3}t$
Small drain's work: $\frac{1}{6}t$
Equation: 1 pool $= \frac{1}{3}t + \frac{1}{6}t$
Solve: $1 = \frac{1}{2}t$    $t = 2$ hours

3) 1 hour
1st worker's rate: 1/2 job per hour
2nd worker's rate: 1/3 job per hour
3rd worker's rate: 1/6 job per hour

1st worker's work: $\frac{1}{2}t$
2nd worker's work: $\frac{1}{3}t$
3rd workers work: $\frac{1}{6}t$
Equation: 1 job $= \frac{1}{2}t + \frac{1}{3}t + \frac{1}{6}t$
Solve: $1 = \frac{12}{12}t$    $t = 1$ hour

4) 1 hour  30 minutes
1st line's rate: 1/2 pond per hour
2nd line's rate: 1/6 pond per hour

1st line's work: $\frac{1}{2}t$
2nd line's work: $\frac{1}{6}t$

Equation: 1 pond $= \frac{1}{2}t + \frac{1}{6}t$
Solve: $1 = \frac{2}{3}t$    $t = 1\frac{1}{2}$ hours

5) 12 hours
Hose's rate: 1/3 pool per hour
Drain's rate: – 1/4 pool per hour

Hose's work: $\frac{1}{3}t$
Drain's work: $- \frac{1}{4}t$
Equation: 1 pool $= \frac{1}{3}t - \frac{1}{4}t$
Solve: $1 = \frac{1}{12}t$    $t = 12$

### Level 2

1) 1 hour  52.5 minutes
1st bulldozer's rate: 1/3 job per hour
2nd bulldozer's rate: 1/5 job per hour

1st bulldozers work: $\frac{1}{3}t$
2nd bulldozer's work: $\frac{1}{5}t$
Equation: 1 job $= \frac{1}{3}t + \frac{1}{5}t$
Solve: $1 = \frac{8}{15}t$    $t = 1\frac{7}{8}$ hours

2) 18 hours  45 minutes
Lamar's rate: 1/50 house per hour
Claudia's rate: 1/30 house per hour

Lamar's work: $\frac{1}{50}t$
Claudia's work: $\frac{1}{30}t$
Equation: 1 house $= \frac{1}{50}t + \frac{1}{30}t$
Solve: $1 = \frac{8}{150}t$    $t = 18.75$ hours

3) 1 hour  36 minutes
Gregg's rate: 1/2 pile per hour
Co-worker: 1/8 pile per hour

Gregg's work: $\frac{1}{2}t$
Co-worker's work: $\frac{1}{8}t$
Equation: 1 pile $= \frac{1}{2}t + \frac{1}{8}t$
Solve: $1 = \frac{5}{8}t$    $t = 1\frac{3}{5}$ hours

4) 40 days
Sine's rate: 1/50 tunnel per day
Tangent's rate: 1/200 tunnel per day

Sine's work: $\frac{1}{50}t$
Tangent's work: $\frac{1}{200}t$
Equation: 1 tunnel = $\frac{1}{50}t + \frac{1}{200}t$
Solve: $1 = \frac{5}{200}t$    $t = 40$ days

5) 3 hours
Worker 1 rate: 1/2 car per hour
Worker 2 rate: 1/4 car per hour
Worker 3 rate: 1/8 car per hour
Worker 4 rate: 1/8 car per hour

Worker 1 work: $\frac{1}{2}t$
Worker 2 work: $\frac{1}{4}t$
Worker 3 work: $\frac{1}{8}t$
Worker 4 work: $\frac{1}{8}t$
Equation: 3 cars = $\frac{1}{2}t + \frac{1}{4}t + \frac{1}{8}t + \frac{1}{8}t$
Solve: $3 = 1t$       $t = 3$ hours

## Einstein Level
1) 4 hours
Amount of time 1 brick wall: $2\frac{2}{5}$ hours
Lennox's rate: 1/6 wall per hour
Dad's rate: $n$

Lennox's work: $\frac{1}{6}$ x $2\frac{2}{5}$
Dad's work: $n$ x $2\frac{2}{5}$
Equation: 1 wall = $(\frac{1}{6}$ x $2\frac{2}{5}) + 2\frac{2}{5}n$
Solve: $1 = .4 + 2\frac{2}{5}n$       $n = .25$
Dad's rate is 1/4 wall per hour

2) 3 hours
Time unload 1 truck: $2\frac{1}{10}$ hours
Alomar's rate: 1/7 truck per hour
Jon's rate: $n$

Alomar's work: $\frac{1}{7}$ x $2\frac{1}{10}$
Jon's work: $n$ x $2\frac{1}{10}$
Equation: $1 = (\frac{1}{7}$ x $2\frac{1}{10}) + 2\frac{1}{10}n$
Solve: $1 = .3 + 2\frac{1}{10}n$       $n = .33$
Jon's rate is 1/3 truck per hour.

3) 2.5 hours
Hose A rate: 1/4 pool per hour
Hose B rate: 1/5 pool per hour
Leak's rate: –1/20 per hour

Hose A work: $\frac{1}{4}t$
Hose B work: $\frac{1}{5}t$
Leak's work: $-\frac{1}{20}t$
Equation: 1 pool = $\frac{1}{4}t + \frac{1}{5}t - \frac{1}{20}t$
Solve: $1 = .4t$       $t = 2.5$ hours

4) 1 hour  16 minutes
Derek's rate for 25 pancakes:
1/2 pile per hour
Teammate's rate for 25 pancakes:
2/7 pile per hour

Derek's work: $\frac{1}{2}t$
Teammate's work: $\frac{2}{7}t$
Equation: 1 pile = $\frac{1}{2}t + \frac{2}{7}t$
Solve: $1 = \frac{11}{14}t$       $t = 1\frac{3}{11}$ hours

5) 10 minutes
Lenny's rate: 2 floors per hour
Abe's rate: 1 floor per hour
Melody's rate: 3 floors per hour

Lenny's work: $2t$
Abe's work: $t$
Melody's work: $3t$
Equation: 1 floor = $6t$
Solve: $t = 1/6$ hour

## Chapter 17: Simultaneous Equations

### Page 192

1) x = 8        y = 12
$$4x + y = 44$$
$$x + y = 20$$

After subtracting:    3x = 24        x = 8

2) x = 7      y = 20
Add:  3x + 2y = 61
$$9x - 2y = 23$$

12x = 84      x = 7

3) x = 14      y = 13
Add:  x + y = 27
$$x - y = 1$$

2x = 28        x = 14

4) x = 50      y = 17
$$\tfrac{1}{2}x + 3y = 76$$
$$1\tfrac{1}{2}x + 3y = 126$$

After subtracting up:        x = 50

5) x = 0        y=9
$$x + 2y = 18$$
$$x + y = 9$$

After subtracting:            y = 9

6) Pencil $.17        Pen $1.29
Add:  2 pencils + pen = $1.63
$$10 \text{ pencils} - \text{pen} = \$.41$$

12 pencils = $2.04
Pencil = $.17

7) $89
Add:  Coat + Mountain Boots = 112
$$\text{Coat} - \text{Mountain Boots} = 66$$

2 Coats = 178
Coat = $89

8) $7.50
Mouse + Porcupine = $12.50
2 Mice + Porcupine = $20

After subtracting up:  Mouse = $7.50

9) First is 11 Second is 1
Add:  2x - y = 21
$$2x + y = 23$$

4x = 44        x = 11

10) Ryan is 13 years old
Add:  Ryan + 3 Steve = 34
$$7 \text{ Steve} - \text{Ryan} = 36$$

10 Steve = 70        Steve = 7

### Page 195

1) x = 32      y = 47
(Multiply by 3)      x + y = 79
$$3x + 4y = 284$$

New equations:      3x + 3y = 237
$$3x + 4y = 284$$

After subtracting up:        y = 47

2) x = $\tfrac{1}{2}$      y = 4
(Multiply by 3)      4x + 3y = 14
(Multiply by 4)      3x + 4y = 17.5

New equations:      12x + 9y = 42
$$12x + 16y = 70$$

After subtracting up: 7y = 28        y = 4

3) $x = \frac{3}{4}$　　　$y = 3$
(Multiply by 2)　　$x + y = 3.75$
　　　　　　　　$14x - 2y = 4.5$

New equations:　　$2x + 2y = 7.5$
　　　　　　　　$14x - 2y = 4.5$

Add:　　　　　$16x = 12$　　$x = \frac{3}{4}$


4) $x = 6$　　　$y = 12$
(Multiply by 3)　　$2x - y = 0$
　　　　　　　　$4x + 3y = 60$

New equations:　　$6x - 3y = 0$
　　　　　　　　$4x + 3y = 60$

Add:　　　　　$10x = 60$　　$x = 6$


5) $x = 7.5$　　$y = 8.5$
(Multiply by 3)　　$2x + 3y = 40.5$
(Multiply by 2)　　$3x + 2y = 39.5$

New equations:　　$6x + 9y = 121.5$
　　　　　　　　$6x + 4y = 79$

After subtracting:　　$5y = 42.5$　　$y = 8.5$


6) $15
(Multiply by 4)$4c + 3d = 135$
(Multiply by 3)$3c + 4d = 145$

New Equations:　　$16c + 12d = 540$
　　　　　　　　$9c + 12d = 435$

After subtracting:　　$7c = 105$　　$c = 15$


7) Stacy 21　　　　Lindsey 12
(Multiply by 2) 2 Stacy + Lindsey = 54
　　　　　　　　Stacy + 2 Lindsey = 45

New equations:　　$4 S + 2 L = 108$
　　　　　　　　$S + 2 L = 45$


After subtracting:　　$3 S = 63$　　$S = 21$

8) $6.35
(Multiply by 2)　　$2t + 2p = 13.08$
　　　　　　　　$3t + 4p = 19.81$

New equations:　　$4t + 4p = 26.16$
　　　　　　　　$3t + 4p = 19.81$

After subtracting:　　　　$t = 6.35$

9) $x = 7$　　　$y = 8$
(Multiply by 2)　　$3x + 2y = 37$
(Multiply by 3)　　$2x + 3y = 38$

New equations:　　$6x + 4y = 74$
　　　　　　　　$6x + 9y = 114$

After subtracting up: $5y = 40$　　$y = 8$

10) $1.29
(Multiply by 3)　　$6A + 2G = 9.52$
　　　　　　　　$2A + 6G = 7.92$

New equations:　　$18A + 6G = 28.56$
　　　　　　　　$2A + 6G = 7.92$

After subtracting:　　$16A = 20.64$　　$A = 1.29$

## Level 1

1) A pair of shoes cost $35.50
Add:　Shoes + Socks = 39.75
　　　Shoes - Socks = 31.25

　　　2 Shoes = 71　　Shoe = $35.50


2) A science book cost $28.50
Add:　$M + 2S = 80.50$
　　　$5M - 2S = 60.50$

　　　$6M = 141$　　Math = 23.50

So:　Math + 2S = 80.50
　　　23.50 + 2S = 80.50

Solve: 2S = 57      S = 28.50

3)  Luke weighs 145 pounds
(Multiply by 2)      $\frac{1}{2}$E + L = 250
                     $\frac{1}{2}$L + E = 282.5

New equations:       E + 2L = 500
                     $\frac{1}{2}$L + E = 282.5

After subtracting:
$1\frac{1}{2}$L = 217.5  L = 145

4) Jay has $29
(Multiply by 2) Donna + Jay = 54
                2 Donna + 3 Jay = 137

New equation:        2 D + 2 J = 108
                     2 D + 3 J = 137

After subtracting up:        J = 29

5) Weight 82 pounds          Height 62"
Add:  w + h = 144
      3w - h = 184

      4w = 328      w = 82

6) Ben's allowance is $8
                B + F = 11.25
                3B + F = 27.25

After subtracting up: 2B = 16      B = 8

7) Height is 62 inches
Add:  height + weight = 155
      weight - height = 31

      2w = 186      w = 93
If Maria's weight is 93 pounds, then her
height is 62 inches.

8) Rosa' age 9          Mother's age 48

Add:   Rosa + Mother = 57
       Mother - Rosa = 39

2 Mother = 96       Mother's age = 48

9) x = 2       y = 16
                x + y = 18
                x + 2y = 34

After subtracting up:        y = 16

10) Width = 11 inches
(Multiply by 2)      L - W = 24
                     2L + 2W = 92

New equations:       2L - 2W = 48
                     2L + 2W = 92

                     4L = 140      L = 35
If the length is 35 inches, then the width is 11
inches.

## Level 2
1) One cat cost $22
We want to get rid of the dogs in the
equations.
(Multiply by 5) 3 dogs + 5 cats = 365
(Multiply by 3) 5 dogs + 3 cats = 491

New equations:       15d + 25c = 1825
                     15d + 9c = 1473

After subtracting:   16c = 352    c = 22

2) Computer game cost $82.50
Add:   Game - Mug = 75
       Game + Mug = 90

       2 Games = 165      G = $82.50

3) x = $-8\frac{1}{3}$
Add:  2x + 18 = y

$x + 7 = -y$

$3x + 25 = 0$

$3x = -25$     $x = -8\frac{1}{3}$

4) $x = 12$

(Multiply by 7)     $3\frac{1}{2}x + 2y = 43$

(Multiply by 4)     $2x + 3\frac{1}{2}y = 25\frac{3}{4}$

New equations:     $24.5x + 14y = 301$

$8x + 14y = 103$

After subtracting:     $16.5x = 198$     $x = 12$

5) 93

The tens column will be x and the units column will be y.

Add:  $x + y = 12$

$2x - y = 15$

$3x = 27$     $x = 9$

6) 110 children attended

$4A + 3C = 2778$

(Multiply by 4)     $A + C = 722$

New equations:     $4A + 3C = 2778$

$4A + 4C = 2888$

After subtracting up:     $C = 110$

7) Amadeus bought 12     3-cent stamps

$1.26 equals 126 cents

$1.14 equals 114 cents

(Multiply by 3)     $5x + 3y = 126$

(Multiply by 5)     $3x + 5y = 114$

New equations:     $15x + 9y = 378$

$15x + 25y = 570$

After subtracting up: $16y = 192$  $y = 12$

8) Jordan had $1640

(Multiply by 2)     $L + J = 2850$

$2L + 3J = 7340$

New equations:     $2L + 2J = 5700$

$2L + 3J = 7340$

After subtracting up: $J = 1640$

9) 20 nickels

Number of coins:     $n + d = 83$

Value of coins:     $5n + 10d = 730$

(Multiply by 10)     $n + d = 83$

$5n + 10d = 730$

New equations:     $10n + 10d = 830$

$5n + 10d = 730$

After subtracting:     $5n = 100$     $n = 20$

10) 37 horses

Number of animals: $h + c = 100$

Value of animals: $500h + 200c = 31,100$

(Multiply by 200)     $h + c = 100$

$500h + 200c = 31,100$

New equations: $200h + 200c = 20,000$

$500h + 200c = 31,100$

After subtracting up: $300h = 11,100$

$h = 37$

## Einstein Level

1) 80 cows

The number of duck legs is 2d

The number of cow legs is 4c

Number of animals: $d + c = 97$

Number of legs:     $2d + 4c = 354$

(Multiply by 2)     $d + c = 97$

$2d + 4c = 354$

New equations:     $2d + 2c = 194$
                   $2d + 4c = 354$

After subtracting up: $2c = 160$     $c = 80$

2) Regular cost of a saddle $10
$h + s = 960$
$.7h + .75s = 672.5$

(Multiply by 7)    $h + s = 960$
(Multiply by 10)   $.7h + .75s = 672.5$

New equations:     $7h + 7s = 6720$
                   $7h + 7.5s = 6725$

Subtract up:  $.5s = 5$          $s = 10$

3) 37 hours
Hours worked: x
Bonus: y

Mike:      $6x + y = 333$
Juanita:   $10x + y = 481$

After subtracting up: $4x = 148$     $x = 37$

4) Bike cost $70
Cost of bike: x
Cost of hiking boots: y

Cost of bike with tax: 1.05x
Cost of hiking boots with tax: 1.05y

Equations:   $1.05x + 1.05y = 116.13$
             $2x + y = 180.60$

You need to get the y's the same so you can subtract and have them disappear.

(Multiply by 40) $1.05x + 1.05y = 116.13$
(Multiply by 42) $2x + y = 180.60$

New equations:     $42x + 42y = 4645.2$
                   $84x + 42y = 7585.2$

After subtracting up:     $42x = 2940$
                          $x = 70$

5) 30 quarters
Number of nickels: x
Number of dimes: x
Number of quarters: y
Number of half-dollars: y

Value of nickels:      5x
Value of dimes:        10x
Value of quarters:     25y
Value of half-dollars: 50y

Value of nickels and half-dollars=1635
Equation:     $5x + 50y = 1635$

Value of dimes and quarters=1020
Equation:     $10x + 25y = 1020$

(Multiply by 2)    $5x + 50y = 1635$
                   $10x + 25y = 1020$

New equations:     $10x + 100y = 3270$
                   $10x + 25y = 1020$

After subtracting:   $75y = 2250$     $y = 30$

6) Brianna's savings account is $1360
Brianna's savings: x
Sister's savings: y

15% of sister's savings: .15y
10% of Brianna's savings: .10x

The problem says that Brianna's savings in combination with 15% of her sister's savings will pay off Brianna's $1660 debt.
Equation: $x + .15y = 1660$

The problem also says that if the sister combined her savings with 10% of Brianna's savings, the sister will have enough to pay off her $2136 debt.

Equation: y + .10x = 2136

x + .15y = 1660
y + .10x = 2136

|                  |                      |
| (Multiply by 10) | x + .15y = 1660      |
|                  | y + .10x = 2136      |

New equations:    x + .15y = 1660
                  10y + x = 21,360

After subtracting up:9.85y = 19,700
                           y = 2000

The sister has a savings of $2000. We can find Brianna's savings by placing the 2000 into the equation in place of y:

y + .10x = 2136
2000 + .10x = 2136
.10x = 136
x = 1360

7) $15,000 in Bank A
Money in Bank A: x
Money in Bank B: y

Interest from Bank A: .04x
Interest from Bank B: .05y

Because the total amount of money to invest was 100,000 , you can write the following equation:
        x + y = 100,000

Because you know the amount of interest earned in a year was 4850, you can write the following equation:
        .04x + .05y = 4850

Two equations:    x + y = 100,000
                  .04x + .05y = 4850

                  x + y = 100,000
(Multiply by 20)  .04x + .05y = 4850

New equations:    x + y = 100,000
                  .80x + y = 97,000

After subtracting:  .20x = 3000
                    x = 15,000

8) The bike cost $80
Bike: x
Helmet: y

Remember that if something is discounted 25% off the regular price, its cost is 75% of the regular price.

Cost of discounted bike: .75x
Cost of discounted helmet: .60y

Latisha's total cost was $105 and Amanda's total cost was $75 so we can write the following equations:

x + y = 105
.75x + .60y = 75

(Multiply by 6) x + y = 105
(Multiply by 10).75x + .60y = 75

New equations:    6x + 6y = 630
                  7.5x + 6y = 750

After subtracting up:      1.5x = 120
                           x = 80

9) x = 60°     y = 60°
Because there are 180° in each triangle, we can write the following equations:

2x + y =180
2y + x = 180

(Multiply by 2)    2x + y =180
                   2y + x = 180

New equations:     4x + 2y = 360
                   2y + x = 180

After subtraction: $3x = 180$

$x = 60$

10) $x = 12$   $y = 13$

Small rectangle perimeter:

$2x + 2y = 50$

Large rectangle perimeter:

$2y - 5 + 2y - 5 + x + 4 + x + 4 = 74$

(Collect):   $4y - 10 + 2x + 8 = 74$

$4y + 2x = 76$

Equations:   $2x + 2y = 50$

$4y + 2x = 76$

After Subtracting up:   $2y = 26$

$y = 13$

## Chapter 18: Fun With Variables

## Level 1

1) pear = 2 cherries

Add:  2 Apples + Cherry = Pear

3 Cherries - 2 Apples = Pear

4 cherries = 2 pears

Pear = 2 cherries

2) 2 apples = 3 pears

You want to get rid of the bananas.

(Multiply by 3) Banana + Pear = Apple

3 Bananas = Apple

New equations:   $3B + 3P = 3A$

$3B = A$

After subtraction:   $3P = 2A$

3) snail = 6 ants

You want to get rid of snakes

Equations:   3 snails = snake

18 ants = snake

After subtraction:   3 snails - 18 ants = 0

Solve for snail:   3 snails = 18 ants

snail = 6 ants

4) tomato = 5 grapes

You want to get rid of peaches

Equations:   $2T = G + P$

$9G = P$

After subtraction:   $2T - 9G = G$

Solve for T:  $2T = 10G$

$T = 5G$

5) dog =10 hamsters

$D + C = 12 H$

$5C = D$

You need to get rid of the cat in the first equation. If the one cat was 5 cats, it would be easy to get rid of because we know that 5 cats equal one dog. You can change the one cat to five cats in the first equation by multiplying the equation by 5.

(Multiply by 5) $D + C = 12H$

New equation: $5D + 5C = 60H$

Trade D for 5C: $5D + D = 60H$

$6D = 60H$            $D = 10H$

## Level 2:

1) x = 6z

You want to get rid of the y's

Add equations:   $2y + 4z = 2x$

$3x - 2y = 10z$

$3x + 4z = 2x + 10z$

Solve for x:   $x = 6z$

2) cat = 9 parrots

Take two equations and get rid of the dogs.

cat - 3 parrots = 3 dogs
dog + 7 parrots = cat

We want three dogs in the bottom equation so we will multiply by 3.

(Multiply by 3) dog + 7 parrots = cat

New equation: 3dogs+21parrots=3cats

3 dogs=cat - 3 parrots

After Subtraction:
21 parrots=2 cats + 3 parrots
Solve for cat: 2 cats = 18 parrots

cat = 9 parrots

3) camel = 2 deer
You want to get rid of the turtles.

3 camels - 2 deer = turtle
2 deer + camel = turtle

After subtraction:    2 camels -4 deer = 0
Solve for deer:       2 camels = 4 deer
                      camel = 2 deer

4) 2 math books = 7 science books
2S + E = M
3E = M + S
5S = E + M

Take the top and bottom equations and get rid of the English.

2S + E = M
5S = E + M   (Switch equation around)

2S + E = M
E + M = 5S

After subtraction: 2S - M = M - 5S
Solve for 2 math books: 7S = 2M

5) One Mays would equal 3 Garcias
Equations:

6G = 4R
2R = M

Because one Mays equals two Robinsons, then two Mays would equal four Robinsons. Because two Mays equal 4 Robinsons, two Mays would equal 6 Garcias.

One Mays would equal 3 Garcias

**Einstein Level**
1) rectangle = 11 triangles
2 squares + triangle = rectangle
2 circles - triangle = square
3 circles + 2 triangles = rectangle

We will get rid of the squares in the first two equations:
2 squares + triangle = rectangle
2( square = 2 circles - triangle)

New equations:
2 squares + triangle = rectangle
2 squares = 4 circles - 2 triangles

After subtracting:    T = R - 4C + 2T which equals 4C = R + T

Now use this equation with the third equation:

3C + 2T = R
4C = R + T

We need to get rid of the circles.

(Multiply by 4)3C + 2T = R
(Multiply by 3)4C = R + T

New equations:       12C + 8T = 4R
                     12C = 3R + 3T

After subtracting: 8T = R - 3T

R = 11T

2) 2 worms = 5 salamanders
3 worms + salamander = lizard
snake + salamander = worm
lizard - 5 snakes = salamander

We will get rid of snakes in the last two equations. We need to multiply the middle equation by 5.

5( snake + salamander = worm)
lizard - 5 snakes = salamander

New equations:
5 snakes + 5 salamander = 5 worms
lizard - 5 snakes = salamander

After adding:
5 salamanders + L = 5 W + salamander
Which equals:4 salamanders + L = 5 W

We now need to get rid of the lizards from this equation plus the top equation.

3 W + salamander = L
5 W = 4 salamanders + L

After subtracting up:  2W - S = 4S
                        2W = 5S

3) z = 7x
2x + 2y = z
y - 3r = x
2x + 10r = z

We need to make the y's disappear from the first two equations.

$$2x + 2y = z$$
(Multiply by 2)   $$y - 3r = x$$

New equations:   $$2x + 2y = z$$
                 $$2y - 6r = 2x$$

After subtracting: 2x + 6r = z - 2x
Which equals:        4x + 6r = z

Now we take this equation and place it with the third equation and get rid of the r's.

(Multiply by 10) 4x + 6r = z
(Multiply by 6) 2x + 10r = z

New equations:      40x + 60r = 10z
                    12x + 60r = 6z

After subtracting:   28x = 4z
                      z = 7x

4) 3 termites = 4 ants
We need to get rid of the beetles
(Multiply by 2) 2 termites - ant= beetle
          2 beetles - termite = 2 ants

New equations:      4T - 2A = 2B
                    2A = 2B - T

After subtracting: 4T - 4A = T
                   3T = 4A

5) 6 bats = 7 bees
2 bats + bees = 4 mosquitoes
5 bees = 6 mosquitoes

We need to get rid of the mosquitoes. We will do this by multiplying the top equation by 3 and the bottom equation by 2.

6 bats + 3 bees = 12 mosquitoes
10 bees = 12 mosquitoes

After subtracting: 6 bats – 7 bees = 0
                   6 bats = 7 bees

## Chapter 19: Order of Operations

### Level 1
1) 59
2) 12
3) -35
4) 6
5) 0

6) 22
7) 2
8) 0
9) 27
10) 2.5

## Level 2

1) (8 − 4) x 5 + 10 = 30

2) 5 x (7 + 3) = 50

3) 6 x (5 + 5) ÷ 1 = 60

4) (2 x 49) + (6 x -2)     98 −12 = 86

5) 6 x (5 + 12) - 3 = 99

6) 2 x $(25)^2$ = 2 x 625  = 1250

7) 130     $(5 ÷ \frac{1}{5} = 25)$

8) -27

9) 1

10) 1

## Einstein Level

1) $n = 1\frac{1}{5}$
$5n = 54 ÷ 9$

$5n = 6$
$n = 1\frac{1}{5}$

2) 40
16 ÷ 2 + 8 x 4     8 + 32     40

3) 5 x (2 + 1000) x 4 = 20,040

4) -25

5) -75

6) $-57\frac{1}{7}$
$100 ÷ \frac{1}{4} ÷ (2 - 9) = 400 ÷ -7 = -57\frac{1}{7}$

7) 791
$100 ÷ (\frac{1}{4} ÷ 2) - 9 = 791$

8) 1
$1 ÷ 1 \text{ x } \frac{1}{4} + \frac{3}{4} = 1$

9) 10

10) 100

## Chapter 20: Fun With Formulas

## Level 1

1) 52.5 kilometers
$3.5 \sqrt{225} = 3.5 \text{ x } 15 = 52.5$

2) 20°C
$\frac{110 + 30}{7} = 20$

3) 10.5 slugs
Mass $= \frac{336}{32} = 10.5$

4) Temperature is 98.6° No concern
F = 1.8 x 37 + 32
F = 32

5) 842.8 newtons
Newtons = 9.8 x 86
Newtons = 842.8

## Level 2

1) 71° Celsius
           159.8 = 1.8C + 32

Solve for C: 1.8C = 127.8
                      C = 71°

2) 100 meters
$35 = 3.5 \sqrt{h}$
Solve for $h$: $\sqrt{h} = 10$
                      $h = 100$

3) 96 chirps
$$\frac{18}{1} = \frac{Chirps + 30}{7}$$
Cross-multiply:      Chirps + 30 = 126
                     Chirps = 96

4) 50 kilograms
                     490 = 9.8 Kilograms
Solve for kilograms: K = 50

5) 1 pound
$$\frac{.03125}{1} = \frac{weight}{32}$$
Cross-multiply: Weight = 1

## Einstein Level

1) 1.296 kilometers
$126 = 3.5\sqrt{h}$
Solve for $h$: $\sqrt{h} = \frac{126}{3.5} = 36$
            $h = 1296$ meters

2) 3.575 slugs
Change kilograms to pounds:
52 x 2.2 = 114.4
Mass = $\frac{114.4}{32} = 3.575$

3) 890.91 newtons
Change pounds to kilograms:
200 ÷ 2.2 = 90.91

Newtons = 9.8 x 90.9090
Newtons = 890.91

4) -40 degrees
If both temperatures are the same, then you can write the following equation:

$$C = 1.8C + 32$$

Solve for C:  .8C = -32
             C = -40

5) $F = \frac{1.8 \; chirps + 278}{7}$

$$\frac{F - 32}{1.8} = \frac{Chirps \; per \; minute + 30}{7}$$

Cross-multiply:
7F -224 = 1.8 chirps +54
7F = 1.8 chirps+ 278
$F = \frac{1.8 \; chirps + 278}{7}$

## Chapter 21: Function Machines

### Page 227
1) 299

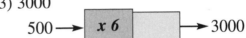

2) 11,988

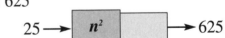

3) 3000

500 → x 6 → 3000

4) 625

25 → $n^2$ → 625

5) 175

### Page 228
1) 48th term

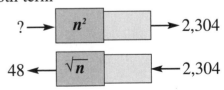

2) 810th term

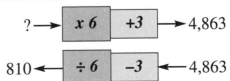

3) 4789th term

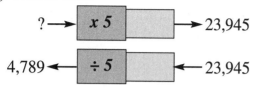

? → [x 5] → 23,945

4,789 ← [÷ 5] ← 23,945

4) 1000th term

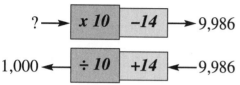

? → [x 10] [−14] → 9,986

1,000 ← [÷ 10] [+14] ← 9,986

5) 9th term

## Level 1
1) 3001

1,000 → [x 3] [+1] → 3,001

2) 25

5 → [n²] → 25

3) 500th term

? → [x 4] [+2] → 2,002

500 ← [÷ 4] [−2] ← 2,002

4) 5,000,000

1,000,000 → [x 5] → 5,000,000

5) 3125
Multiply the preceding term by 5

6) 7.9
The amount between each number grows by .1 each time

7) 5 squares
(Don't forget the large square.)

8) 693

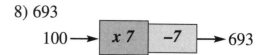

100 → [x 7] [−7] → 693

9) 90 mosquitoes

30 → [x 3] → 90

10) -31

10 → [x(−6)] [+29] → −31

## Level 2
1) 125

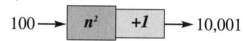

5 → [n³] → 125

2) 10,001

100 → [n²] [+1] → 10,001

3) 999,999

1,000 → [n²] [−1] → 999,999

4) 14 squares

5) 85

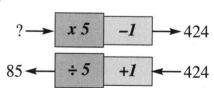

? → [x 5] [−1] → 424

85 ← [÷ 5] [+1] ← 424

6) 6 hours   50 minutes
(Remember it triples every 10 minutes)

7) 1024
To find the next number, multiply the previous number by 4.

8) The area is 16 times as large.
Try any sample radius.

9) 1490

500 → **x 3** **−10** → 1,490

10) 85th term

? → **x 6** **−12** → 498

85 ← **÷ 6** **+12** ← 498

## Einstein Level

1) 10,100

100 → **$n^2$** **+n** → 10,100

2) $10,737,418.24

31 → **$2^{n-1}$** → $10,737,418.24

3) 204
There is a pattern that makes it possible to know how many squares there are without the tedious counting.

1 small square: 1 total
4 small squares: 5 total
9 small squares: 14 total
16 small squares: 30 total

Notice the pattern to 1,5,14,30 by looking at the pattern in the amount
of space between each number: 4,9,16
Because these are perfect squares, the next amount of space will be 25 then 36 and so forth. The pattern of total squares will continue as shown below:
1,5,14,30,55,91,140,204

4) 81st year
The function machine takes the square root of the number of books read.

5) 36°
Burn-through is doubling for each drop of 5° of temperature.

6) 252.5

500 → **x .5** **+2.5** → 252.5

7) 1,000,007

1,000 → **$n^2$** **+7** → 1,000,007

8) 17,640 total interior degrees

100 → **x 180** **−360** → 17,640

9) -2480

500 → **x (−5)** **+20** → −2,480

10) 20 weeks

## Chapter 22: Math Contests

## Math Contest 1:
1) 20 cents
Algebra and Proportions

Two ratios: $\frac{50,000,000,000}{100,000,000} = \frac{100}{n}$

Cross-multiply:
50,000,000,000n = 10,000,000,000
Solve: $n = .2$ or $.20

2) 3368 votes
60% of 5613
.60 x 5613 = 3367.8

3) 10:45 A.M.

D = R x T:   673.75 = 55 x $n$

Solve:        $n$ = 12.25 hours

4) Angle B = 110    Angle A = 120

Angle A: $n$ + 10

Angle B: $n$

Equation: $2n + 10 + 60 + 70 = 360$

Solve: $2n + 140 = 360$

    $n = 110$

5) 16 quarters

Number of nickels: $n$

Number of dimes: $4n$

Number of quarters: $8n$

Value of nickels: $5n$

Value of dimes: 10 x $4n$ or $40n$

Value of quarters: 25 x $8n$ or $200n$

Equation: $5n + 40n + 200n = 490$

Solve: $245n = 490$

    $n = 2$

## Math Contest 2

1) $6 per hour

Sara earns per hour: $n$

Claudia earns per hour: $2n$

Karen earns per hour: $3n$

Equation: $6n$ x 500 = 18,000

Solve: $3000n = 18,000$

    $n = 6$

2) 379 no votes

$$\frac{568}{(\textit{total votes})\ n} = \frac{60}{100}$$

Cross-multiply: $60n = 56,800$

Solve: $n = 946.66$

If there are 947 total votes, then the no votes must equal 947-568 = 379

3) 74 beats per minute

$$\frac{21\ (\textit{beats})}{17\ (\textit{seconds})} = \frac{n\ (\textit{beats})}{60\ (\textit{seconds})}$$

Cross-multiply: $17n = 1,260$

Solve: $n = 74.12$

4) 89 cents

You need to get rid of the pencils so you will multiply the bottom equation by 4.

        4 pencils + pen = 1.65

(Multiply by 4)  pencil + 4 pens = 3.75

New equations: 4 pencils+pen = 1.65

        4 pencils + 16 pens = 15

After subtracting up: 15 pens = 13.35

        Pen = .89

5) 4.5 mph

You will use blocks of time to find the average speed. The block you will use is 9.

| 3 | 3 | 3 | 9 |

$$\frac{3 + 3 + 3 + 9}{4\ \textit{blocks of time}} = 4.5$$

## Math Contest 3

1) $2066.67

The ratio of good apples to the total is 75:90 while the ratio of paying for good to paying for all is $n$: 2480. We set up these two ratios and then solve.

$$\frac{(\textit{good apples})\ 75}{(\textit{total})\ 90} = \frac{(\textit{pay for good})\ n}{(\textit{pay for total})\ 2480}$$

Cross-multiply:     $90n = 186,000$

Solve:          $n = 2066.666$

2) $24.25
Cost of book without tax: $n$
Equation:     $1.08n = 26.19$
Solve:        $n = 24.25$

3) 111
Smallest number: $n$
Next: $n + 1$
Next: $n + 2$
Largest: $n + 3$

Equation: $4n + 6 = 450$
Solve: $n = 111$

4) 19 inches
Smallest side: $n$
Next: $n + 2$
Next: $n + 5$
Largest: $n + 8$
Equation: $4n + 15 = 59$
Solve: $n = 11$

5) 15.4 mph
3 minutes and 53.43 seconds is equal to
233.43 seconds and there are 3600 seconds in
an hour so we can set up the following ratios:

$$\frac{1 \ (mile)}{233.43 \ (seconds)} = \frac{n \ (miles)}{3600 \ (seconds)}$$

Cross-multiply: $233.43n = 3600$
Solve:                 $n = 15.42$

## Math Contest 4
1) 6.4 feet
weight x distance from fulcrum = weight x
distance from fulcrum

Equation:     $60 \times 8 = 75 \times n$
Solve:        $n = 6.4$

2) $165.24

Discount:  $.15 \times 180 = 27$
New price: $180 - 27 = 153$
Price with tax: $1.08 \times 153 = 165.24$

3) $2.50
Ball: $n$
Glove: $n + 45$

Equation:     $2n + 45 = 50$
Solve:        $n = 2.5$

4) 101

5) 28 miles shorter
We will use the Pythagorean Theorem to find
the distance from Westown to Eastown.
Equation: $91^2 - 35^2 = a^2$
Solve: $8281 - 1225 = a^2$
          $a^2 = 7056$
          $a = 84$

The direct route is 91 miles while the indirect
route is $35 + 84$ or 119 miles.

## Math Contest 5
1) 10.3 gallons
$$\frac{92 \ (miles)}{6 \ (gallons)} = \frac{158 \ (miles)}{n \ (gallons)}$$

Cross-multiply:     $92n = 948$
Solve:              $n = 10.3$

2) 1 hour  15 minutes
Cyclist 1 distance: R x T or 24t
Cyclist 2 distance: R x T or 20t

Equation: $24t - 20t = 5$
Solve: $4t = 5$
          $t = 1.25$

3) .1n
One page: $300 \div 50 = 6$ minutes
Change to hours: $\frac{6}{60}$ hours

Ten pages: (300 x 10) ÷ 50 = 60 minutes

Change to hours: $\frac{60}{60}$ hours

$n$ pages:(300 x $n$) ÷ 50 = 6n

Change to hours: $\frac{6n}{60}$ or .1n

4) No

If this is a right triangle, then the following must be true:

$16^2 + 13^2 = 20^2$

256 + 169 = 400

425 does not equal 400

5) 7 inches

Call each side of a square $n$. It is now easy to see that the perimeter is made up of 12 $n$'s.

Equation: $12n = 84$

Solve: $n = 7$

## Math Contest 6

1) 1 hour  20 minutes

We first need to find each person's rate.

Steve's rate: $\frac{1}{2}$car per hour

Jill's rate: $\frac{1}{4}$ car per hour

Next, we need to find the amount of work each person does. Remember that

W = R x T.

Steve's work: $\frac{1}{2}t$

Jill's work: $\frac{1}{4}t$

We now need to find how long it will take when Steve and Jill work together to paint one car.

Equation: $\frac{1}{2}t + \frac{1}{4}t = 1$

Solve: $\frac{3}{4}t = 1$

$t = 1\frac{1}{3}$

2) 28 kilometers

Equation: Kilometers = $3.5\sqrt{64}$

Solve: Kilometers = 3.5 x 8

K = 28

3) 350 kilometers

Equation: Kilometers = $3.5\sqrt{10{,}000}$

Solve: K = 350

4) 30° C

Equation: $\frac{C}{1} = \frac{180 + 30}{7}$

Cross-multiply: 7C = 210

Solve:          C = 30

5) No chirps. Crickets couldn't live at 100°C. 100°C is the boiling point of water.

This is how you would find the answer if you used the equation:

Equation: $\frac{100}{1} = \frac{Chirps + 30}{7}$

Cross-multiply: Chirps + 30 = 700

Solve: Chirps = 670

## Math Contest 7

1) 87.5%

7 parts out of a total of 8 are below water.

Equation: $\frac{7\ (amount\ below\ water)}{8\ (total)} = \frac{n}{100}$

Cross-multiply: 8n = 700

Solve:          n = 87.5

2) $\frac{n}{6}$

Amount in 1 day: $\frac{1}{6}$

Amount in 5 days: $\frac{5}{6}$

Amount in $n$ days: $\frac{n}{6}$

3) 127.5°

There are 24 total parts. There are 180 total degrees in a triangle. You can solve the problem by making the following equation:

Equation: $\frac{17}{24} = \frac{n}{180}$

Cross-multiply: 24n = 3060

Solve:          n = 127.5

4) $5.92

You can solve this problem by making two ratios.

Equation: $\frac{11.5 \ (Sam)}{17 \ (Janelle)} = \frac{n}{8.75}$

Cross-multiply: $17n = 100.625$

Solve: $n = 5.92$

5) $.49

10Apples + 20 Oranges = 12.70
20 Apples + 10 Oranges = 13.70

We are trying to get rid of the oranges. The first thing we need to do is multiply the bottom equation by 2.

New equations:
10Apples + 20 Oranges = 12.70
40 Apples + 20 Oranges = 27.40

After subtracting up:30 Apples = 14.7
Apple = .49

## Math Contest 8

1) No, the tree is over 97 feet.

Equation: $\frac{36 \ (stick)}{23 \ (shadow)} = \frac{n \ (tree)}{62 \ (shadow)}$

Cross-multiply: $23n = 2{,}232$

Solve: $n = 97.04$

2) 350 miles

Number of miles driven: $n$
First company charge: $.08n + 20$
Second company charge: 48
Equation: $.08n + 20 = 48$
Solve: $.08n = 28$
$\qquad n = 350$

3) 39

4) 165 pounds

Steve: $n + 20$
Tom: $n + 35$
John: $n$

Equation: $3n + 55 = 490$
Solve: $3n = 435$
$\qquad n = 145$

5) 6 feet

Distance Tonya is from fulcrum: $n$
Distance Donna is from fulcrum: $14 - n$

Equation: $\quad 60 \times n = 80 \times (14 - n)$
Solve: $60n = 1{,}120 - 80n$
$\qquad 140n = 1120$
$\qquad n = 8$

## Math Contest 9

1) When a $50 book is on sale for 75% off, the discount is .75 x 50 which is $37.50. The new price is $12.50.

When there is an additional 20% off, the new discount is .20 x 12.50 which is $2.50. The price with all discounts is $10.

2) $36.77

$\frac{1.37 \ (Canadian)}{1.00 \ (American)} = \frac{n \ (Canadian)}{26.84 \ (American)}$

Cross-multiply: $n = 36.7708$
Solve: $n = 36.77$

3) 48,49,50

Smallest: $n$
Next: $n + 1$
Largest: $n + 2$

The sum of the first two numbers minus 47 would equal the third number.

Equation: $2n + 1 - 47 = n + 2$
Solve: $n = 48$

4) 12 years old

Jane: $n$

Julie: $2n$

Jan: $3n$

Jack: $3n + 1$

Equation: $9n + 1 = 109$

Solve: $9n = 108$

$n = 12$

5) $\frac{1}{512}$ slugs or .002 slugs

Formula: Mass $= \frac{Weight}{32}$

Because an ounce is $\frac{1}{16}$ of a pound, we can write the following equation:

Equation: $Mass = \frac{\frac{1}{16}}{32}$

Solve: $Mass = \frac{1}{512}$ slugs

## Math Contest 10

1) 35 triangles pointing up

1st row: 1 triangle pointing up

1st and 2nd row:

4 total triangles pointing up

1st, 2nd, and 3rd row: 10 total triangles pointing up

1st,2nd,3rd and 4th row: 20 total triangles pointing up

1st,2nd,3rd,4th and 5th row: 35 total triangles pointing up

2) $40

Original price of book: $n$

Discount: $.15n$

New price:

Regular price minus discount

Equation: $n - .15n = 34$

Solve: $.85n = 34$

$n = 40$

3) 120°

Because all of the sides in the hexagon are equal, the angles are all equal. The interior angles inside a 6-sided polygon add up to 720°.

Equation: $6n = 720$

Solve: $n = 120$

4) 3 mph

Block of time is 6.

| 2 | 2 | 2 | 6 |

Equation:

$$\frac{2 + 2 + 2 + 6}{4 \ blocks} = 3$$

5) $50

Frame: $n$

Painting: $n + 900$

Equation: $2n + 900 = 1000$

Solve: $n = 50$